D1249286

GRANT'S TOMB

Also by Louis L. Picone

The President Is Dead!
Where the Presidents Were Born

GRANT'S TOMB

THE EPIC DEATH OF ULYSSES S. GRANT
AND
THE MAKING OF AN AMERICAN PANTHEON

LOUIS L. PICONE

Arcade Publishing • New York

First Edition

Arcade Publishing books may be purchased in bulk at special discounts for sales promotion, corporate gifts, fund-raising, or educational purposes. Special editions can also be created to specifications. For details, contact the Special Sales Department, Arcade Publishing, 307 West 36th Street, 11th Floor, New York, NY 10018 or arcade@skyhorsepublishing.com.

Arcade Publishing® is a registered trademark of Skyhorse Publishing, Inc.®, a Delaware corporation.

Visit our website at www.arcadepub.com.
Visit the author's site at www.LouisPicone.com.

Grandmaster Flash Words and Music by Edward Fletcher, Clifton Chase, Sylvia Robinson and Melvin Glove. Copyright © 1982 SUGAR HILL MUSIC PUBLISHING LTD. and TWENTY NINE BLACK MUSIC. All Rights Controlled and Administered by SONGS OF UNIVERSAL, INC. All Rights Reserved Used by Permission. *Reprinted by Permission of Hal Leonard LLC.*

10 9 8 7 6 5 4 3 2 1

Library of Congress Cataloging-in-Publication Data is available on file.
Library of Congress Control Number: 2020945361

Cover design by Erin Seaward-Hiatt
Cover photographs: © John Parrot/Stocktrek Images/Getty Images (Grant portrait); courtesy of the National Park Service, Manhattan Historic Sites Archive (Grant's Tomb)

ISBN: 978-1-950691-70-8
Ebook ISBN: 978-1-951627-55-3

Printed in the United States of America

Dedicated to my fellow members of the #Sweet16
Francesca, Vincent, Leonardo, Mom, Dad, Rosemarie, Gerry,
Ralph, Margie, Joseph, Danielle, Maggie, Katrina, Mary, and Olivia

and

My father-in-law, Mel Leipzig

CONTENTS

INTRODUCTION

THE FINAL RESTING place of Ulysses S. Grant, the victorious Civil War general and eighteenth president of the United States, is a colossal, 150-foot-tall neoclassical tomb located in the most important city in the country. It is larger than the final resting place of any other president—in fact, it is larger than the final resting place of any other person in America. There is nothing like it in the United States or in our neighbor nations. Ulysses S. Grant's tomb is the largest in North America, but sadly, many people—too many—are completely unfamiliar with it.

Grant's Tomb harkens back to the sacred and immense burial wonders of the Roman emperors and Egyptian pharaohs. But while millions travel great distances to see the pyramids, Rome's Castel Sant'Angelo, and the Taj Mahal, a mere fraction of those have climbed into a minivan or stepped onto a subway to visit Grant's Tomb. In fact, many Americans (including a surprising number in New York) could not even say where it is. And more than a few do not realize that Grant's Tomb is Grant's final resting place! This is because what most people *do* know, unfortunately, is the tired old Groucho Marx gag, "Who is buried in Grant's Tomb?" a joke first used on his TV game show *You Bet Your Life* as a softball question for those hapless contestants who could answer no others correctly.

But this was not always the case. At the end of the Civil War, Grant was among the most admired Americans, if not *the* most admired, especially in the North. He epitomized the country's highest aspirations: Grant's presidential campaign slogan was "Let us have peace," and he personified the reunification of North and South. When he died in 1885, Grant had become one of the most popular men in the world and undoubtedly the most beloved in America. His death was deeply mourned by people both north and south of the Mason-Dixon line. "Let us have peace" became his inspiring epitaph.

What followed his death is a story of honor, glory, drama, and intrigue as well as controversy, which began almost the moment Grant passed away. Many cities vied for the privilege of hosting his burial place. The honor was awarded to New York City, leaving many outside the state infuriated, jealous, and resentful. Construction of Grant's Tomb was almost canceled before the cornerstone was laid, due to a lack of organization and funding and an abundance of dithering and resistance. When the tomb was finally completed twelve years later, it immediately became the most popular destination in New York City.

But it was never just the tomb of one man. Even before it was completed, there were persistent questions: What does Grant's Tomb mean? What is its significance? The answer, as we will see, has evolved over the years and continues to change to this day.

In the decades immediately after death, Ulysses S. Grant was as adored as Abraham Lincoln and George Washington. His grave became a sacred and revered shrine to which hundreds of thousands made a pilgrimage each year, many of them Union and Confederate veterans who gathered to celebrate reunification. During this same period, Confederate monuments also began to proliferate in the South.

For two decades Grant's Tomb remained the top attraction in New York City. But as the Civil War generation passed into history, the visitors dwindled. A hundred years after the Civil War ended, Grant's reputation had declined, he slipped from public memory, and his neglected tomb fell into disrepair. It was vandalized, desecrated, and besieged by junkies, prostitutes, and gang members until only the bravest souls ventured to see it.

But like the man, Ulysses S. Grant's Tomb is resilient, and it has endured. Today it is again different—not the revered site it once was nor the disgraced one it later became. Most dismiss it as an out-of-the-way attraction among the plethora of tourist sites located throughout the city, or just another historic site managed by the National Park Service, or the grave of another president whose accomplishments have long since been forgotten, to be visited by school groups, scout troops, and people who are "into that kind of stuff." But it is more, much more, and people should know its story.

One logistical note: the site was not and never has been officially known as "Grant's Tomb." While it was called that by some from the outset, it was also referred to as "Grant Monument" or "Grant Memorial." Today its official name is the "General Grant National Memorial," but "Grant's Tomb" remains its most recognized moniker, and I use it throughout this book to make it easy for the reader.

GRANT'S TOMB

I

"GENERAL GRANT IS DOOMED"

AMERICA'S EIGHTEENTH PRESIDENT, Ulysses S. Grant, left office on March 4, 1877 after two tumultuous terms. As a Civil War general, his accomplishments were unquestioned and his accolades well-deserved. Along with Abraham Lincoln, Grant was heralded as one of the two men most responsible for restoring the Union and abolishing slavery. But because Lincoln was tragically assassinated on the verge of victory, it was Grant alone who survived to receive the nation's adulation. Grant never forgot his enemy were fellow Americans, and in accepting the surrender of Confederate General Robert E. Lee at Appomattox, he was generous and accommodating. Grant shared rations with the starved Confederate soldiers and allowed them to return to their homes with dignity. For this, he earned the respect of the defeated Southerners. In subsequent history, he has been widely admired as a "magnanimous warrior of mythic status to whom the people of the United States turned for leadership time and again in the years after Lincoln's assassination," as Joan Waugh has written.[1]

As a president, however, he was often lambasted as a novice politician whose trust in his cabinet and those in his inner circle was misguided and abused. The list of scandals during his administration is extensive and relentless, and the subject is worthy of a book of its own. Among the most notorious was the Black Friday gold panic of September 1869, when two acquaintances, financiers and railroad magnates James Fisk and Jay Gould, conspired with Grant's brother-in-law Abel Rathbone Corbin to corner the gold market. In the early 1870s, there was corruption in the post office involving inflated or fictitious mail routes on the Pacific coast. The scheme that became known as the Star Route postal ring implicated Postmaster General John Creswell. In 1872, several Republican senators and Grant's vice president, Schuyler Colfax, were accused of accepting bribes in exchange for favorable legislation that benefited the Crédit Mobilier of America railroad company. The Whiskey Ring scandal, exposed in 1875, involved (among others) Grant's private secretary, Orville Babcock, who was indicted for conspiring to defraud the government of millions in liquor excise tax. Other scandals involved the Department of the Interior, the Department of Justice, the Department of War, the Department of Navy, and the New York Custom House. While General Grant basked in glory, President Grant wallowed in corruption. Despite his failings, he remained beloved by many, and his legacy as General Grant, more than President Grant, would be most enduring.

Historians generally accept that Grant was not corrupt himself, nor did he profit from any of the scandals that rocked his presidency, but rather that he was guilty of being a poor judge of character. This fatal flaw would come back to haunt him in spades later in his life. But through all his ups and downs, Grant comported himself with the dignity, persistence, and self-assurance of a man who somehow knew he would come out on top in the end.

Hiram Ulysses Grant was born to Jesse and Hannah Simpson Grant in Point Pleasant, Ohio, on April 27, 1822. Ulysses (who rarely used his first name) was mild-mannered, loved horses, and enjoyed reading. He grew up in a fervently antislavery family, and his parents' views strongly shaped him as he grew into adulthood. His father was a tanner, but Ulysses wanted to forge his own path, explaining, "I'd like to be a farmer, or a down-the-river trader, or get an education."[2] Without consulting Ulysses, his father Jesse enrolled him in West Point Academy, where he could receive a free education and possibly launch a career in business. By mistake, his application, which was completed by someone else on his behalf, gave his name as Ulysses Simpson Grant, assuming that his mother's maiden name had been used as the child's middle name, as was customary. After initial hesitation, Ulysses took to the new name; he had never liked his initials "HUG" anyway. He also grew to love the military and decided to pursue a life as a soldier. After graduation, he was commissioned as a brevet second lieutenant and stationed at Jefferson Barracks outside of St. Louis, Missouri. There he met the sister of a fellow West Point graduate, Julia Dent. Ulysses was immediately smitten, but she was less certain. Julia slowly warmed to him, but military life was not always conducive to romance. During their courtship, Ulysses left to fight in the Mexican-American War in 1846, where he served under future president Zachary Taylor. Enthralled with the beauty of the Mexican countryside, especially Monterrey, he gushed in a letter to Julia, "This is the most beautiful spot that it has been my fortune to see in the world."[3]

Grant's life story consistently shows a thoroughly decent man of good intentions, but his early years followed a course of continual ups and downs, success followed by inevitable failure. Grant excelled in the military, where he discovered a sense of purpose and rose through the ranks. After the Mexican-American War, he was stationed on the farthest edges of the United States, first in the Oregon Territory and later in California. Without Julia and with a lot of time on his hands, he took to drinking. While stationed at Fort Humboldt in northern California, he was promoted to captain by Secretary of War Jefferson Davis. Grant responded to Davis with two letters, both written on April 11, 1854. The first was to proudly accept the commission. In the second he wrote simply, "I very respectfully tender my resignation of my commission as an officer of the Army." The reason for the quick switch was rumored to be the result of a drinking binge at Fort Humboldt, after which his senior officer gave him an ultimatum: resign and receive an honorable discharge, or face court-martial. After Grant left the military, attempts at business and farming met similar fates, as early promise ended in failure.

For Grant, as for so many other Americans, the Civil War changed everything. Given his ignominious departure from the military, Grant was at first hesitant to enlist, but soon, in April 1861, the former soldier was convinced to volunteer for the Union cause. Urged to enlist as a captain, Grant demurred, having departed the military at that same rank seven years earlier. Instead, Grant reentered the military at a much lower rank, as an aide to the adjutant general's office, and focused on training volunteers. He again quickly rose in the ranks and was promoted to colonel of the 21st Illinois Volunteers in June 1861 and brigadier general in September 1861. As his sphere of command increased, he amassed victory after victory on the battlefield. In February 1862, Grant had Confederate general and old West Point friend Simon Bolivar Buckner cornered at Fort Donelson, Tennessee. Buckner sought to negotiate a surrender, but Grant was defiant. On February 16, the message he sent Buckner in response earned him the name that would define his career: "Sir: Yours of this date proposing Armistice, and appointment of Commissioners, to settle terms of Capitulation is just received. No terms except unconditional and immediate surrender can be accepted. I propose to move immediately upon your works." Ulysses Simpson Grant, better known as U. S. Grant, had now become "Unconditional Surrender" Grant.[4] After the victory, President Lincoln promoted Grant to the rank of major general.

Later that year, in December 1862, Grant issued his notorious General Order No. 11. The order was in response to Northerners participating in an illegal cotton trade with Southerners using Confederate currency—which had the effect of devaluing US Treasury notes—along the Southern borders. Jewish traders were

Ulysses S. Grant, photograph taken 1864 to commemorate his promotion to Commanding General of the United States Army. (Courtesy of the National Park Service, Manhattan Historic Sites Archive)

among the guilty, though they were by no means the only participants in the illicit commerce. However, Grant's order stated narrowly, "The Jews, as a class violating every regulation of trade established by the Treasury Department and also department orders, are hereby expelled from this department [of the Tennessee, the territory that included parts of Kentucky, Mississippi, and Tennessee] within 24 hours from the receipt of this order." Within a few weeks, the order was revoked by President Lincoln, who objected not to its intent but rather its sweeping implication of "an entire religious class." The order haunted Grant for the rest of his public career and remains a stain on his legacy.[5]

Grant continued to win not only brutal and bloody battles but also the admiration of President Lincoln. Still, rumors of Grant's drinking plagued the president. Confronted with the accusations and saddled with generals like George B. McClellan, who would rather march in formation than engage the enemy, Lincoln defended Grant by shooting back, "I can't spare this man, he fights!" Lincoln promoted Grant to Commanding General of the United States Army in March 1864. His ascendancy over three years, from a failed businessman to the most powerful military leader in the United States, was nothing short of staggering. The following year he defeated Confederate General Robert E. Lee's army to bring the bloodiest war in American history to a conclusion.

After the Civil War, Grant conquered the battlefield of politics when he was elected president in 1868. Though plagued by scandal, Grant's administration had several notable successes. The Treaty of Washington strengthened relations with Great Britain, and he ushered in the conservation movement with the Yellowstone National Park Protection Act. He also advocated for the rights of Native Americans and African Americans. In his inaugural address, Grant declared, "The proper treatment of the original occupants of this land—the Indians—[is] one deserving of careful study. I will favor any course toward them which tends to their civilization and ultimate citizenship."[6] When former Confederate soldiers formed the Ku Klux Klan to terrorize free blacks in the South and reverse the gains made during Radical Reconstruction, Grant attacked the organization with the same ferocity he had demonstrated in Vicksburg and Shiloh years earlier. Thousands of Klan members were arrested and the terrorist organization was dismantled. But during his second term, his enthusiasm for Native American rights faded, and Reconstruction became less of a priority, as his administration grew mired in scandal and corruption.

Two months after leaving the presidency, in May 1877, Grant arrived in Philadelphia, where he stayed with his good friend George W. Childs. After being feted for a week, including a reception at

Independence Hall on May 14, Ulysses and Julia departed for a tour around the world.[7] Grant had nurtured a passion for travel since his time as a soldier during the Mexican-American War, and despite his tarnished presidency, he remained a beloved figure around the globe. While many of his larger expenses, such as a vacation home in Long Branch, New Jersey, had been funded by wealthy admirers, the trip was paid for by Grant himself. In the years after the Civil War, Grant had invested in the Consolidated Virginia Mining Company, based in Virginia City, Nevada, purchasing twenty-five shares. Riding the success of the Comstock silver and gold mines, he had made a profit of $25,000. Grant estimated that the fortune gained from his successful investment would cover two and a half years of travel.[8]

Fifteen years earlier, in 1862, a young reporter named Samuel Langhorne Clemens had arrived in the bustling mining town. In February 1863, writing for the *Territorial Enterprise* newspaper, Clemens penned his first article under the alias that would shine in the annals of American literature: Mark Twain. It was under his nom de plume that he had met Grant in 1866 in Washington, DC. On Grant's eleven-day transatlantic journey in 1877, he read Mark Twain's *The Innocents Abroad*. Destiny would bring these two together again in the years to come.

Grant was no typical American tourist. In England, crowds cheered and held banners that read WELCOME TO THE LIBERATOR and his campaign slogan of reunification, LET US HAVE PEACE.[9] In France, he visited the studio of Frédéric Auguste Bartholdi. The sculptor was hard at work on the historic gift to America that would one day rival Grant's Tomb as the top tourist destination in New York, the Statue of Liberty.

In Spain, the Grants visited the Royal Chapel of Granada. Built in the early 1500s, the building serves as the final resting place of the Spanish monarchs who sponsored Christopher Columbus's voyage to the New World, Queen Isabella I and King Ferdinand. The coffins are inside two sarcophagi that rest side by side in the chapel. Reportedly, on viewing the memorial, Grant turned to his wife and said, "Julia, this is the way we should rest in death."[10]

At every exotic locale, Grant was bathed in adulation. In China, Grant met Viceroy Li Hung-Chang. Despite the cultural chasm, the two quickly bonded. Li was so impressed with Grant's diplomatic skills that he asked Grant to help negotiate a treaty between China and Japan over the disputed Ryukyu Islands. (President Hayes authorized Grant's participation.) Japanese leaders, apparently as impressed as Li, agreed to the terms.[11]

Grant was accompanied on his voyage by *New York Herald* reporter John Russell Young, who later wrote about his experiences in the book *Around the World with General Grant*. While on the journey, Young published conversations with Grant in a regular *Herald* feature he called "Table Talk." Grant biographer Ronald C. White recounts, "Americans thrilled to Grant speaking in his own voice

Ulysses S. Grant and Viceroy Li Hung-Chang in China in January 1879 during Grant's two-and-a-half-year world tour. After Grant's death, Li visited his old friend's temporary tomb shortly before the permanent memorial was completed. (Courtesy of the Library of Congress)

about the important persons and episodes of his military and political career."[12] These articles whetted the appetite of the American public, who craved more from Grant in his own words. Later Grant succumbed to the demands and wrote short accounts of battles for *Century Magazine*. Once the public heard the authentic Grant voice, their demands increased for a full-length treatment, but that would not come for years yet.

Finally, two and a half years after leaving the United States, the Grants boarded the iron steamship *City of Tokio* in Japan on September 20, 1879, to return home. As the famous passenger approached the American west coast, yachts and steamboats met his ship to escort it into San Francisco Bay. Only three decades after the discovery of gold, San Francisco was still flush with cash, and the citizens doled out their riches to welcome Grant home. In the bay, he boarded the *St. Paul*, where he was greeted by a welcoming party of four hundred guests. After a luncheon of "quail in aspic, *foie gras* and ices washed down by a Niagara of Mumm's best champagne," he disembarked and was given a grand escort to the luxurious Palace Hotel.[13]

After several more celebrations in San Francisco, Grant embarked upon a meandering journey east. He settled briefly in his hometown of Galena, Illinois, in November. Later in the month, he continued east to Chicago, where he was feted with a grand affair. After reviewing a parade of 80,000 marchers, the dignitaries made their way to the Palmer House. There Grant was toasted repeatedly and sat, composed, through fourteen speeches rife with praise. The fifteenth and final man at the podium that evening was Mark Twain. Standing on a table so all could hear his sharp wit, he delivered his toast to "The Babies—As they comfort us in our sorrows, let us not forget them in our festivities." In the early morning hours, Grant laughed throughout Twain's tongue-in-cheek tribute.[14]

On December 16, 1879, the Grants arrived in Philadelphia. During the previous thirty-one months, they had circled the globe.

Everywhere they went, Grant was heralded as a hero and liberator of four million enslaved people. He left America a national hero; he returned as global royalty.

His popularity at an apogee, Grant was once again considered for the highest office in the land. Despite a scandal-ridden two-term presidency, his handlers believed Americans were willing to overlook his failings and elect him a third time in the 1880 election.[15] Worried that his popularity might peak too soon, advisers suggested another trip, calculating that the adoration could be prolonged to coincide with the upcoming campaign. Fortunately, the Grants were not yet cured of the travel bug, so they escaped the northern winter with a trip south. The couple traveled to Florida, Cuba, and Mexico, the land Grant had fallen in love with more than three decades earlier during the Mexican-American War.

The Grants returned to the United States in March 1880. While the former president did not publicly seek the presidency, he wasn't aloof to the possibility of another shot at it, and when he learned that his name would be submitted as a Republican candidate, he did not forbid it. With his hat once again in the ring, Grant remained publicly uninterested but was privately active in the campaign. Yet it was another Civil War veteran—although one not nearly as illustrious—James A. Garfield, who won the Republican nomination and was elected. While the mysteries of fate can never be fully unraveled, perhaps the loss was a blessing for Grant. Barely four months after taking office, on July 2, 1881, Garfield was shot by Charles J. Guiteau as he walked casually through the Baltimore and Potomac Railroad station in Washington, DC. After enduring excruciating medical treatment, he perished on September 19, 1881, at the New Jersey shore town of Long Branch. Garfield was the second president assassinated in only sixteen years.

Failing to get a nomination he had not publicly pursued, Grant abandoned further ambitions of public office. He did, however, actively campaign on Garfield's behalf. He spoke in Hartford, Connecticut,

hometown of Mark Twain, a member of the welcoming committee. Before the appearance, Twain spoke with Grant's son Fred, and
the subject of his father's finances arose. In his autobiography, Twain
recalled that, in their discussion, "it gradually came out that the
General, so far from being a rich man, as was commonly supposed,
had not even income enough to enable him to live as respectably as
a third-rate physician."[16] But through the generosity of friends and
other means, the Grants got by.

The Grants moved to New York City after the election, settling
into opulent accommodations at the Fifth Avenue Hotel. Built in
1859 at 200 Fifth Avenue, the hotel had become "the grandest and
most glamorous hotel of the Gilded Age."[17] Grant was familiar with
it, having stayed there before, and it had also served as Republican
national headquarters. The Fifth Avenue Hotel was where the
movement to nominate Grant for the presidency had been launched,
at the elegant and much talked about "Peabody dinner," hosted by
millionaire philanthropist George Peabody on March 22, 1867.[18]
While at the hotel, Grant was frequently visited by Mark Twain, as
the two grew from casual acquaintances to close friends—ironically,
for Twain had briefly served in the Confederate Army. Twain later
confessed to being an unabashed admirer, going so far as to call himself "Grant intoxicated."[19] As many others had before him, Twain
suggested to Grant that he write his memoirs. Grant demurred,
claimed he was not a talented writer, and added that he did not need
additional income.[20] Twain continued to visit Grant after the former
president relocated to permanent accommodations in a brownstone
at 3 East Sixty-Sixth Street in August 1881. (This building no longer exists, but there is a marker at the entrance of the current building at that location.) The luxurious home in the most well-to-do
area of the city was given to him by wealthy friends, including J.
Pierpont Morgan, Anthony Drexel, Thomas Scott, Hamilton Fish
(his former secretary of state), and George W. Childs.[21]

In New York, the popular former president stayed politically active. After Garfield's death two months after he was shot, Grant attended his funeral in Washington, DC, in September 1881. Wealthy friends continued to support him financially and assembled a quarter-million-dollar trust fund to provide him an annuity. But despite his generous friends, Grant was not a wealthy man and focused on building his own portfolio. His son, Ulysses Simpson "Buck" Grant Jr., and an associate, Ferdinand Ward, founded a brokerage house named Grant & Ward in 1880. Buck had attended Harvard University and Columbia Law School but had seemed to find his true talents as an investor.[22] However, the real brains of the operation was Ward; at only twenty-eight, he had realized impressive, almost unbelievable profits for his investors. A Wall Street peer described Ward as "magnetic" and "deceitfully unassuming."[23] Between that financial success and the family relation, the two were easily able to convince Grant to invest heavily in their firm.

Initially sizable profits silenced Ward's most vocal skeptics. Grant's wealth grew to $1.5 million, and any concerns about his family's financial security abated. But Ward was not quite what he appeared to be. His own father once wrote of him, "It is hard to trust his word or confide in him as to anything."[24] He was right; Grant should have been more discerning. His friend and former aide-de-camp, Horace Porter, tried to warn him in early 1884. Even during the Gilded Age, a period of tremendous economic expansion when some amassed previously unheard-of wealth, the profits Ward claimed were beyond belief.[25] The era's name was coined by Mark Twain in his novel *The Gilded Age: A Tale of Today*, published during Grant's presidency. (Grant was familiar with Twain's novel, for he attended a play based on the book in the fall of 1874.[26]) Corruption was also hallmark of the era, and Grant's scandal-plagued administration was emblematic of that. As historian Ronald C. White writes, "scandals and skullduggery . . . were becoming part of the business and politics [of the age]."[27]

Despite inexplicably large gains, Grant was undeterred and his faith in Ward unshaken. On May 4, 1884, Ward arrived at Grant's home unannounced. A bashful Ward apologized for the intrusion and asked Grant if he could borrow $150,000 immediately. The Marine Bank, which held Grant & Ward's funds, was in danger of closing due to the city's unexpected withdrawal, which would cause great embarrassment to the firm. Ward eased Grant's concerns and promised there was no risk and he would be repaid within a day. Since Grant's riches were all on paper, and not in cash, he approached William H. Vanderbilt for a loan. Vanderbilt was suspicious of Ward and his miracle profits and told Grant, "What I've heard about that firm would not justify me in lending it a dime."[28] He added, "I care very little about Grant and Ward. But to accommodate you personally I will draw my check for the amount you ask. I consider it a personal loan to you and not to any other party."[29] Vanderbilt was right. Just like Bernie Madoff 130 years later, Ward was running what would become known as a Ponzi scheme. His clients' "profits" were, in actuality, investments from other clients. The house of cards inevitably tumbled on May 6, 1884, and the failure of Grant & Ward and the Marine Bank would help precipitate what would become known as the Panic of 1884. Grant lost everything. Now he was not only bankrupt but also deep in debt to Vanderbilt.

That was not even the worst thing that happened to Grant that year.

In general, Grant had enjoyed good health, despite still suffering from a hip injury he had incurred on Christmas Day 1883, when the sixty-one-year-old Grant stepped out of a carriage in front of his home and slipped on a frozen sidewalk. He fractured his hip and was required to use crutches. Soon he was to experience a much more serious medical crisis. Grant was a prolific cigar smoker, a habit that began as he emerged a national hero in the Civil War. Grant had been a pipe enthusiast, but at the Battle of Fort Donelson an admiral handed him a cigar, which he absently kept with him throughout the fighting, alternating between holding it in his hand

and chewing on the stump. After the victory, a newspaper printed a potent image of a calm Grant, with cigar in mouth, as the battle raged.[30] Soon people responded by flooding the postal service with boxes of cigars for the general. Most were from grateful citizens, but more than a few gifts came from opportunistic manufacturers hoping Grant would be seen smoking their product. In a short time, Grant amassed an astounding arsenal of more than 11,000 cigars.[31] In an attempt to match demand with supply, Grant dropped the pipe and was soon on his way to a lifelong habit of twenty stogies a day. It was therefore not surprising when he began to suffer from a sore throat.

On May 30, 1884, Grant left New York for his three-story, twenty-eight-room vacation cottage at 995 Ocean Avenue, Long Branch, New Jersey. The town was a popular spot for the rich and famous of the day. Grant had first visited Long Branch in 1868 as a guest of George W. Childs, co-owner of the Philadelphia *Public Ledger*, whom he had met during the Civil War. In 1869, Childs, along with railroad magnate George Pullman and New York banker Moses Taylor, purchased the home and, like his New York brownstone years later, gave it to Grant as a gift. While today a group of millionaire businessmen purchasing a home for the sitting president would surely raise ethical eyebrows, in the Gilded Age such a favor barely caused a stir. Grant's arrival transformed Long Branch. As one author wrote years later, "the resort rose steadily in eminence until it reached a peak with the arrival of President Ulysses S. Grant."[32]

On June 2, Grant sat with Julia in the pantry. He picked up a peach and took a bite, but to his surprise he experienced a sharp, searing pain. At first, thinking it was a bee or wasp, Grant cried out, "Oh my, I think something has stung me from that peach." He drank some water, but it only exacerbated the pain and burned like "liquid fire" as he swallowed.[33] The discomfort slowly subsided, but Julia remained concerned and urged him to seek medical care, at which Grant assured her, "No it will be all right directly, and I will not have a doctor."[34]

Grant did, however, tell Childs of the pain in his throat. Childs suggested that an internist who was staying in Long Branch at the time, Dr. Jacob M. Da Costa from Philadelphia, take a look. Da Costa found a lesion and advised Grant to schedule an appointment with his regular New York physician, Dr. Fordyce Barker, for a more thorough examination. As the pain became more bearable, Grant's sense of the urgency dimmed, and he didn't schedule the appointment until his summer vacation had ended. But he may have been aware that he had serious health issues.

Two months after the peach incident, on August 4, Grant attended a reunion of the Army Chaplains of the Civil War in the great auditorium in Ocean Grove, New Jersey. In the crowd were thousands of Union and Confederate veterans who had benefited from the spiritual and medical care of the Christian and Sanitary Commissions in attendance at the convention. The event was presided over by Childs, who was also president of the Christian Commission during the war.

Grant was introduced to the crowd by Union veteran Reverend A. J. Palmer, who proclaimed, "no combination of Wall Street sharpers shall tarnish the luster of my old commander's fame."[35] Grant, still using crutches from his hip injury eight months earlier, struggled from his chair and was assisted to the podium. The crowd erupted in applause and Reverend E. H. Stokes described the scene: "Moved by the united impulse of full hearts, [the crowd] rose to its feet and, with cheers and waving handkerchiefs, gave the wounded chief such a greeting and welcome as has perhaps never before been accorded to any visitor on these grounds. It was indeed . . . an ovation that defied description."[36] Grant, overcome with emotion, struggled to gain his composure. He spoke in a faltering voice: "Ladies and gentlemen—under all circumstances it is a difficult matter for me to speak, and how much more difficult under the present circumstances. An hour ago, I might have said something about the Sanitary and Christian commissions. I witnessed the good done. They did a great deal by way of consolation, writing letters to friends at home for the sick and wounded and found where their dead were buried." A distracted Grant added, "I hope you are all having a good time here today," then struggled as he began another thought, "I appreciate . . ." but could not continue.

Grant broke into sobs before the concerned audience. Unbeknownst to those in the crowd, but as perhaps Grant was painfully aware, this would be his last public appearance. He had never been a renowned orator, but his final showing ended with him falling back into his chair and weeping uncontrollably. Reporters blamed it on his bad

Dr. Fordyce Barker, who was the first physician to treat Grant for the pains in his throat that were later diagnosed as cancer. (Courtesy of The National Library of Medicine)

Dr. George Frederick Shrady, a noted microbiologist, who diagnosed Grant with throat cancer. He continued to treat Grant until his death. (Photo from his 1908 memoir *General Grant's Last Days*)

leg and the financial crash.[37] But what they didn't know, and what even Grant had yet to confirm but surely suspected, was that he was gravely ill.

On September 5, Grant signed his last will and testament. It was drawn up by his lawyer, William A. Purrington, who was a friend of Buck. It was witnessed by Childs and his guest, Reverend Henry J. Morton of Philadelphia.[38] At the end of the summer, Grant returned to New York, but it was not until October 20 that he finally met with Dr. Fordyce Barker. Barker was an accomplished physician, a member of medical associations in Europe, and president of the

New York State Medical Society.[39] After examining him and finding an inflammation, Barker sent Grant to the foremost throat specialist on the East Coast, Dr. John Hancock Douglas. Grant had known the handsome, gray-haired Douglas since 1862; they had first met during the Civil War, when Douglas served on the United Sates Sanitary Commission. On October 22, Douglas discovered three small growths at the back of the roof of Grant's mouth and a swollen gland on the right side. But the most concerning was a scaly, inflamed growth at the base of Grant's tongue.[40]

Grant asked Douglas bluntly, "Is it cancer?" Douglas later wrote about his thoughts at that moment: "The question having been asked, I could give no uncertain, hesitating reply . . . I realized that if he once found that I had deceived him, I could never reinstate myself in his good opinion."[41] Douglas delivered his sobering prognosis of advanced tongue and throat cancer. In his memoirs, Douglas added that his response to Grant was "qualified by hope," but he knew it was bad. In 1884, cancer was a veritable death sentence. Douglas called upon Dr. Barker and two additional specialists, Dr. Henry Sands and Dr. T. M. Markoe, to review his prognosis. Douglas also took a biopsy and sent the frozen sample to a noted microbiologist, Dr. George Frederick Shrady.

Shrady was no stranger to presidents. Three years earlier, he was consulted by Dr. Willard Bliss as he cared for a dying President James Garfield after he'd been shot by Charles J. Guiteau. Following Garfield's death from his wounds two and a half months later and Guiteau's execution for his crime, Dr. Shrady played a part in both of their autopsies.[42] But now, the noted physician was unaware he was once again tasked with the care of a president. Grant's identity was concealed so Shrady could make an impartial examination, and his confirmation was disheartening: "The tissue comes from the base of the throat and tongue, and is affected with cancer." Shrady was then told that the specimen came from Ulysses S. Grant. The doctor bluntly responded, "Then General Grant is doomed."[43]

2

"IT IS ALL OVER"

WITHIN A MATTER of five months, Grant's world had shattered. In May 1884, he was wealthy and healthy, though still nursing a fractured and mending hip; by October he was bankrupt and mortally ill. Dr. Douglas, having concluded Grant was beyond a cure, instead shifted attention to making him as comfortable as possible. He administered cocaine for the pain and had Grant return twice a day for a dose of iodoform, a medication similar to chloroform, to treat the infection. (Later, he showed Julia how to administer the medicine from home.) The medication would, at least for a while, reduce the pain so Grant could eat and sleep. But Douglas understood what the next few months held for Grant, and it was grim: the cancer would spread to his neck, and eventually Grant would struggle to eat and breathe. Aware his time was limited, Grant focused on regaining financial security for his family.

Grant was a loyal friend (to a fault, some would claim), and now that he was in need, his wealthy friends offered their assistance. But while he was diminished in some ways, his pride was not, and he chose not to accept their generosity. Though his situation was dismal, a heroic and famous man like Grant was not without options.

Many times, he had received offers to publish his memoirs. His "Table Talk" interviews with John Russell Young during his voyage around the world had whetted the public's appetite for more. In the intervening years, Grant had written several articles about select

Civil War engagements for *Century Magazine*, which netted him $500 each, but he had repeatedly declined to expand his experiences into a full memoir. Grant did not believe himself to be a disciplined writer—and regardless, he humbly doubted the public was interested. While today presidential memoirs are commonplace, if not obligatory, this was not the case in the 1880s, when there was little precedent for such a book. Only James Buchanan had published his memoirs, *Mr. Buchanan's Administration on the Eve of The Rebellion*, a year after the Civil War. It was an unconvincing effort to salvage his legacy and hardly a bestseller. Martin Van Buren started working on an autobiography when he was seventy-one, but he died eight years later, before it was completed.[1]

As soon as Grant learned of his diagnosis, he left Douglas's office and immediately went to the office of the Century Company at 3 East Seventeenth Street on Union Square. He told them he was now ready to consider a full-length book. By 1885, Civil War personal memoirs and battlefield accounts had become somewhat of a cottage industry. Many were written by privates, both to deal with post-traumatic stress and to supplement their meager military pensions. Tomes authored by generals, both Union and Confederate, were more profitable and in demand, and many of them were first featured in the pages of *Century Magazine*.[2] Grant, as the top military official and most beloved figure of his era, had always been the most sought-after prize of publishing houses. Needless to say, Century representatives were elated that he had reconsidered their previous offers. But that appreciation did not mean they were prepared to offer special contract arrangements, and they proposed a standard 10 percent royalty on expected sales of 25,000 units. Grant decided to think about the offer and left the office without signing a contract.

Grant discussed the terms of the contract with his friend, Mark Twain. While Twain was a great admirer of Grant, he was also a businessman and knew that someone of Grant's stature should command much better terms. Earlier in 1884, Twain had started his own publishing house, Charles L. Webster & Company, and was in the process of publishing its first book, *The Adventures of Huckleberry Finn*. He proposed that the company's second book be Grant's memoirs. After some negotiating and discussions with Century, Twain and Grant agreed on a much more generous publishing contract, one that was guaranteed to provide his family with sufficient income after he was gone. Century Company publishers would still reap some benefits. They had paid Grant for the serialization rights, so portions of the memoirs would first appear in *Century Magazine*. Once published, the rights would revert to Grant to include in his book.[3]

Grant went to work. From November 1884 through the winter, he could most likely be found working at his desk. His preferred position was one leg crossed over the other and his body twisted to the right, so he faced the desk. He wore horn-rimmed glasses as well as a shawl and wool cap to keep warm. Grant preferred a pen over a pencil and wrote on manila sheet paper. Assistants, including his Civil War aide-de-camp, Horace Porter, helped with the writing and research, but the words on the page were all his.

Grant was attended by his African American valet Harrison Tyrrell, who accompanied Grant to medical appointments and knew as well as anyone the pain he endured. As November turned to December, Grant struggled to sleep. He could endure the pain, but the insomnia was the most difficult for him. During a visit, Porter reminded Grant how during the war the general could sleep under the most terrifying conditions. "Ah, yes," Grant recalled, "it seems strange that I, who always slept so well in the field, should now pass whole nights in the quiet of this peaceful house without being able to close my eyes."[4] As the weeks dragged on, an exhausted Grant sank into depression and struggled to write. Instead, he would sit by the fire and play solitaire, alone in his thoughts, for hours on end. But by Christmas, Grant's spirits improved, and he resumed writing on a regular basis.

Grant's physical condition remained a secret from the general public for several months. In January 1885, a Philadelphia newspaper reported Grant was suffering an illness, although the reporter did not know the specifics. Grant's doctors did their best to keep up the façade, telling pesky reporters, "The General is cheerful and comfortable."[5] Even Twain was fooled. When he told Grant how happy he was to read of the good prognosis, Grant lamented, "Yes—if it had only been true."[6]

As his cancer progressed, Grant struggled to speak, and when he swallowed it felt like "molten lead" going down his throat.[7] Doctors limited his diet to soup, milk, and oatmeal, and his weight plummeted (eventually he would lose a staggering seventy-five pounds). He was administered morphine and a mixture of liquid cocaine and disinfectant. The powerful narcotics provided him temporary relief from pain, but Grant was always concerned about becoming addicted.[8] During the day, he feared he would choke to death. At night, he was haunted by demons as nightmares invaded his sleep. In these sinister dreams, he relived the most harrowing moments of the Civil War, awash with symbolism of what bankruptcy would do to his beloved wife. He experienced excruciating pain in his face and ears. His doctors removed all of Grant's rotted teeth to alleviate his throat pain. "Most of his food is in liquid form and once in a while he takes a little meat cut up very fine," Dr. Douglas later noted.[9] In February 1885, Grant's son Fred confided to Twain that his father might only have weeks to live.

But Grant was a fighter, and he found much-needed distraction and purpose in writing. His memoirs became his reason to live, and he labored six to eight hours a day to complete them before his death. His doctor warned Grant's son, "I fear the worst the day the General completes his book."[10] The saga of Grant's final months is an epic final chapter in the life of one of America's most extraordinary men.

On February 28, Grant's son Fred could keep up the charade no longer. A week earlier, a "rose-colored report" was published in a medical journal about Grant's health that proved to be his final straw. It was all a ruse; Fred told an Associated Press reporter, "My father is a very sick man. There is no use in longer denying the fact."[11] The next day, the *New York Herald* splashed the dramatic headline across the page: GRANT IS DYING.

Immediately, a deathwatch began as reporters set up camp outside the home. Doctors, no longer burdened with evading the press, released updates twice a day. Within a week of the headline, New York police were stationed outside Grant's home to control the reporters and gawkers. Eventually, the newsmen coalesced in a headquarters nearby on Madison Avenue that was equipped with telegraph lines to file their reports. Reporters stoked the country's worst fears when they reported, "Grant is dying and may be dead tomorrow."[12] Soon afterward, *Harper's Weekly* would print full front-page engravings of Grant in three consecutive issues, each showing him in a weaker condition than in the previous one.[13] The attention the press paid to Grant at this time was extraordinary and would abate only somewhat throughout the next dozen years. This was not only because Grant was a national hero. In modern parlance, the period between his illness and when his tomb was finally dedicated, in 1897, was a very long slow news cycle. For one thing, it fell in the midst of a twenty-year stretch during which no sitting presidents had died—from James Garfield's death in 1881 to William McKinley's in 1901—the longest since William Henry Harrison became the first president to die in office in 1841. In addition, the press did not have the distraction of a major American war. The years 1884–1897 fell roughly in the middle of a thirty-three-year stretch without American involvement in a significant conflict, which began with the end of the Civil War and ended the year after Grant's Tomb was dedicated with the outbreak of the Spanish American War in 1898. During this extended period of peacetime and uneventful presidential succession, Grant's health, death, public remembrances, and memorial tomb were given extraordinary coverages.[14]

Now that the public knew the truth of Grant's health and imminent death, some suggested a gesture of American appreciation. In addition to proclamations of sympathy, there were sporadic calls for a public memorial. On February 21, 1885, a week before news of Grant's health broke, the Washington Monument was dedicated by President Chester Arthur. While fundraising had started more than fifty years earlier, the mammoth structure symbolized the monumental ostentatiousness of the Gilded Age. At over 555 feet, the obelisk was the tallest building on earth and to this day remains the tallest stone structure in the world. Washington was the father of the Union, but Grant had saved it. Surely, a comparable memorial was appropriate for Grant. But for now, he was still alive, and Grant had one last request from his country.

When he had become president, Grant was stripped of his title of "general," as was customary and appropriate for the civilian leader of the nation. Now, as he approached the end of his life, he asked President Arthur to restore his military title. His presidency had been rife with scandal, and Grant himself had conceded in his farewell address, "Mistakes have been made, as all can see and I admit." But that was not the case with his Civil War accomplishments. "General" was the title he cherished, and it was as General Grant, not President Grant, that he wanted to die. But his request was not just sentimental or symbolic. As general, he would receive a $13,500 annual pension, while as an ex-president he received none. (This was the case until President Dwight Eisenhower signed the Former Presidents Act into law on August 25, 1958.) More importantly, Julia would receive $5,000 a year as a general's widow.[15] These funds would be desperately needed by his wife until royalties from the book began to arrive (and whether the book would ever generate a profit was not at all certain).[16] President Arthur made the bill granting this wish one of his top priorities. The Senate consented unanimously, and on March 4, 1885, in his last official act as president, Arthur ordered Grant to be notified by telegram of his reinstatement.

Moments later, President Arthur escorted Grover Cleveland to his inauguration.[17] In New York, the telegram was received with great joy and rendered an appreciative Grant speechless. But Julia spoke eloquently for both when she said, "They have brought us back our old commander."[18]

As the weeks progressed, Grant's energy faded, and his writing slowed. Toward the end of March, a series of violent coughing spells seemed to indicate the end was near. On March 25, he suffered a violent spasm of coughing and was administered cocaine and morphine, though Grant disliked the latter, as it clouded his mind and made writing difficult. On March 30, he suffered another coughing spell so severe his doctors believed he might not live through the night. Even if he did, they grimly surmised, he would surely be dead within ten days. Fearing he could not survive another similar attack, they contemplated removing his tongue but refrained, suspecting that he could not endure such an operation. Grant's physicians were running out of treatment options as the cancer metastasized and spread throughout his throat and neck.

When Fred confessed Grant's condition to the press, he expressed fears that "there would be hundreds of letters coming with every mail, and this would only excite him."[19] Of course, he was right. In addition to generous offers, home remedies, and miracle cures, letters of goodwill and best wishes also poured in. One of the more intriguing came from California. Several wealthy citizens, led by Civil War veteran General Francs Darr, offered to buy Grant a home to live in on a vineyard "under the direction of a skilled viticulturist." Grant politely declined.[20] A class of young girls from Brooklyn's Clinton Avenue Institute, who had recently studied the Civil War, expressed "their heart-felt sympathy . . . in your suffering illness."[21] The Excelsior Club of Hackensack, New Jersey, also offered sympathy, but closed with the temerity to ask for a receipt as a keepsake.[22] On March 29, local children wrote Grant, "We little ones of the 'Children's Hour' of the Sixty First Methodist Church New York have heard that you are sick. We are very sorry and pray to God to make you well again. . . . We shall remember you when the big people now living are dead. . . . Please accept our hearty love, good wishes and prayers."[23] But a cure for Grant was not to be found from the letters or quack remedies suggested to him.

Julia, fearing Grant was close to death, sent for Reverend John Philip Newman from Washington, DC. Newman was pastor at the church where Grant worshipped as president and chaplain of the Senate from 1869 to 1874. With Ulysses and Julia in the audience, he also preached at Dedication Day at Metropolitan Methodist Church four days before Grant's inauguration in 1869.[24] To Julia's dismay, Grant had never been baptized, so she implored Newman to convince her husband it was not too late. Grant was skeptical of Newman, but for Julia's sake he was polite to the reverend. On April 1, Grant suffered yet another violent coughing spasm. Newman baptized Grant while he drifted in and out of consciousness at a moment when doctors thought he might only have minutes left to live. Shortly after the sacrament was completed, Doctors Shrady and Douglas injected Grant with brandy in hopes to revive him. When his choking spasms continued unabated, they administered a second injection and his pain began to ease.[25] Three days later, Mark Twain wrote an entry in his diary, morbid in its simplicity: "Gen Grant is still living, this morning."[26]

Amazingly, after the doctors had predicted his imminent demise, Grant defied expectations and improved. On Easter Sunday, April 5, Grant dozed by the fire. As he slept, thousands of people gathered outside his window on Sixty-Sixth Street and stood in silence. When Grant awoke, he saw the crowd and told his doctor, "What a beautiful day it is." Told how fond they were of him, he replied, "I am very grateful for them, very. I am sure I should like them to know that I am appreciative." Months earlier Grant feared his writing was substandard, but now it was his primary method of communication, so he took his pen to paper. He offered thanks to all those who showed him heartfelt love and enduring support. Only the day before, Grant

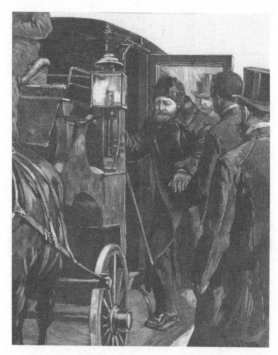

Harper's Weekly, *April 11, 1885. As evidence of his unrivaled popularity, an image of an enfeebled Grant taking a carriage ride is front-page news.* (Courtesy of the National Park Service, Manhattan Historic Sites Archive)

had received a "very friendly and condolatory letter" from his former adversary, Confederate President Jefferson Davis.[27] Now he thought of the Confederates as he wrote his message. Grant's wishes were not only for those close to him, but also to "Those who have not hitherto been regarded as friends." Grant, with no more malice in his heart or time for enemies, was at peace. His "Easter Message," as it became known, was printed in *Century Magazine* and newspapers across the globe. Southern newspapers in particular received his message with kindness and sympathy. This was the opening salvo of the spirit of reunification and reconciliation that became a hallmark of Grant's final struggle and would persist after his death.

On April 9, twenty years after Lee's surrender at Appomattox,

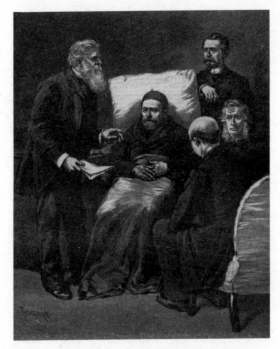

Harper's Weekly, *April 18, 1885. Grant sur-
rounded by his physicians (Douglas, Sands, Shrady,
Barker).* (Courtesy of the National Park Service,
Manhattan Historic Sites Archive)

Grant made a request of his doctors. Could he enjoy his beloved
vice just once more and have a few puffs of a cigar to celebrate the
anniversary? With nothing to lose, the doctors agreed, and Grant
indulged for the last time.

Expressions of sympathy were published in newspapers across the
country. As a testament to the magnanimous warrior, his former
enemies expressed their concerns when the Confederate Survivors
Association from Augusta, Georgia, wrote on his birthday, April 27,
"Remembering him now as the generous victor who . . . conceded
liberal and magnanimous terms of surrender, do we—standing by
the graves of our Confederate Dead . . .—respectfully tender to
General Grant assurances of our sincere and profound sympathy in
this season of his direful extremity."[28]

On May 23, Grant penned his dedication in broad, eloquent script: "These volumes are dedicated to the American soldiers and sailors." A week later, a group of those soldiers reciprocated their support and dedication for Grant. Four hundred from the Grand Army of the Republic (GAR), a fraternal organization of Union veterans that formed shortly after the Civil War, marched past his home as a band played "Marching through Georgia." Upon hearing the song, Grant moved to his window, drew back the curtain, and saluted the veterans.[29]

As the warm spring turned to a sweltering summer, the city heat further aggravated Grant's health. His doctors suggested a change of climate might improve his condition. Upon learning of the doctor's advice, Grant's good friend and staunch Republican Joseph W. Drexel offered his modest cottage in Mount McGregor, a remote location in the Adirondacks of upstate New York, north of Saratoga Springs. The son of an Austrian immigrant, Joseph Drexel had entered the banking business with his father in Philadelphia. Following his father's death in 1871, he came to New York and joined his brother, Anthony, at Drexel, Morgan, and Company.[30] While old money fraternized in Newport, Rhode Island, one reporter disparagingly remarked, the new rich "are very fond of frequenting the watering places of Saratoga."[31] Grant, as a member of that class of nouveau riche, was familiar with Saratoga Springs, known as the Spa City. He had visited it six times since the end of the Civil War, including three as president, and was last there in 1882.[32]

Drexel's offer to Grant, however, was not entirely altruistic. As owner of the nearby Balmoral Hotel (which would provide meals and services during Grant's stay), Drexel believed that, in life, Grant would draw throngs to the area. But more substantially and inevitably, in death the home would be forever memorialized. Drexel's business partner was blunt: "If [Grant] should die [at Mount McGregor], it might make the place a national shrine—and incidentally a success."[33] Drexel's motives aside, Grant's doctors concurred that the home provided the fresh air and solitude that Grant so desperately needed. After a grateful Grant accepted the offer, work got underway at the cottage to make it suitable for his stay. Arrangements were made for Dr. Douglas to stay with Grant while Shrady boarded nearby. Initial plans were for the Grants to depart on June 23, but the date was moved up a week as Grant's health rapidly declined. Grant was optimistic, however, and planned a return trip for two months hence, on September 15.

On June 16, 1885, as the temperature in New York City approached 100 degrees, an emaciated Grant emerged from his home at 8:00 a.m., bundled in a wool cap, coat, and scarf. This was the first time many reporters had seen him since the announcement of cancer several months earlier. "His body is wasted almost to a skeleton and the bones of his hands and wrists show through the tightly drawn skin," a journalist for the *Salt Lake Evening Democrat* grimly reported.[34] Grant rode a carriage to Grand Central Station and boarded a special 9:30 a.m. train. The train had been graciously provided by William H. Vanderbilt, who a year earlier had loaned Grant money that he suspected he might never see again. But Grant was determined to repay his loan. Without the cash, he sent Vanderbilt a treasure trove of historic artifacts accrued throughout his life, such as battle maps and swords from the Civil War and gold coins and gifts from his worldwide travels. Vanderbilt initially refused, but Grant was adamant. In the end, Vanderbilt accepted the repayment so as not to embarrass his friend but vowed to donate them to the Smithsonian upon Grant's death. With that sad event inevitably approaching, Vanderbilt was able to offer his train as a small token of his admiration.

Grant adjusted his wool cap and settled into his seat. Crowds could be seen gathered along the tracks as the train meandered north through the Hudson Valley. As the train slowed at a station along the way, railroad workers waved their arms, but one was missing a hand. "Thank God I see you alive, General Grant," the track worker cried.

Looking at the stump on his wrist, he added, "I lost that with you at the Wilderness, an' I'd give th' other one to make you well." An emotional Grant saluted in reply.[35]

At 10:15 a.m., the train passed West Point, prompting a nod and faint smile to cross Grant's lips as he saw his alma mater. The only stop on the way to Saratoga was in Albany, so one journalist on board the train, eager to get timely reports of Grant's condition to his publisher for the afternoon edition, instructed Western Union operators to "watch for copy to be thrown off the train as it went through . . . Tarrytown, Peekskill, Poughkeepsie, Rhinebeck, and Hudson."[36]

The train arrived in Saratoga Springs at approximately 2:45 p.m., where Grant was greeted by a small crowd at the station.[37] He slowly walked to another train on the Saratoga, Mount McGregor & Lake George Railroad line. After twelve miles, he was welcomed at the cottage by a committee that included Drexel. Grant tried to walk, but after a few steps he stumbled and could not continue and was carried the remaining distance. He sat outside for about an hour enjoying the mountain view before stepping inside to rest. The next day, June 17, two hundred miles south but a world away, a disassembled Statue of Liberty arrived from France in New York City harbor.[38]

At Mount McGregor, expressions of sympathy and admiration continued to arrive from across the country, including "feelings of deep solicitude and anxious concern at his condition" from the Colored Citizens of Chicago.[39] Many people also traveled to the cottage to see Grant, understanding it might be his final stand. An elderly Union veteran, Sam W. Willett, volunteered to keep the visitors from bothering Grant and set up a small white tent outside the home to keep guard. Some who traveled to the cottage were soldiers hoping to see their former commander one last time; more than a few were peddlers and medicine salesmen trying to gain entrance to the home and sell their wares; many were tourists,

Grant and his family with and Dr. Douglas on the porch at Mount McGregor. (Courtesy of the Library of Congress)

lured by Drexel's advertising. One newspaper reported, "Placards and handbills have been widely distributed in Saratoga and elsewhere announcing excursions . . . containing the big-type name of Grant to catch the eye."[40] The visitors slowly walked past the home in hopes of a glimpse of Grant on the porch, where he often sat wearing a wool cap with a blanket on his lap despite the eighty-degree temperatures. Their most sought and treasured reward was a silent nod from Grant. Julia, on the other hand, was annoyed by the gawkers. She wanted them driven away, but the hotel management resisted any such discouragement. It was, after all, a large part of the reason why Drexel offered the cabin to Grant in the first place.

Some special visitors were granted private moments with Grant, who conversed in a low hushed voice. Later, when speaking became too difficult, Dr. Shrady advised Grant to stop talking. Instead, he wrote thoughtful notes in response. Union General William Tecumseh Sherman, who had once told Grant, "You are now

Washington's legitimate successor," was one such visitor.[41] Another old friend who came to the cottage was Confederate General Simon Bolivar Buckner, the former classmate at West Point whom Grant defeated, and treated honorably, at Fort Donelson.[42] Bolivar stopped at Mount McGregor after visiting Niagara Falls on his honeymoon with his young wife, Delia Clairborne. He wanted to see his old friend and, as his wife later wrote, "assure [Grant] that the southern people appreciated the magnanimity at Appomattox."[43] Perhaps the two spoke of old times at West Point or of the Mexican–American War, or maybe they discussed when Grant defeated Buckner at Fort Donelson. Buckner would only say their chat was private, while offering Grant's comment that "the war has been over for a long time." Buckner spoke aloud, and Grant conversed through notes, which Buckner tucked away and saved as a memento of their final time together.[44]

Grant continued to write his memoirs at Mount McGregor, often while enjoying the mountain air on the porch. Reporters who had been on deathwatch in New York City followed Grant north to chronicle his final days, and their observations from a distance were fodder for daily reports.[45] They reported what they saw and speculated on its meaning. A journalist from Indianapolis reported on June 22: "When General Grant arose from his chair on the piazza yesterday afternoon he was observed to shrug his shoulders, as though he felt a sharp pain about the body."[46] Whereas in New York they leaned pessimistic, now they looked closely for any encouraging sign: "At about 11 o'clock the general rose. He seemed to be refreshed by his rest and brightened by the cool, clear air."[47]

Grant was aware that he was now in the final phase of his suffering. He attempted to discuss plans for his burial with his family several times. Julia, too distraught at the prospect of a life without her husband, refused to talk about the matter. Unbeknownst to Grant, however, his family had begun to inquire about burial arrangements, including the Soldiers' Home in Washington, DC.

On June 24, Grant wrote a note to his son, methodically detailing three options for his final resting place along with his rationale for each:

West Point.—I would prefer this above others but for the fact that my wife could not be placed beside me there.

Galena, or some other place in Illinois.—Because from that State I received my first General's commission.

New-York.—Because the people of that city befriended me in my need.[48]

Grant left his son for a few moments, but then returned. Perhaps having considered the grand public funerals of Lincoln and Garfield, Grant now handed Fred a second note:

It is possible that my funeral may become one of public demonstration, in which event I have no particular choice of burial-place; but there is one thing which I would wish you and the family to insist upon, and that is that, wherever my tomb may be, a place shall be reserved for your mother at my side.[49]

This was not the first time Grant had mentioned his burial. In a letter to his son Fred, written the day after arriving at Mount McGregor, Grant stated, "We own a burial lot in the cemetery at St. Louis, and I like that city, as it was there I was married and lived many years and there three of my children were born. We also have a burial lot in Galena, and I am fond of Illinois, from which state I entered the Army at the beginning of the war. I am also much attached to New York, where I have made my home for several years past and through the generosity of whose citizens I have been enabled to pass my last days without experiencing the pains of pinching want."[50] But now, a week later, he had eliminated St. Louis from consideration. With his thoughts clarified, he no longer discussed the topic. The final decision would be Julia's to make.

On June 30, Dr. Douglas released a statement: "General Grant's life has been prolonged by the invigorating air here."[51] But shortly afterward, any beneficial effects of the mountain air faded as Grant's health began a final decline. The cancer that riddled his throat had spread to the back of his jaw and neck. Grant's weight had plummeted to about a hundred pounds, and comfortable sleep proved increasingly elusive. But he continued to work, even as frequent cocaine treatments lost their effectiveness to temporarily numb the pain. On July 1, he wrote the five-hundred-word preface. The next day, Grant wrote a lengthy and eloquent note to Dr. Douglas. In the letter, which Grant requested not be shared until after his death, he confided to his trusted physician, "I am very thankful to have been spared this long, because it has enabled me to practically complete

Grant working on his memoirs on the porch at Mount McGregor, June 27, 1885. (Courtesy of the Library of Congress)

the work in which I take so much interest." But Grant conceded, "1 cannot stir up strength to review it and make additions and subtractions." He knew his time was near and was at peace. "If it is within God's providence that I should go now, I am ready to obey His call without a murmur. I should prefer going now to enduring my present suffering for a single day without hope of recovery."[52]

As his health further declined, Grant continued to make small changes to the book, and on July 19, he put the finishing touches on it. The 400,000-word manuscript, which would be published in two volumes as *Personal Memoirs of U. S. Grant*, was complete. Grant's final battle was victorious. He could now die in peace, and he was ready. That same day, he wrote this note to Dr. Douglas: "There is nothing more I should do to [the book] now, and therefore I am not likely to be more ready to go than at this moment."[53] Twain later opined, "I think his book kept him alive several months. He was a very great man and superlatively good."[54]

On the same day Grant finished his memoirs, he sat on the porch in a top hat and read the papers. His photograph was taken—the last one.[55] The next day, Dr. Shrady administered morphine twice. Grant was uncomfortable, but the narcotic eased him to sleep. The doctor telegraphed Grant's son Buck in New York to come to Mount McGregor to see his father before the end. On Wednesday, July 22, Grant spoke in a hushed whisper to his family, "I don't want anybody to feel distressed on my account." This was the last significant verbal statement he would ever make.

Grant had been lying in his chair, as he had every night for several months, but now he asked his doctors to move him to his bed. Lying flat on his back, he drifted in and out of consciousness. Doctors expected he would pass that evening, but around 10:00 p.m. on July 22, Grant indicated to those gathered around him to go to sleep, implying death would not take him just yet. He struggled to breathe, and in a final desperate attempt to offer relief, his doctors opened his throat. The operation allowed air to flow to his lungs but also left his throat pitifully exposed as it filled with mucus. Speech was no longer possible, and Grant was now reduced to hushed, strained monosyllabic words.

Since George Washington, Americans have been obsessed with the presidents' final words. They have been featured on popular lithographs of deathbed scenes, printed in newspapers across the nation, and often repeated in eulogies and speeches for years thereafter.[56] But Washington left little to inspire. When he uttered his final words, "'Tis well," the first president was responding to his personal secretary Tobias Lear's reassurances that he would follow Washington's final command to "not let my body be put into the vault in less than three days after I am dead." (Washington dreaded being buried alive.) Some presidents have reserved their final utterances for family, such as Andrew Jackson, who calmed his brood with, "Oh, do not cry—be good children and we will all meet in heaven," and James K. Polk, who professed to his beloved wife, "I love you Sarah, for all eternity, I love you." Others departed with a civics lesson to encourage the public in the national moment of despair, particularly the first two to die in office. William Henry Harrison, who met his end after only a month in the White House, uttered, to no one in particular, "Sir, I wish you to understand the true principles of the government. I wish them carried out. I ask nothing more." Zachary Taylor, who died after little more than a year in office, definitively stated, "I am not afraid to die. I have done my duty. My only regret is leaving those who are dear to me." Still others declared a profession of faith before departing for the afterlife, such as Martin Van Buren, who stated, "There is but one reliance, and that is upon Christ, the free Mediator of us all," and James Buchanan praying, "Oh Lord, God Almighty, as Thou wilt."[57]

Grant, no longer able to speak, left no dramatic or reassuring final declaration to his family, country, or savior. At about 3:00 a.m. on July 23, the general appeared agitated and wanting. His nurse,

Henry McSweeny, leaned close to hear Grant whisper his final word, "Water."

An hour later, mucus that had accumulated in his lungs caused a death rattle in his throat. Dr. Shrady could offer comfort, but nothing more, and applied hot cloths and mustard and injected Grant with brandy. At 5:00 a.m., Dr. Douglas released a statement to reporters: "He is conscious, that is, he has not lost his power of recognition. He breathed; his heart lives; his lungs live; his brain lives . . ." He then added hopelessly, "and that is about all."[58]

Doctors remained with Grant as the family rested. At around 7:45 a.m., Dr. Shrady summoned the family. Dr. Douglas sat on one side of the bed, and Julia on the other. A moment later, Fred entered the room and Douglas stood to allow him to sit beside his father. As Fred stroked his father's forehead, Julia grasped her husband's hand. The room was silent as Grant opened his eyes one last time. He slowly looked around the room and saw his wife and four children surrounding the bed; his three daughters-in-law at the foot; his physicians, Doctors Douglas, Sands, and Shrady; Nurse McSweeny in

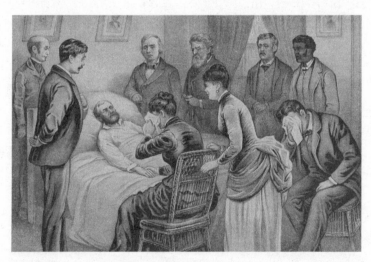

Currier & Ives lithograph, The Death of General Grant: At Mount McGregor, Saratoga Co. New York, July 23rd 1885. (Courtesy of the Library of Congress)

the corner; and his loyal companion Harrison Tyrrell (alternatively spelled "Terrell") by the doorway. "The rays of the morning sun stole quietly into the death chamber," recalled Dr. Shrady.[59] The *New York Times* captured the final moments: "Only the fluttering throat, white as his sick robe, showed that life remained. The face was one of peace. There was no trace of the present suffering. The moments passed in silence . . . [then] a startled, wavering motion of the throat, a few quiet gasps, a sigh and the appearance of dropping into a gentle sleep followed."[60] Ulysses S. Grant closed his eyes and took his last breath. It was 8:06 a.m., Thursday, July 23, 1885.

The group stood in silence. Finally, Dr. Shrady whispered, "At last." Dr. Douglas solemnly added, "It is all over."[61] Nurse McSweeny closed Grant's eyes, and each family member approached to kiss Grant on the head.[62] Fred stopped the clock, a Victorian custom to ensure it remained forever frozen at the moment Grant died.[63]

3

"Mother Takes Riverside"

HAD GRANT ENJOYED perfect health and financial security, writing his memoirs in under ten months would have been a formidable accomplishment. That he was able to do so while bankrupt and cancer-ridden is nothing less than heroic. Dr. Douglas, who was with him throughout the ordeal, released a statement: "If he was great in his life, he was even greater in death. Not a murmur, not a moan, from first to last. He died as he had lived, a true man."[1] Moments after his death, soldiers at Mount McGregor fired their guns to salute their fallen leader, and reporters raced down the mountain road to the nearest telegraph office. Within minutes, people across the globe learned the sorrowful news. Twenty minutes after he died, Karl Gerhardt, an artist from Hartford, Connecticut, and a good friend of Mark Twain, created a death mask, forever capturing Grant's gaunt features.[2] Later that day, President Grover Cleveland released a proclamation:

> The President of the United States has just received the sad tidings of the death of that illustrious citizen and ex-President of the United States, General Ulysses S. Grant, at Mount McGregor, in the State of New York, to which place he had lately been removed in the endeavor to prolong his life. In making this announcement to the people of the United States the President is impressed with the magnitude of the public loss of

a great military leader, who was in the hour of victory magnanimous, amid disaster serene and self-sustained; who in every
station, whether as a soldier or as a Chief Magistrate, twice
called to power by his fellow-countrymen, trod unswervingly
the pathway of duty, undeterred by doubts, single-minded and
straightforward. The entire country has witnessed with deep
emotion his prolonged and patient struggle with painful disease and has watched by his couch of suffering with tearful
sympathy. The destined end has come at last, and his spirit has
returned to the Creator who sent it forth. The great heart of
the nation that followed him when living with love and pride
bows now in sorrow above him dead, tenderly mindful of his
virtues, his great patriotic services, and of the loss occasioned
by his death. In testimony of respect to the memory of General
Grant, it is ordered that the Executive Mansion and the several Departments at Washington be draped in mourning for a
period of thirty days and that all public business shall on the day
of the funeral be suspended; and the Secretaries of War and of
the Navy will cause orders to be issued for appropriate military
and naval honors to be rendered on that day. In witness whereof
I have hereunto set my hand and caused the seal of the United
States to be affixed. Done at the city of Washington, this 23d
day of July 1885, and of the Independence of the United States
the one hundred and tenth.[3]

Doctors suggested an autopsy, but the family demurred, as there was
no reason to further desecrate Grant's cancer-ravaged body.[4] The
Stephen Merritt Burial and Cremation Company of New York City
was hired for the funeral arrangements. Handlers dressed Grant in a
black suit and placed his body in an ice coffin, but this was only a temporary measure. Two hundred and thirty miles away in Rochester,
New York, a new casket was being built by the Stern Manufacturing
Company. The Style E State casket was extolled as "one of a kind"

The death mask created by Karl Gerhardt, an artist from Hartford, Connecticut, twenty minutes after Grant's death. (From Portraits in Plaster: From the Collection of Laurence Hutton (From "Grant and Lincoln in Bronze," McClure's Magazine, October 1895)

and "the finest ever made in this country."[5] The coffin was six feet long, cloth-covered polished oak lined with polished copper, adorned with "the finest purple silk velvet," and framed in silver. The inside was lined with light cream-colored satin, and it had solid silver handles and a gold nameplate engraved, simply, U. S. GRANT.

Even before the coffin was delivered, proud and curious locals clamored to see it. On July 26, like a surreal dry run of the public viewing, a staggering 15,000 people were permitted inside the factory to file past the empty coffin. It was then placed aboard a train bound for New York City, where it was brought to the Stephen Merritt Burial and Cremation Company at 241–243 West Twenty-Third Street.[6] The next day Merritt, also a Methodist minister, put the coffin on display. This time, a mind-boggling 70,000 New Yorkers in their Sunday best lined up to see the casket.[7]

To add weight to this number, compare the number of attendees to the actual public viewing of another Republican president held in the same city, eighty years later. After President Herbert Hoover passed away at the age of ninety on October 20, 1964, his public viewing was held at St. Bartholomew's Church over two days, on

Grant's death was mourned across the world. This embroidered silk features symbolic figures of the North and South shaking hands. The name "K. Shiwomasu. No.6 Nishi- Furukawamachi. Nagasaki, Japan" is stitched at the bottom. During World War II, the silk was removed from public view, as well as "whatever else there is from Japan." (Courtesy of the National Park Service, Manhattan Historic Sites Archive)

October 21 and 22. During that period, the doors remained open for sixteen and a half hours, but a mere 22,000 people filed in to pay their respects. More than three times as many New Yorkers went to see the *empty* coffin of President Grant than went to see the coffin that actually held President Hoover's remains. This comparison is even more remarkable when one considers that when Hoover died in 1964, the population of New York was almost *six times* what it was when Grant died in 1885.[8] In death as in life, Grant was the most celebrated man in America.

After the viewing, the well-traveled casket was placed in an oak case and put aboard a northbound train, arriving at Mount McGregor on July 29. Grant's remains were dressed one last time in a black Prince Albert coat, white starched shirt, gold cufflinks, black scarf, and black slippers. Handlers gently placed him in the coffin. His right hand was set over his heart, while his left lay by his side.[9] Fred offered some special mementos for his father. First, Fred placed a ring on his finger. The ring had once belonged to Grant, but when it no longer fit him, he gave it to his wife. Now Fred slipped it on his withered finger with ease. Next, he placed a lock of Julia's hair and a note from her in his pocket that read, "Farewell till we meet again in a better world."[10] Grant's coffin was set on a catafalque and placed in the parlor beneath a black broadcloth and silk canopy.

Expressions of sympathy poured in from all corners of the globe. They arrived from American expatriates in Berlin, Germany, and Melbourne, Australia; from French Canadians from Worcester, Massachusetts; and from officials of the Royal Burgh of Scotland in Inverness. The London *Post* reported the sad news: "The American public has lost one of its most illustrious citizens," before adding that Grant was "not a Napoleon or a Wellington".[11] Robert Todd Lincoln, Abraham Lincoln's eldest son, who had served with Grant at the end of the Civil War and witnessed his magnanimity toward Lee at Appomattox, sent a letter to Julia: "It will always be a satisfaction to me that I was permitted for a time to be sufficiently near General Grant, not only to see the daily exercise of the noble characteristics for which he is honored by the world, but also some of the private virtues and qualities which make his death so crushing a blow to you and your children."[12]

Letters arrived from across the United States—they were notarized, typed on official stationery, and handwritten on rough paper; written by prominent officials and ordinary citizens, by patriotic and fraternal organizations, and by local governments; official and ceremonious as well as informal and sincere sentiments from regular people. Some included rolls of signatures in solidarity with the author's solemn proclamations and resolutions. From Iowa, the Woman's Relief Corps quoted scripture to comfort the widow.[13] From New Jersey, ten thousand people signed a resolution of sympathy from the Essex County Trades Assembly of Newark.[14] Condolences were also offered from the Ohio Association of Union Ex-Prisoners of War; the Knights of Pythias of the State of Pennsylvania; the Sons of Temperance; the Board of Indian Commissioners; and the National Tanners and Hide and Leather Dealers Association, which referred to Grant's "brief career as a tanner" when he worked with his father Jesse Root Grant.[15] Many of these were later compiled in a book bound in blue velvet by D. T. Ames & Company. The volume weighed in at a hefty thirty-five pounds and was later presented to the widow.[16]

Pastors across America feverishly rewrote their sermons to pay homage to the fallen hero at their Sunday, August 2 services. Each searched for a unique angle, and throngs crowded places of worship to hear their tributes and mourn in community. At the Spring Street Presbyterian Church, Reverend Woodruff Halsey's sermon was titled "Grant, the Ideal American." While the "typical American," Halsey preached, sought fortune and riches, he "will ruin us if we do not take care." Instead, proclaimed Halsey, his congregation should emulate Grant's "spirit of simplicity, of downright honesty, and of unflinching integrity." At the James Methodist Episcopal Church on Madison Avenue in New York City, Reverend Henry Baker focused on Grant's presidency and his ability to keep the post–Civil War peace after "Lincoln's pacific policy, cut short before proved, and four years of the crazy administration by Johnson."[17] Across the ocean, a service was held in Westminster Abbey in London. On his global tour, Grant's first stop was in England, and years later he still held a place in British hearts. Canon Frederic Farrar boasted that Grant preferred "a pair of shirt sleeves" to a coat of arms and added that he fought for "the unity of a great people, the freedom of a whole race."[18]

In addition to letters, floral arrangements arrived at the cottage in abundance. Some were sent by Grand Army of the Republic members, including a five-foot piece from the Meade Post of Philadelphia. Soldiers at Mount McGregor paid their respects and each day placed fresh flowers at the foot of the coffin. Soon the home overflowed, and the air filled with their pungent aroma.

In the South, citizens reacted to Grant's death with respect and reverence. At a Confederate reunion in Fort Worth, Texas, fifteen thousand people gathered for the event, which included a barbecue of twenty cattle and sixty lambs. In a speech at the opening ceremony, former Confederate States Secretary of the Treasury John H. Reagan reminded the crowd "to never forget the services he had rendered to the conquered soldiers of the South."[19] In Montgomery, Alabama, a reporter wrote, "No man since Washington has better illustrated the genius of American institutions or the temper of Americans as a people. The close of his military career was in a generous treatment of his fallen foe that sent a thrill of grateful recognition through the heart of the south."[20] Former Confederate President Jefferson Davis had wished Grant "repose of his mind and comfort of his body" in the missive sent before his death.[21] Davis was invited to a memorial service for Grant in New Orleans but declined, responding, "My health does not permit me to be present."[22] Confederate General James Longstreet added, "He was a great general, but the best thing about him was his heart."[23]

In Charleston, South Carolina, a reporter astutely observed, "Had his life ended but a few years since the mourning for the great leader would have been more or less sectional in its manifestation. Dying as he now dies, the grief is widespread as the Union, as the sorrow is as national as his fame."[24] This is a critical point about Grant's death. When Lincoln died, the Civil War was still being fought. It was a nation divided—his extraordinary twenty-day funeral pageant was witnessed, and Lincoln was mourned, only by Northerners. Through the next two decades, amid the tension and tragedy of

Grant's death in 1885 provided the perfect time and the ideal subject to usher in a national celebration of reunification. In this Puck *cartoon from August 5, 1885, the caption reads, "Peace, and the good will of all men." The wreaths placed by the statue of Grant read "Southern Soldiers" and "Northern Soldiers," and the one in the hands of the prostrate African American man reads, "Our Friend."* (Courtesy of the Library of Congress)

Reconstruction, Northern and Southern whites progressed slowly toward reunion. Grant's death in 1885 provided the perfect time and the ideal subject to usher in a national celebration of reunification. Consider the proclamation from Columbia, South Carolina, a city that burned to the ground after its surrender to Union forces in 1865: "The death of General Grant will be honestly felt as a national affliction all over the wide union without reference to section or party."[25]

Meanwhile, a week passed, and Grant's corpse was still in the cottage. The delay was not unexpected. Several weeks before his death, as Grant suffered in excruciating pain, he continued to anticipate his family's comfort and well-being. Should he die during the summer, Grant suggested his body remain at the cottage until the weather cooled, "to spare his family a sad and fatiguing journey in sultry weather."[26] But the more pertinent reason that the body was still at Mount McGregor was the lack of a burial location. Having avoided the subject during his illness, the family could no longer delay a decision.

Reporters asked Grant's friend, George W. Childs, if he knew of the intended burial place. He did not but added that Grant had told him years earlier he wished to be buried in West Point or at the Old Soldiers' Home in Washington, DC.[27] Indeed, an offer from Lieutenant General Philip Sheridan from the Old Soldiers' Home was sent the day of Grant's death, offering the grounds for burial.[28] Sheridan, whom Grant made commander of the Army of the Potomac's Cavalry Corps during the Civil War, proposed a "suitable spot for the final interment where the surroundings may be made in keeping with the grandeur of the character of the man whose remains are there left to repose."[29] The family, however, never seriously considered the offer. Grant was adamant he wanted to rest beside Julia, and women were forbidden to be buried at the Old Soldiers' Home. Another offer was made by city officials from Springfield, Illinois, where Abraham Lincoln's remains lie. In addition, the trustees of

Oakwood Cemetery in Troy, New York offered a plot overlooking the Hudson River.[30]

New York City mayor William Grace wasted no time and telegraphed the family at 1:00 p.m. on the day Grant died to make a play for his city. Grace was both the first Irish and first Catholic mayor of the city as well as an entrepreneur, a wealthy shipping magnate, and a conservative Democrat elected in the years after Tammany Hall corruption was exposed and its leader, William M. "Boss" Tweed, arrested. Mayor Grace immediately followed up on his telegram with a formal letter reiterating his offer, adding, "I might say, as a matter for your consideration, that the prominent height of Riverside Park, on the banks of the Hudson, has been suggested as an appropriate site for a great national monument which will undoubtedly be built."[31] This was the first suggestion of the little-known Riverside Park on the west side of Manhattan as Grant's final resting place. The narrow strip of land extended to 125th Street, miles beyond the cultural and residential heart of the city. Central Park, on the other hand, was only a minute's walk from the Grant's home on Sixty-Sixth Street. If it was to be New York City, the family had already assumed it would be Central Park.

Fred responded to the telegram, asking Mayor Grace to send a representative to the home to discuss the arrangements in person. The next day, chief clerk William L. Turner boarded a train for Mount McGregor. New Yorkers were confident, as the *Brooklyn Daily Eagle* boasted, "There is now little doubt that General Grant's remains will be buried in Central Park, New York."[32] As expected, the *New-York Tribune* offered an endorsement: "It is here in the vernal beauty of Central Park, [where the tomb would be] surrounded by the most peaceful and tender woodland scenery, yet lapt in the arms of this great population; here, where every holy day and holiday workingmen and women, in scores of thousands, will bring their children to gaze upon his monument, and will teach them the lesson of duty it imparts."[33] Central Park, designed in the 1850s and completed in 1876, was frequented by New York's elite. Grant himself very much enjoyed visiting the park and spending time with people there. Other suggestions were offered, including a few who preferred Union Square.[34] Even some who agreed with the mayor's proposal of Riverside Park offered specific recommendations, including one who suggested between Seventy-Ninth and Eighty-Fourth streets for its "esthetic, artistic, and practical" assets.[35] In short, almost everyone had an opinion about the matter.

Julia's primary concern, like her husband's, was that they be permitted to rest side by side in death. This caused a delay for several days, since Grace's proposal was for Grant's remains only. The requirement was well publicized before Grant's death, and it is surprising that Grace had not addressed it previously. But after some administrative formalities, the matter was resolved when Park Commissioner John D. Crimmins approved the request on July 27. That same day, Fred departed for New York City.

New York City in 1885 was much different than the city it would become, but the seeds of growth were already bearing fruit. A post–Civil War boom had solidified New York's claim as the business capital of America, and recent years had seen many companies settle in the city. To meet the real estate demands, "there was a dramatic enlargement—both horizontally and vertically—of the city's business district." "Sky buildings" were pushing the city architecture farther and farther into the air. Recently completed buildings like the Produce Exchange at Bowling Green Park and the headquarters of the Standard Oil Trust at 22–24 Broadway towered ten stories tall.[36] The city was by far the largest in America, with a population of 1.4 million souls (compared with about one million in Philadelphia). While the privileged few Gilded Age luminaries lived in mansions along Fifth Avenue as far north as the upper fifties, most of the population, including hundreds of thousands of recent immigrants who sought opportunity in America, having recently arrived from Germany, Ireland, Russia, Greece, and Italy, were crammed downtown, many in overcrowded tenement buildings. The oasis in the middle of this hustle and bustle of city streets was the bucolic 842-acre Central Park, which stretched from Fifty-Ninth Street to 110th Street and from Fifth Avenue to Eighth Avenue.

While the family preferred Central Park for Grant's final resting place, they were open to other locations. Before he departed, Julia gave Fred instructions: if the group came to an agreement on a location, he was empowered to commit on behalf of the family.[37] Mayor Grace and the commissioners took Fred to see three sites within Central Park. Accompanying them were Horace Porter, General William Tecumseh Sherman, and former Colorado senator and Buck's father-in-law, Jerome B. Chaffee.[38] The first location they reviewed was near the Fifty-Ninth Street entrance to Central Park, but Fred rejected the busy location. They next traveled to an area known as "The Mall," a beautiful parcel in the middle of Central Park that spans Sixty-Sixth to Seventieth streets (it is also the only straight path in the park). Dense with flora, the parcel was shadowed by a canopy of American elm trees. This was nearest to Grant's home and most favored by the family. But Fred was dissuaded by Mayor Grace, who felt the full-growth horticulture would force designers to integrate the memorial into its surroundings as opposed to a more barren landscape, where they would have freer rein. The group continued north to Watch Hill on the west side near Eighth Avenue by 106th Street (today called the Great Hill). It was—and still is—one of the more beautiful locales in Central Park. Fred ascended the hill to get a firsthand look at the view and spotted a building under construction on the perimeter of the park. He asked what it was and was told it was New York Cancer Hospital. An awkward view indeed, and Fred pondered aloud how it might feel for a patient to look out their window and see the tomb of a man who had succumbed to the very disease they were fighting. With that, Watch Hill was swiftly eliminated from consideration.

After Central Park, the contingent continued to the northern end of Riverside Park, a relatively new park designed by Frederick Law Olmsted in 1873. It encompassed a strip of land along the Hudson River from Seventy-Second to 125th Streets. The group stopped at 122nd Street. It was unarguably a scenic location on the West Side of upper Manhattan, but twelve years after the park was formed, the site was still undeveloped. However, Grace argued, the barren landscape provided designers a clean slate to create a memorial that would not need to conform with its surroundings. He noted its prominent height and location on the banks of the Hudson and added that it would make "an appropriate site for a great national monument." In addition, while Central Park was a completed work, Riverside was a blank canvas "hardly touched by art."[39] Mayor Grace concluded, "Everything must be subordinated in order to give it a commanding effect."[40]

After viewing the site, the group ate dinner and then returned south back through Central Park. They stopped at Belvedere Castle, in the middle of the park at Seventy-Ninth Street, to review the site for a temporary tomb location. The whimsical structure was designed in 1865 by British architects Calvert Vaux, who taught Frederick Law Olmsted, and Jacob Wrey Mould, who at the time was an assistant New York City architect. *Belvedere*, Italian for "beautiful view," was "intended to be a Victorian Folly, a fantasy structure that provides a great backdrop and views, but without a real intended purpose."[41] After the tour was concluded, Fred boarded a train and returned to Mount McGregor without having committed to any site.

Riverside Park was favored by many of the city's politicians and businessmen, who aggressively lobbied for Grant to be buried there. The *New York Times* suggested that it "will probably be rechristened" as "Grant Park." As the population of New York continued to move north, the newspaper predicted Riverside Park "will soon be virtually in the heart of the city, while Central Park . . . will no longer be uptown."[42] Commissioner Crimmins proudly suggested that the

"park is growing in popularity every year, and in a short time promises to take the place of Central [Park]."[43] The family, however, was
unconvinced. Riverside Park was hardly a household name. Indeed,
as was written at the time, "'Where is Riverside Park?' was the
question asked by thousands of New York's own intelligent citizens
. . . and outside of the city this park was a myth."[44]

The question was a valid one. Modern-day readers would find it
difficult to imagine the New York landscape of the 1880s. Riverside
Park lies six miles north of the downtown southern tip of Manhattan
Island, where much of the population was crammed. The park is
located on the western shore of the island on the Hudson River.
To the east, the island extends for approximately two miles to the
banks of the Harlem River. Indeed, the site chosen for Grant's Tomb
was relatively remote in addition to being largely undeveloped, and
even today is an area where few tourists venture. Standing on the
highest point of the park, which would eventually be the site of the
tomb, one could see New Jersey to the west and to the east an unob-
structed view of the Long Island Sound, as few buildings had been
erected along the expanse. As the mayor had, one reporter suggested
the barren landscape would prove an asset, as "the proposed monument will be exceptionally conspicuous from many points of view,
while opportunity for the display of taste in ornamental terraces and
grounds about it is unequaled."[45]

Back in Mount McGregor, Fred laid out maps and described the
options to his family. They weighed multiple factors: Julia could rest
by her husband's side when she died; it would be easy for family and
the public to visit; the city official's prompt and aggressive offer; and
it was, of course, one of the sites that Grant himself had requested.

The next afternoon, July 28, Fred sent Mayor Grace a curt telegraph. It read: "W. A. Grace. New York: Mother takes Riverside.
The temporary tomb had better be in the same place. F. D. Grant."[46]

4

"A Colossal and Memorable Demonstration"

Shortly after the Grant family telegraphed Mayor Grace to accept Riverside for the tomb, their decision was made public. There were immediate outcries in opposition. The most vocal dissenters came from people in Washington, DC, who believed Grant's remains belonged in a location of national distinction. New York, they argued, was not representative of the entire country and did not have sufficient national identity. Other protesters accepted New York but did not agree with Riverside Park as the location.[1] One Baptist minister asked how Grant could be buried "in the most unsuitable of places—a pleasure park, where gaiety and abandon abound?"[2] Reverend John P. Newman, a family confidant, publicly expressed his disappointment and lamented, "Oh. It is such a lonely place there; and he was thoroughly a man of the people."[3] Many held out hopes that the family would reconsider, and telegrams arrived at Mount McGregor urging them to do so. An appeal was made to George W. Childs to travel to Mount McGregor and intervene with the family's decision. Childs diplomatically responded to their plea: "The family, as well as all the intimate friends, have received numerous letters from army and navy officers urging Washington as the proper place; but Riverside Park has been selected and there is no probability of a change." He then added, "It is a delicate matter to discuss with the family, and I think nothing more should be said on the subject."[4]

In the days after the decision was made, however, there were also scattered voices of support from across the country. From Chicago, an editorial from the *Inter Ocean* newspaper praised New York in that they "bid high in testimony of appreciation and in evidence of warmest affection for the right to name his burial place." The reporter added, "It is not inappropriate that Grant's remains should rest in the metropolis of the nation."[5] From Boston, a reporter from the *Traveler* called Washington, DC's claim disingenuous and argued, "We have no historic burial place at the national capital like to that which the English in London have Westminster Abbey."[6] Indeed, even to this day, only President Woodrow Wilson is interred in Washington, DC. These few voices of support outside of New York, however, would soon be drowned out by the more vocal opposition.

With Riverside Park chosen, plans could proceed to remove Grant's body from Mount McGregor. Denied a national tomb, President Cleveland was eager to have a national funeral, similar to those of Lincoln and Garfield. The president assigned Major General Winfield Scott Hancock to travel to Mount McGregor and assist the family with the arrangements. Hancock's responsibilities included the solemn task of transporting the body back to New York City and organizing the funeral events.[7] Hancock had first met Grant when the two were students at West Point Military Academy (Grant was one year ahead of Hancock, who graduated in 1844). He was known as "Hancock the Superb" due to his handsome appearance and striking features, gained national fame at the Battle of Gettysburg in 1863, and was nominated by the Democratic Party to run for president in 1880.

Grant's death is often celebrated as ushering in a spirit of reunification between Northerners and Southerners, but what is often overlooked is how his passing also brought about, albeit temporarily, a convergence of people across the political divide, unified in their obligation to the nation and respect for Grant. During Hancock's 1880 presidential run, Grant actively campaigned against him and instead supported another Civil War figure, the Republican candidate James Garfield, who won the election by a narrow margin.[8] For the Democratic Party, retaining white supremacy in the South, which had been achieved after the end of military Reconstruction, remained an imperative if not explicitly a plank in the party platform.[9]

The responsibility for the funeral arrangements were assigned to the "tall and gaunt" Major General Alexander Shaler.[10] First there would be a public viewing in the state capital of Albany, followed by a massive public demonstration in New York City. In the meantime, Hancock stationed a guard of honor at Mount McGregor under the command of Colonel Roger Jones. Fred had assigned special responsibilities to the Grand Army Post 327 of Brooklyn and notified Jones of their privileged role. They were one of the last groups that Grant had met with when he reviewed them on Decoration Day the previous year while on crutches. (At the event, daughters of the veterans presented flowers to Grant, who "accepted the gift, with thanks, and kissed the six young ladies."[11]) The day Grant died, the veterans met to formally rename their group to U. S. Grant Post 327. Thirteen of the members were assigned by Fred as special honor guard for the duration of the funeral.[12] In appreciation of their "prompt kindness," the Saratoga Wheeler Grand Army Post was also assigned a special responsibility.[13] While the Brooklyn group was granted access to the cottage, the Wheeler Post veterans were assigned porch detail.

On the afternoon of Monday, August 3, Reverend Newman conducted a small memorial service in the home. He read from the book of Job: "Because thou shall forget thy misery, and remember it as water that pass away."[14] That same day, Major General Hancock arrived at Mount McGregor with eight hundred National Guardsmen.

The next morning, August 4, began as overcast and rain appeared imminent, but the sun soon broke through the clouds and brought with it a picture-perfect day. At long last, twelve days after Grant's death, the public memorial was underway. At about 9:00 a.m.,

General Hancock arrived at the cottage and Fred ushered him inside. Thirty minutes later, the doors were opened, and the public entered to pay their respects. It was a brief period of public display, and by 10:00 a.m. the doors were closed. A funeral service followed before a crowd of a thousand people on the lawn. Some had traveled for hundreds of miles, including Grant's friend and aide-de-camp, Horace Porter, who took a seat on the porch beside General Sherman and Chief Quartermaster of the Army of the Potomac Rufus Ingalls.[15] After Psalm 90 was read, Bishop W. L. Harris of the Methodist Episcopal Church of New York said a prayer and was followed by the hymn, "My Faith Looks Up to Thee." Reverend Newman, who had been working on his sermon for several days, quoted from Matthew: "Well done, thou good and faithful servant, enter thou into the joy of thy Lord." The brief ceremony was done.

The thirteen honored members of the Brooklyn U. S. Grant Post hoisted the coffin and solemnly marched to the train station. As the procession passed, people respectfully doffed their hats. Julia remained inside the Mount McGregor home. She was too distraught to leave the cottage but was also adhering to a Victorian custom. Just like Mary Todd Lincoln, Julia would not attend any of the public bereavement ceremonies for her beloved husband. Instead, she remained in the comfort and solitude of the Mount McGregor cottage, finally departing at 11:30 a.m. on August 31, more than three weeks after Grant's funeral.[16]

At 1:00 p.m., soldiers fired their guns in salute as the engineer, Martin, started the seven-car train and it slowly departed Mount McGregor. People stood by the tracks to watch as it slowly passed. The train arrived in Saratoga Springs a half hour later. At the request of the family, the coffin was removed by an honor guard without ceremony or fanfare and transferred to the nearby New York Central Railroad line. The pallbearers placed it on a catafalque inside a special funeral car, the *Woodlawn*.[17] The car was draped in mourning and adorned with an American flag. Dignitaries including New

York governor David Bennett Hill filled the seven cars behind the *Woodlawn*. Shortly after 2:00 p.m., Thornton gave the signal and the funeral train began to chug slowly south. Crowds of people had gathered along the route to pay their respects.[18]

The presidential funeral train was a tradition that dated back to John Quincy Adams's death in 1848.[19] It afforded a personal way for those unable to attend ceremonies in the cities to pay their respects. Beside the tracks, they wept, prayed, sang hymns, and caught a fleeting glimpse of the funeral car that held Grant's remains. The forty-mile journey was completed in a little over an hour and a half, and the train pulled into Albany at 3:40 p.m.

Pallbearers removed the coffin and placed it on an ornate caisson drawn by six black horses, each led by an honorary member from GAR Posts 5 and 21. A procession of four thousand marchers included police, members of Fifth Artillery and the Company E Infantry, and nine hundred members of the Grand Army of the Republic. They wound through the city; Spencer Street to North Pearl Street, State Street, Eagle Street, Washington Street, Knox Street, and then back on State Street to the Capitol building. The throngs of people that crowded the parade route prompted concerns for a city that had a population of only 93,000 at the time. One newspaper warned, "Thieves and pickpockets are said to be here in countless numbers." But the police were also prepared, and few incidents were reported.

The coffin was placed in the Senate chamber on an impressive catafalque. Within the previous few days, a canopy had been built over the catafalque and the room draped in black crepe. Overhead, eight electric lights were hung, each with the power to "give a flood of light of the magnitude of 320 candles."[20]

The Merritt undertakers opened the coffin to review the body before allowing the public inside for an open-casket viewing. It would be the first test for Merritt's skills as embalmers. The practice dated back five thousand years to the ancient Egyptians, who

STEPHEN MERRITT BURIAL CO.,

241-243 West 23d St.,

New York City.

Undertak-
ers. ☩
Embalm-
ers, and ☩
Funeral
Directors.

REV. STEPHEN MERRITT,
President of the Stephen Merritt Burial Co.

The Largest, Most Magnificent and Complete Undertaking
Establishment on this Continent.

Elegant and Commodious Funeral Parlors for the Use of
Our Patrons.

Clerical and Musical Attendance Provided, when Desired.

The Best Service and Equipment in All Departments.

- - MODERATE CHARGES. - -

Special and Prompt Attention Given to All Calls whether Day
or Night, in City or in the Suburbs.

Business done in all parts of the U. S. and Canada and in Europe

OPEN ALL NIGHT AS WELL AS DAY.

Telephone 14—18th Street. Cable—Undertaker, New York

*Advertisement for the Stephen Merritt Burial Co.
Merritt was hired to handle the burial arrangements,
including embalming Grant's body. Decades later
they would proudly proclaim in their advertising,
"We Conducted His Funeral!" beneath a picture of
Grant's Tomb. (From* Monthly Echo of the Original
5 Points Mission, *August 1898)*

sought to preserve the bodies for the afterlife. During the Civil
War, embalming had become a widely used method to help preserve fallen soldiers' remains so they could be returned home from
the battlefield (it also became a highly profitable business). After
Abraham Lincoln was assassinated in 1865, he became the first president to be embalmed, and his remains were put on public display
for a spectacular twenty-day pageant that covered 1,700 miles from
Washington, DC, to Springfield, Illinois, with public open-casket
viewings held in major cities along the way. It had not gone well.

When his remains were put on display in New York City Hall, where Grant would lie in state the following day, a repulsed reporter noted, "The discolored face of the President was not desirable. . . . The features were so very unnatural, the color so thoroughly turned, and the general appearance so unpleasant, that none could regard the remains with even a melancholy pleasure."[21]

Now Grant's funeral directors faced a similar challenge, as seventeen days would elapse from death until placement in a temporary crypt, during which time hundreds of thousands would get a close-up view of their handiwork. By 1885, the practice of embalming had improved, but it was still not perfected, and perhaps even for the most talented of embalmers, making Grant's cancer-riddled remains presentable was too tall a task.

When they opened the casket, the startled funeral directors discovered, "the body had been so jarred by the journey over the pavements that it had been disarranged and the features were almost repulsive."[22] For twenty minutes they toiled before they placed a plate glass over the remains. General Sherman and Governor Hill stepped inside to spend a few moments beside the coffin in private, followed by a score of Albany officials and dignitaries. At 6:45 p.m., the doors were opened and the public surged inside. Despite Merritt's efforts, many were repulsed by what they saw. A horrified reporter for the *Ithaca Democrat* wrote, "The appearance of the remains was not natural. The skin of the face has the appearance of having been enameled in a bungling manner. The skin is a ghastly hue and has a scaly appearance." The reporter placed blame on Merritt's men: "The face was powdered without reference to the probable effect of the brilliant light to which the remains were subjected."[23]

Almost as soon as the doors were opened, dark clouds gathered overhead, a strong wind prevailed, and a light rain began to fall. But the sizable crowd was undeterred. In the first hour, 7,400 people somberly shuffled past on both sides of the coffin. If someone dallied, honor guardsmen from the U. S. Grant Post coaxed them along. At 9:00 p.m., the crowd was held back for a few moments to allow Grant's sons, Governor Hill, and Dr. Douglas to view the remains. Throughout the night into the early hours of Wednesday, August 5, the crowds continued unabated. The *Brooklyn Daily Eagle* reported: "all callings and all conditions of life were represented, but all were decorous and orderly, and all were decently attired." Some came with babies in arms or little children by the hand to show them the face of the American hero.[24] At midnight, three hundred German singers serenaded the mourners waiting outside. At 1:00 a.m. the line began to thin and then slowed to a trickle.

As the dark sky began to lighten, a few early risers joined the line of mourners, including farmers who had just arrived from the countryside. Starting at sunrise, cannons were fired every half hour. By 6:00 a.m. the count reached 51,200 mourners, and when the doors closed at 10:30 a.m., 77,200 people had viewed the remains.[25] The caretakers then tended to Grant's body once again. Aware of the startled complaints from the night before, they judiciously toiled to make Grant more presentable. Albany was just the opening act; the main event was in New York City later that day.

At 11:30 a.m., August 5, the guard of honor carried the coffin outside. It was a bright, clear, but intensely hot day, and businesses had closed throughout Albany for the occasion. Trumpeters played a solemn dirge as the pallbearers slowly descended the steps. They placed the coffin into the funeral carriage as guns boomed. A massive crowd watched a military procession of 6,400 veterans march down State Street to Broadway to Steuben Street. Thousands crowded the Albany Central Depot and nearby rooftops were filled with people who watched the honor guard place the casket onto the funeral train. The Jackson Corps played a solemn dirge and a thirty-eight-gun salute was fired as the train slowly departed south to New York City.

The train rolled through Poughkeepsie at 2:45 p.m., passing

dozens of New York Central Railroad workers with their hats in hand. Surely they had gathered out of respect for Grant, but it also happened to be payday, and many had come to pick up their checks. Among them was a single elderly veteran with one leg who bowed his head as the train passed. Traveling through Fishkill at 3:11 p.m., the train slowly rolled over coins on the tracks, placed by people seeking a flattened keepsake. Ten minutes later the train passed through Cold Spring. At 3:27 p.m. it rolled through Grant's alma mater, West Point Military Academy. Soldiers fired their guns every five seconds, cadets presented arms, and officers stood bareheaded to salute their greatest alumnus.[26]

Finally in New York City, the train passed through Harlem at 4:48 p.m., and precisely at 5:00 p.m., right on schedule, it pulled into Grand Central Station. Church bells pealed throughout the city to announce the arrival of Grant's funeral train. Minutes earlier, there had been a driving rain, but as soon as the train arrived, the skies cleared and dark clouds dissipated. Surely, most witnesses surmised, the sudden change in weather was a sign of providence. The coffin was transferred onto a funeral hearse and set beneath a canopy topped with ornate black plumes that peaked seventeen feet in the air. The elaborate hearse was draped in black and pulled by twelve horses, each led by an African American groom. To avoid the horses running off with the coffin, the hearse was weighed down with three tons of pig iron ballast. General Hancock gave the order at 5:30 p.m., and the marchers began a slow walk. The parade was led by mounted police and included two companies of Marines and eight regiments of soldiers. Members of the Fifth Artillery Company A and Twelfth Infantry Company E marched before the hearse. Following the hearse walked the undertaker Merritt, "his clerical dress attracting much attention."[27] Along the route, troops lined Fifth Avenue on both sides, and as the hearse passed a church its bells tolled.[28] The marchers passed flags at half-mast and stores draped in black. At Forty-Third Street and Fifth

Avenue additional marchers joined the procession. Crowds packed the streets, people looked out every available window, and some scaled lamp and telegraph posts for a better view. Those in the crowd chatted eagerly but fell silent when the hearse passed. As they stood still and watched respectfully, the only sounds that could be heard were boots on the cobblestone and the solemn dirges. At Twelfth Street, about a dozen African American bystanders joined the marchers from the sidelines. As they were not part of the official procession, police removed them and disbanded their spontaneous demonstration of affection.[29]

The closed coffin in New York City Hall after the first day's public viewing. Image by "Hugh Montgomery Hill," and the caption reads, "Made by electric light, 1 a.m., Aug. 6." (Courtesy of the National Park Service, Manhattan Historic Sites Archive)

Thousands had gathered at City Hall to await the arrival of the procession. Much like the rest of the New York's government buildings, City Hall had been decorated in solemn mourning. City commissioner of public works Rollin M. Squire oversaw the decorations, for which he contracted the Unexcelled Fireworks Company. One adornment he adamantly insisted upon was a display that featured lines from a poem about Grant. When the cortege arrived at 7:00 p.m., night had fallen, and the large crowds had created a dangerous and confusing scene. In the melee, women and children were crushed and "screamed aloud from pain or fright."[30]

The casket was unfastened from the catafalque and carried inside. The driver departed, but a moment later, a plume, caught in an overhead electric wire, detached and fell to the ground. The overzealous crowd scrambled for the treasure, but a groom picked up the plume before it could be appropriated. The plume was the first sought prize of the "relic hunters" who enthusiastically tried to abscond with anything related to the death of Grant, sometimes resorting to extreme, illegal, and bizarre measures to obtain their plunder.

Inside City Hall, the coffin was set on the same catafalque used in Mount McGregor, which had arrived earlier that day. A wreath of oak leaves that Grant's granddaughter Julia had made at Mount McGregor was placed upon it. The coffin sat in the corridor beneath heavy black drapes, "making it seem like a giant tent."[31] Electric lights were hung to allow mourners to see Grant's features. A massive guard of honor, including fifty New York policemen, protected the remains. Mayor Grace, who must have beamed with pride at the fruits of his hard work and persistent efforts, was present to formally receive the remains. After the transfer ceremony, the coffin was removed to the Board of Aldermen room. Inside, undertaker Merritt once again inspected the body. He found the face to be "very hard and very pale, but in an excellent state of preservation, only a slight discoloration being noticeable around the eyes."[32] Merritt applied marble powder to smooth over the imperfections and only after he was satisfied did he consent to an open-casket viewing. The coffin was returned to the vestibule, where it was adorned with elaborate floral arrangements. Grant was not the first deceased president whose remains were viewed by the public in New York City

Hall, having been preceded by James Monroe in 1858 and Abraham Lincoln in 1865. To date, however, he would be the last.

At 9:00 p.m., New York Superintendent Murray bellowed, "Let them come in!" The doors were opened, and people shuffled past the coffin over a rubber mat to deaden the sound. Mourners came from all walks of life. The *New York Times* colorfully described them to include "Chinamen, colored men . . . young men with their sweethearts, young girls without escorts and lonely looking matrons." In later hours the crowds also featured "bootblacks with their boxes swung over their shoulder" and "newsboys with unsold papers under their arms." The *Times* also identified those who came from outside the city by their "countrified headgear" and expressed amusement that they "were slow to fully comprehend the preemptory orders of the police."[33] At midnight the lines were halted for a few minutes when an electric light burned out and the noxious smell of carbon filled the air. At 1:00 a.m. the doors closed to the public. In those four hours, 40,000 people had viewed the remains, including "special mourners" sent by the Army of the Potomac, who had included fellow West Point graduate Abner Doubleday.[34] After the last of the public departed, the U. S. Grant Post took over as honor guard for the evening.

On Thursday, August 6, the public viewing began at 6:00 a.m. Inside the hall, mourners passed a fifteen-foot-tall "superstructure" floral arrangement, a gift from the city council that had been brought in overnight.[35] There was one additional change to City Hall's decor. Someone had discovered that the verses hung at the city commissioner's insistence were actually from Squire's own poem "War and Freedom," which he had written twenty years earlier. New York residents were infuriated, officials were embarrassed, and Squire's egregious self-promotion had been removed.[36] By the end of the day, another 150,000 people had viewed the remains. On Friday, a hundred thousand more paid their respects as the public viewing came to an end. All told, almost 300,000 people had solemnly walked past Grant's remains.

Saturday, August 8, was mild and sunny, ideal for a funeral procession. Throughout the city, businesses were closed and buildings adorned in mourning, including the United States Treasury;
the Stock Exchange; Brown Brothers; Mills Building; and the
Incandescent Gas Light and Fuel building, which was fronted with
a two-story black curtain with thirty-one stars that spelled out "His
Name and Fame Will Abide Forever."[37] Some reporters judged the
quality of the decor as if it were a competition (the Herald Building,
for instance, was criticized as "sloppy").[38] Private residences were
also decorated in mourning. The displays of grief were most sincere

*On the day of Grant's funeral, buildings throughout New
York City were decorated in mourning. The Incandescent
Gas Light and Fuel Company is covered in black bunting
and thirty-one stars that spell out "His Name and Fame Will
Abide Forever." (Courtesy of the National Park Service,
Manhattan Historic Sites Archive)*

and heartfelt in the homes of the poorer residents. In the sparsely populated area in the upper west side of the city, it was reported that a "poor colored boot-black" hung a roughly painted sign that read, HE HELPED TO SET ME FREE.[39] This humble man powerfully expressed the appreciation many African Americans held for Grant. Not only did he provide the military fortitude to win the Civil War, but he also fought the Ku Klux Klan just as vigorously during his presidency. Renowned abolitionist Frederick Douglass had praised Grant: "In him the negro found a protector, the Indian a friend, a vanquished foe a brother, and imperiled nation a savior."[40]

Houses of the well-to-do were often left unadorned, however, since their owners were away at their summer vacation homes. While many New Yorkers had bought their somber decorations once they had learned that burial would be in their city, others—both optimists and pragmatists—had made their purchases months earlier. Even if Grant was buried in another city, they would not go to waste. Across the nation, buildings were adorned with similar decorations of mourning, including the McLean house at Appomattox, where Grant accepted Lee's surrender.

The funeral brought a significant boost to the New York economy. Hotels were booked, restaurants ran a brisk business, and entrepreneurs sold trinkets, including black mourning ribbons, Grant busts, and other assorted tokens. The day marks the first instance of such mass commercialism at a presidential funeral. There were a few entrepreneurs in 1865 at Lincoln's twenty-day pageant and in 1881 at Garfield's funeral, but decorum for the murdered presidents kept many salesmen at bay. Other presidents who had died in recent years—James Buchanan (1868), Franklin Pierce (1869), Millard Fillmore (1874), and Andrew Johnson (1875)—did not generate the patriotism, enthusiasm, or commercialism to motivate vendors to set up shop. The combination of Grant as an iconic figure in American history; his expected, albeit tragic, death; a funeral in the most populated, and most popular, city in America; and the length of time vendors had to prepare for the event after Grant's death gave New York merchants license to put out their wares and profit handsomely.

Benches were erected, and seats were on sale along the funeral procession route, some for as much as $5, a handsome sum at a time when the annual average salary was approximately $400.[41] But the entrepreneurs overestimated demand and many parade viewers preferred to stand, leaving rows of unsold seats.

The day featured more gestures of reconciliation, including one from the highest levels of the military. General Hancock asked Robert E. Lee's nephew, Virginia governor General Fitzhugh Lee, to serve as his aide. "I accept the position," replied Lee, explaining, "because by doing so, I can testify my respect for the memory of a great soldier and thus return, as far as I can, the generous feelings he has expressed towards the soldiers of the south."[42] Fred also asked two ex-Confederate generals to serve as pallbearers, Simon Bolivar Buckner and Joseph Johnston. In his final days, Grant had spoken fondly of both men. Johnston, he noted, "showed wonderful ability," while Grant "always had a good word" for his "old-time friend" Buckner, who had visited Grant at Mount McGregor.[43] The Confederate general's jet-black hair and mustache had turned white with age, and reporters noted Buckner "had grown fleshy as of late." Perhaps tired of answering the repeated question of why he was serving as pallbearer, he released a statement to explain his decision: "He was a great soldier. He possessed the qualities which mark the man of 'stern stuff.' He was persevering, tenacious, and kept right ahead. When he thought he was right, he could not be moved." Buckner added, "I go to bury him as one of the Nation's great men."[44] On the day of the funeral, both Buckner and Johnston wore their Confederate gray uniforms with unabashed pride. The remainder of the pallbearers—Union Generals William Tecumseh Sherman and Philip Sheridan; Grant's former cabinet members, Secretary of State Hamilton Fish and Secretary of the Treasury George S. Boutwell; Navy Admiral David D. Porter; Vice Admiral

Stephen C. Rowan; George W. Childs; senator from Illinois John A. Logan; George Jones; and former member of the Connecticut State Senate (1877 to 1881) Oliver Hoyt—were selected by President Cleveland and Julia.[45] The men carried the coffin outside and placed it on the hearse beneath a black canopy and upon a large catafalque high enough to permit those in the crowd to see it. The hearse was an impressive spectacle. In the driver's seat was Albert Hawkins, an African American coachman who had managed the stables at Grant's White House. But this hearse was unlike anything Hawkins had driven before. Almost seven decades after the funeral, Merritt revealed that they used an Ehret's Brewery truck covered in black crepe. The hearse, the same one used three days earlier to transport the body to City Hall, was pulled by twenty-four Ehret's Brewery horses, each led by an African American groom dressed in black. With the increased horsepower (only twelve horses were used to pull the carriage to City Hall), ten tons of pig iron were now required as ballast to keep the horses from stampeding off with the president's body.[46] Flanking the hearse was the ever-present U. S. Grant Post, who had served as honor guard since Mount McGregor.

At 9:00 a.m., a howitzer was fired, and military bands started to play Schubert's "Geisterchor." At 9:30 a.m., thanks to arrangements made by Western Union, church bells pealed not only in New York, but across the United States at the same moment to usher in the day's solemn activities. General Hancock bellowed, "Forward march!" and the procession departed City Hall. The sea of humanity was enormous. Patriotic and military groups had contacted General Hancock and Fred for permission to participate, including the courageous and flamboyant Duryea Zouaves of the 5th New York Volunteer Infantry. An impressive 60,000 people marched, including 8,000 city workers led by Mayor Grace, dozens of military units, and 18,000 members of the Grand Army of the Republic.[47] They included Marines, Navy, National Guard, Fort Sumter veterans, the Old 79th Highlanders with bagpipes in hand, and regiments from as far away as California.

Some carried instruments, some held armaments, and some had howitzers or Gatling guns. But it was not a haphazard affair, and each unit marched lockstep in formation, and in full regalia, behind officers on horseback. The impressive spectacle of military forces was the largest ever gathered in United States history in peacetime.

Since the founding of the United States, presidential deaths have been used as an opportunity for reconciliation and reunification. When George Washington died on December 14, 1799, the young country was fractured in social upheaval that resulted in the unanticipated formation of political parties. Americans retreated into separate corners: the Federalist Party led by Alexander Hamilton and the Democrat-Republicans led by Thomas Jefferson. Washington's death, mourned across the nation, was a moment for citizens to briefly remember their common heritage and recall Washington's own words from his farewell address warning of the danger of political factions. When Andrew Jackson died in 1845, the divisions between the North and South over slavery and western expansion were escalating. Jackson's words from the 1832 South Carolina nullification crisis were repeated throughout the period of national mourning: "Our Federal Union Must Be Preserved." And only four years before the death of Grant, another Civil War veteran who became president, James Garfield, died. At the time, the Republican Party was divided over political patronage jobs. Garfield supported federal positions based on merit, but the opposition, including his vice president, Chester Arthur, backed a spoils system in which federal jobs were given out to individuals, many grossly unqualified, as a reward for their past political and financial support and to ensure their future support and payments. When Garfield died two and a half months after he was shot, President Arthur went against all expectations of mediocrity and conformity and supported the Pendleton Act, which was a major step of civil service reform.

More examples of national reconciliation following a president's demise can be cited from the years after 1885, but no president has ever brought the country together through his death more than Grant. The most visceral display of reunification was witnessed by thousands in the funeral procession, when Confederate veterans including the Richmond Grays, the Walker Light Guards, and the Stonewall Brigade walked side by side with their former Union adversaries. An astonished reporter noted: "Troops from Virginia and Georgia marched in successive files with the troops from Massachusetts, Minnesota, Connecticut, and the District of Columbia."[48] The symbolism was palpable. In the newspaper accounts of the event, there is no bitterness or vindictiveness in the reporting. Indeed, the *New York Times* declared, "These visible evidences that the war is over will have weight in every household in the land."[49] Seen on banners throughout the city and cited in speeches across the country was Grant's phrase, "Let Us Have Peace." While he had uttered no final words of solace or inspiration at Mount McGregor, a public who yearned to heal the wounds of the Civil War provided Grant the last words they wished he had said.

The procession marched north on Broadway. In addition to the seven miles from Lower Manhattan to Riverside Park, the marchers had to contend with unpaved roads and cobblestone streets in poor condition, often with trolley tracks embedded in them. A decade after the funeral, little had improved when Rudyard Kipling lamented New York was "bad in its paving [and] bad in its streets."[50] At Union Square, the procession turned east onto Fourteenth Street. The crowd of ten thousand was silent as the hearse passed by. The only voice, according to the *Brooklyn Daily Eagle*, was an enterprising "stout young boy yelling 'Lemonade; two cents a glass.'" The reporter added tongue-in-cheek, "No one tried to quiet him. He had the right of way and no one questioned his authority."[51] It is worth noting that silence in New York was different in 1885 than it is today. Even if everyone stood quiet in Union Square on a crowded summer day today, there would still be background noises of automobiles, air conditioners, fans, and airplanes overhead. Even from beneath the streets, noise emanates from passing subway cars. But in 1885 no such white noise existed. The silence experienced when Grant's funeral hearse passed is difficult to fathom today.

The procession continued north on Fifth Avenue and passed the Fifth Avenue Hotel at Twenty-Third Street, where the Grants had lived when they arrived in the city years earlier. Several distinguished guests in town for the funeral were staying there, including President Cleveland, Vice President Thomas Andrews Hendricks, and former presidents Rutherford B. Hayes and Chester Arthur.[52] Hayes and Arthur sat together in a room on the southeast corner of the hotel, or, as Hayes called it, "the ex-presidents room," which afforded a good view of the procession. After about three hours. the dignitaries joined the procession.[53] The parade continued north past the mansions that lined Fifth Avenue. At Forty-Second Street it passed the Croton Distributing Reservoir. Years earlier, the fifty-foot-tall Egyptian structure had held twenty million gallons and supplied water to the city residents, but by 1885 it was no longer in use. At Fiftieth Street the procession passed St. Patrick's Cathedral, which had been dedicated only six years earlier.

The Gilded Age had seen the literal and figurative rise of New York City. Buildings had been constructed taller during the past several years, some towering over ten stories. The telephone had gained wide usage since Alexander Graham Bell exhibited his invention at the Centennial Exhibition in Philadelphia in June 1876; uneven telephone poles and a patchwork of wires hung above the city streets. Crowds stood shoulder to shoulder on the sidewalks, and some brave souls perched atop the poles for a bird's-eye view.[54] The city had changed in other ways besides architecture and infrastructure. During the past two decades, there was an immigration wave from European countries such as Italy, Greece, and Turkey. By 1885, approximately half the population of the city were not born in America. These new immigrants stood among native-born New Yorkers to watch the seven-mile procession. Since the rise of immigration in past years, ceremonies to commemorate the presidents, whether for the dedication of monuments or for funerals, were an opportunity for the newcomers both to embrace their newfound American patriotism and to be criticized as outsiders on the perimeters of American society. Two years earlier, at the dedication of a statue of George Washington at Federal Hall, a reporter for *Harper's Weekly* claimed such celebrations had "an electric national appeal of great national anniversaries, which brings homogeneous communities to their feet with pride and joy." The same reporter also lamented that the spirit of patriotism in a city of immigrants, particularly Irish, "will be wanting here."[55]

But these events could also prove surprisingly unifying. A week later, a *Harper's Weekly* reporter observed that the festivities "would have impressed the importance of the event celebrated upon every man and women native born or foreign" and wondered aloud that the audience "must have been cheered to see the universal glow of patriotism."[56] The dedication was also used as a warning for those who would not assimilate: "the Irish societies may also wisely ponder the act that, while British authority was happily expelled, the glorious British traditions of constitutional freedom remained, and are organized in new forms. It is the tradition of the English-speaking race that still dominates as it has always controlled our civilizations."[57]

While Grant's funeral was an instructive moment for immigrants to learn about America, it was also an opportunity for the foreign-born to prove they deserved to be part of the national identity through participation. This is evidenced by the German singers at the public viewing and the various ethnic groups who marched in the parade, such as the Liederkranz Society and the Italian Rifle Guard. Regardless of where they were born, such a large crowd inevitably invited trouble. To help reduce the chances of any unpleasant incidents, the New York police proactively rounded up many known pickpockets. Whether this was legal is debatable, but the New York authorities prioritized the reputation of their city over suspected criminals' constitutional rights.

The procession continued north and passed the opulent mansions of the rich known as Millionaires' Row, including the home of Cornelius Vanderbilt. The marchers turned east onto Fifty-Seventh Street and, after three blocks, north onto Boulevard, a wide dirt road that today is Broadway. They continued to Seventy-Second Street, where the procession passed beneath an elevated railroad station. The front of the procession continued, but when the opulent hearse reached the overhead tracks, it was found to be too tall to pass beneath. Confusion reigned for almost an hour as telegraph messages were relayed for instructions.[58] Finally, a detour was taken, and the caisson rejoined the parade and continued north onto Riverside Drive. On the left, marchers could see ships that filled the Hudson River for the event. As the procession approached the tomb, a sailor on land signaled and guns from the ships began to boom.

Former presidents Hayes and Arthur sat together in the same carriage and enjoyed each other's company for the five-hour ride.[59] President Cleveland rode alone in a decorative carriage pulled by six horses. Despite the somber occasion, the sight of the president elicited great applause from the crowd, but he remained gracious and dignified and sat in stoic silence, refusing to acknowledge the cheers. In total, there were a staggering five hundred carriages in the procession. Stephen Merritt had obtained nearly every available one in the city as well as Brooklyn and the areas across the river in New Jersey.

Handling the funeral of a president, especially one as beloved as Grant, was certainly a high honor for the company. But they also profited handsomely from the assignment. Their charges included $10 for each carriage, $150 to carry the body from Mount McGregor to New York City, $30 to transport the floral arrangements to the burial site, $243 for scarves for twenty-seven pallbearers, and $500 for ornamentations for the horses. The final bill of $14,163.75 was paid by the United States government in two installments.[60]

The parade kept coming. For an onlooker standing in place that day, it took five hours for the entire procession to pass by. At 2:30 p.m., the first marchers finally arrived in Riverside Park. A temporary vault had been designed by Jacob Wrey Mould, who turned sixty on the day of the funeral and was the official architect of the Department of Parks. Shortly after receiving Fred's telegraph on July 28, Mould sat at his desk to draw up architectural plans for the temporary tomb. Twenty minutes later, he was done. The expeditious effort is apparent, for the tomb was a very simple one, in stark contrast to another of his works, Belvedere Castle, which had also been considered for a temporary tomb.[61] But perhaps with less than two weeks for the design and construction, a more elaborate structure was not feasible. The tomb was built several hundred feet north of 122nd Street.[62] The stout building stood seventeen by twenty-four feet, four feet tall, with an arched roof. It sat on a bluestone base and was built of red brick with bands and trim of black brick. The keystone was white limestone and the cornice was bluestone. The entrance featured two sets of doors. Beneath a squared cross were exterior iron gates that were more elaborate—appropriately for the age, they featured a gilded "G." At the base of three stone steps were interior oak doors on iron hinges. Some found it symbolic that the entrance faced south, toward Grant's former vanquished foe. The thick walls created a claustrophobic interior space of only seven by twelve feet. The interior was of white enameled bricks (made in Leeds, England, by Ingram and Sons), fine porcelain, and marble. In the rear was a small round window to let in sunlight, which reflected off the white interior, illuminating the coffin.

Soon after Mould completed his design, construction proceeded at a fast clip. Men worked all night before the funeral and continued in the morning, even as the procession was underway. Finally, at noon, they laid down their tools. The incomplete tomb, and the nearby piles of material and tools, startled some in the crowd who found the roof covered with wet tar. The *New York Times* reported that it "did not favorably impress many persons who saw the tomb for the first time."[63] While many considered Riverside an unfortunate location, others believed it providential. Nearby was a giant oak tree that had been struck by lightning at almost the same time that Grant had died. Of course, many saw this as a sign from above and visited the location to pick up leaves to save as relics before the tomb had even been constructed.[64] But besides the fallen oak, there was little vegetation in the area. Later, creative artists would draw

Harper's Weekly, *August 15, 1885. Pallbearers carry Grant's coffin to the temporary tomb in Riverside Park on the day of the funeral, August 8, 1885.* (Courtesy of the National Park Service, Manhattan Historic Sites Archive)

the tomb shaded in weeping willow trees, which are both attractive and a traditional symbol of mourning, but which were entirely fabricated.

Given its unimaginative design and hasty construction, it is not surprising that some were critical. One said the structure looked like "a gas retort enclosed in a bake oven."[65] But the critics must have found solace in the fact that it was only temporary. Abraham Lincoln was in temporary crypts (he was actually in three) for six years before a permanent tomb was built; James Garfield was at that time in his fourth year (of an eventual eight) in a temporary tomb. Surely, many surmised, Grant's permanent tomb would be completed in a reasonable amount of time. Few would guess that Grant's remains would reside in Mould's unattractive structure for twelve years.

Around 3:30 p.m., the funeral hearse arrived at Riverside Park. The coffin was placed in a lead-lined cedar case in front of the tomb. The wreath of oak leaves made by Grant's granddaughter in Mount McGregor was placed on top of the coffin before undertaker Merritt screwed the lid on tight. Distinguished guests circled the tomb. Thousands of people in the crowd strained to see the proceedings, while hundreds of daring souls climbed tree branches for a better view. Police tried to get the climbers to come down, but they were insistent. A man perched fifty feet in the air lost his balance, fell to the ground, and hit his head on a stone. He was taken to a nearby hospital but died that night, the funeral's only known casualty.[66]

The military stood at formation, fanning out from the tomb and forming "a kaleidoscope of the most brilliant colors."[67] The tomb itself was so deluged with floral arrangements, including one shaped like a cannon, that it bordered on the absurd. Inside the tomb were so many arrangements that barely any brick could be seen as flowers piled high along the walls, including one from the Woman's Relief Corps and another with an image of a suited Grant with his hand on the head of an emancipated slave.[68] The ceremony was both military and religious, and twenty privileged soldiers were selected by General Hancock to participate. Commander Alexander Reed and the Grand Army of the Republic chaplain-in-chief Reverend J. W. Sayers spoke, and several officers laid flowers at the tomb. Bishop Harris, dressed in striking clerical robes, read the burial rites. Reverend Newman, unsuccessfully fighting back tears, spoke a benediction. Finally, "an old grizzled bugler" who had served under Grant played "Taps" and the hour-long ceremony was over.[69]

As the crowds dispersed and the cedar case was carried inside the tomb, a bold, brazen relic hunter lurched forth and cut a silk tassel off the catafalque![70] But authorities had more sinister miscreants in mind than the tassel-stealing zealot. Nine years earlier, an attempt was made to steal Abraham Lincoln's remains from his tomb in Springfield, Illinois. Fortunately, the plot was foiled, as two in the conspiracy were informants for the Secret Service. But in New York, they were taking no such chances. The case was placed in a steel "air, water and burglar proof" container that workers welded shut with fifty-six steel bolts.[71] In addition to the numerous floral arrangements, a clock was also placed inside the tomb, its hands frozen at 8:06, the moment of Grant's death.[72] The gate was ceremoniously locked and the key handed to Mayor Grace. Responsibility was now in the hands of his city to care for the precious remains.

Even after the ceremony ended, marchers in the procession continued to arrive. While some had decided to bail out of the parade, others persevered and kept arriving at the tomb for hours after the ceremony ended. Reporters heaped superlatives upon the historic event, which was witnessed by 1.5 million people, more than the entire population of the city at the time. It was hailed as "a colossal and memorable demonstration."[73] The procession was praised as "a cortege which has never been equaled in America and rarely in the world."[74] It was not just an American phenomenon but an event of global significance, as a reporter for the *Magazine of American History with Notes and Queries* stated: "Nothing approaching it in magnitude, solemnity or grandeur ever occurred before in the history of the world. It was not imposed on the public by any precedent; it was the spontaneous outcome of the national regard for a man whose generalship had perpetuated the Republic, and who had twice been its President."[75]

5

"A Sacred Duty"

Given Grant's unique place in American history, the public demanded a memorial tomb surpassing any other created before. Karl Gerhardt, who had sculpted Grant's death mask, made an appeal published in the *North American Review*: "As America is the greatest of modern nations, to be a truly national memorial, it should excel in grandeur any existing monument . . . As no one moment of time, therefore, could tell to the future the story of Grant's life, we should erect to his memory the grandest mausoleum or temple of modern times."[1]

But what kind of monument would be built? Was it to be simply a grave or would it ascribe a deeper purpose and meaning? Reverend Newman had suggested the structure include a hall to house gifts given to Grant from countries around the world. "It should be a place that people can visit, not only to gratify an artistic sense, but for instruction of what he was and what the nations of the world thought of him," noted the *New York Times*.[2] The question of the monument's meaning would be one that would persist, and evolve, to this day.

Even before he had confirmation that the tomb would be in his city, Mayor Grace had begun to solicit prominent New Yorkers to assist in the creation of a grand monument. Once it was official, he wasted no time. On July 24, the day Fred had telegraphed his curt acceptance, Mayor Grace sent a letter to "New York's most illustrious citizens"[3]:

In order that the City of New York, which is to be the last resting place of General Grant, should initiate a movement to provide for the erection of a National Monument to the memory
of the great soldier, and that she should do well and thoroughly
her part, I respectfully request you to as one of a Committee to
consider ways and means for raising the quota to be subscribed
by the citizens of New York City for this object, and beg that
you will attend a meeting to be held at the Mayor's office on
Tuesday next, 28 inst., at three o'clock.[4]

Eighty-five wealthy and influential members of New York's gilded
elite responded to Grace's call. The group gathered in the mayor's
office that day included prominent politicians and businessmen, such
as former president Chester Arthur; former senator and Republican
boss Roscoe Conkling; wealthy real estate investor and philanthropist John Jacob Astor; Joseph Drexel, who had offered Grant his
Mount McGregor cottage; railroad and shipping baron Cornelius
Vanderbilt; newspaper publisher Joseph Pulitzer; brewer George
Ehret, who provided Grant's funeral hearse; Grant's secretary of state
and former governor of New York from 1849 to 1850, Hamilton Fish;
Grant's physician Fordyce Barker; former mayor of Brooklyn Seth
Low; and James A. Roosevelt, uncle to future president Theodore
Roosevelt. The minutes of the meeting show the initial stages of
the complex bureaucracy being set up for the ambitious project.
The amiable Chester Arthur, renowned for his fundraising skills for
the New York political machine, was named presiding officer. An
"Executive Committee" was established consisting of "young men,
[with] a strong local organization affiliated with similar organizations in other cities, all united to build a National Monument in the
City of New York worthy of the illustrious dead soldier and patriot;
and worthy of the city itself." The group of twenty was chaired by
former governor of New York Alonzo Barton Cornell and included
Chester Arthur, J. Pierpont Morgan, and Mayor Grace. They would

be the decision-making unit of the association. Another committee of nine worthy gentlemen was established "to prepare a plan of organization" and report back to the Executive Committee at 3:00 p.m. the next day.[5]

On July 29, the nine members of the "Committee on Organization" met at the office of lawyer and Democratic operative Samuel L. M. Barlow at noon. The group included Cornell; Morgan; Grace; former president of the New York Stock Exchange (from 1878 to 1880) Brayton Ives; lawyer and Tammany Hall Democrat Adolph L. Sanger; railroad executive Sidney Dillon; leather merchant and former member of the Connecticut Senate Oliver Hoyt; merchant Cornelius N. Bliss; and vice president of the New York Stock Exchange William Lummis. They moved to name the group "The Grant Monument Association" and affirmed a mission to erect "a great national monument which shall appropriately testify to future ages, the appreciation by the civilized world of the genius, valor and deeds of the grandest character of the century."[6] Additional notables were added to the association, bringing the number of members to "between 100 and 150," including Grant's good friend George W. Childs; the current New York governor, David B. Hill; and the mayor of Brooklyn, D. D. Whitney.[7] The Committee on Organization also made Arthur's position as presiding officer (he would also be referred to as chairman) permanent, while Mayor Grace and Grant's loyal secretary of state, Hamilton Fish (physically imposing at six feet tall), were named vice chairmen. Richard Theodore Greener, the first African American graduate of Harvard University and a prominent attorney, was also confirmed as permanent secretary.

The association also created a committee of subscriptions, which was given the critical task of fundraising and already had received a $5,000 donation from Western Union for a memorial, despite there being no specific plan or concept drawing for the monument yet. J. P. Morgan's investment bank, Drexel, Morgan & Co., was assigned

Richard Theodore Greener was named secretary of the Grant Monument Association and placed in charge of fundraising. This image is from a larger print published by A. Muller & Co. (1883) that features the images of ten prominent African Americans, titled "Distinguished colored men." (Courtesy of the Library of Congress)

as treasurer and Greener as secretary of the subscription committee as well as the association. The forty-one-year-old Greener had entered Harvard as a freshman the year the Civil War ended, in 1865, and later earned his law degree in former Confederate territory at the University of South Carolina. Greener moved afterward to Washington, DC, where he first met Grant. In his own words, Greener "had political relations with him, and enjoyed his friendship during his last illness." Greener later returned to Harvard to become the dean of the department of law and remained active in

Republican politics.[8] For his position, the association paid Greener $200 a month.

The group established the Grant Monument Fund to collect donations. In the days immediately following Grant's death, the public was eager to contribute to a grand memorial tomb. The first recorded donation was made an hour after Grant died, when an Irish woman walked into the office of Rochester mayor Cornelius R. Parsons and handed him a five-dollar bill. The "Native of Ireland," which is the only identification we have of her, had come to America forty-five years earlier and made the anonymous donation because she loved the United States and Ulysses S. Grant.[9] The first donation made after the formation of a monument committee, however, was more unusual. On July 29, Eleanor Fletcher Bishop, mother of popular mentalist Washington Irving Bishop, sent fifty cents to Mayor Grace along with a note on "mourning paper" with a peculiar proposition: "If the people of this city should deny themselves all luxuries in the shape of tobacco, liquor, ice cream and candies, the amount needed for the erection of the monument could be secured at once." She added that if her recommendation was not followed, she would pledge $3,000 herself.[10]

The association was offered an office rent-free at the Mutual Life Insurance Company on the first floor of its elegant building at Liberty and Nassau Streets. They would later move to another Mutual Life Insurance Company building at 146 Broadway.[11]

Early on, there were indications that fundraising would be a challenge, including this prediction from a reporter for the *New York Times*, who wrote a week before the funeral, "Though the American people revere the name of the great soldier and deeply deplore his death, those who expect to see the money for his monument come forth at once and spontaneously will be disappointed."[12] On the same day, another bad omen came from commander in chief of the Grand Army of the Republic General Samuel S. Burdette, who publicly "put himself on record in favor of Washington as the burial place."[13] The Grand Army of the Republic had first formed in 1866 with only twelve members, and by the time Grant died, General Burdette led an organization that approached 400,000 Union veterans.[14] The loss of support from such a massive pool of potential donors was ominous and a sign of problems that lay ahead.

Nonetheless, donations continued to arrive, and the association maintained a meticulous ledger for all, regardless of how small. At the end of July, "A Soldier's Orphan" sent two nickels "and promised to send another each day as long as he could afford it."[15] On August 1, twenty cents was received from "Two Yankee women" and fifteen cents from an eight-year-old boy. On August 4, twenty cents was sacrificed by "A German who gives up his beer." The following day, "Virginia," the daughter of a Confederate general, gave a quarter, and on August 6, a nickel was pledged by "A poor woman with ten children."[16]

Realizing that the funeral would provide a unique opportunity, association members distributed donation sheets to New York hotels to capture the attention of those in town for the event. A week before the funeral they had raised $9,401.70, over half of which had come from Western Union's donation.[17]

As had been done in prior fundraising efforts, the association recruited the city newspapers to solicit donations. The base of the Statue of Liberty was not part of the gift from France, and a year earlier funding for it had been championed by Joseph Pulitzer's daily newspaper, the *World*, which printed the names of contributors regardless of amount. The *New York Times* did the same for Grant's Tomb and sponsored their own fundraising drive, with the amount collected tallied separately in the paper before being forwarded to the Grant Monument Association.[18] The *Times* appealed to their readers' civic pride and national patriotism to support the tomb ("Give what you can and urge your neighbors to do likewise") and dutifully reported the donations on a daily basis.[19] Right away, it was apparent that the readers' donations were not the bonanza the association had hoped it would be. By August 3, the cumulative *New York Times* total was $59. That day only $8 was added to the fund, including $1 from "Mr. and Mrs. H. H. F."[20] By August 5, the total was $77, including $1 from "Mr. and Mrs. George H. Mellish."[21] By August 6, the fund jumped to $143, including a dollar gift from the curiously named "Wisteria Duzy" from Mamaroneck, New York.[22] On August 11, $2 from "A Daughter of a Patriot" brought the paper's total to $220, but no single donation exceeded ten dollars. On August 25, $10 was received from Omaha, Nebraska, from "The Granddaughter of a Revolutionary Officer of Massachusetts."[23] A snarky reporter noted that "the smallest contributions are generally accompanied by the longest letters."[24]

The day after the funeral, on Sunday, August 9, Greener personally appeared before an African American congregation of 1,500 people at the Mount Olivet Baptist Church. He used his own life story to illustrate how far African Americans in New York had come, contrasting the 1863 draft riots, during which protests against the draft turned into a race riot targeting free African Americans, with his elite education and place of honor at Grant's funeral. He made a strong appeal for their support toward the monument.[25]

Efforts were made to form partnerships with business and the community. The executive committee sent circulars soliciting funds to organizations such as groups of clergymen and bankers, and association members were instructed to encourage their own employees and clients to dip into their pockets. Some did, such as Cornelius N. Bliss, who personally donated $500 and collected thousands through his connections with companies such as Upham, Tucker & Co. ($100) and Catlin & Co. ($100); J. P. Morgan and Joseph Drexel, who collected on behalf of their investment bank, Drexel, Morgan & Co.; and A. W. Kingman, who donated $500 from his Brown, Wood, and Kingman dry goods and merchant company and collected another $125 from his employees. Other association members were more reluctant. Trade organizations that formed committees to channel funds to the association included Dry Goods, Book Publishing, Brewers, and the Drug Trade.[26]

Some of the more modest fundraising efforts tugged at New Yorkers' heart and purse strings. Three enterprising young boys aged six to nine from the O'Gormon's Row neighborhood on East 145th street sold fruit, cake, and candy and sent the $2.35 from their sales to the association.[27] Another group of ten children ranging in age from five through eleven from Oriental Point in Long Island held a fair. The group netted an impressive $72, a sum large enough, they believed, to earn them the honor of seeing their names carved in big letters on the tomb. When they were told that was unlikely, they responded with "a flood of tears and howls of dismay."[28]

On August 15, Greener's efforts had brought the tally to $39,552.79. This was hardly the windfall he had wished for. That same day, an unsettling letter arrived at association headquarters from Long Branch, New Jersey. The anonymous author warned, "New-York merchants, bankers, and politicians, who around here, all confess concurrence with the rest of the country that Washington, and not New-York, is the proper resting place for the remains of Gen. Grant, and New-Yorkers are satisfied that the project for a grand monument cannot be successfully out and must be abandoned."[29] While the *New York Times* reported that the "letter failed to have any noticeable effect on the members who read it," they were surely rattled. Long Branch was the site of Grant's vacation home and where Gilded Age elite gathered. While nickels and dimes from children and a teetotaling German were nice, the association needed more sizable checks from the likes of those who vacationed in Long Branch in order to create the majestic memorial that the public expected and the city had promised.

Corporations provided their donation sheets. D. H. McAlpin & Co. Tobacco Manufacturers, for instance, had collected hundreds of small donations, some as little as a nickel, for a total of $1,150.80.[30] By August 18, the ledger had edged to $42,190.24.[31] In addition to the pocket change, sizable donations also began to arrive, such as a $1,000 check from association member John Jacob Astor. On August 22, the ledger stood at $51,983.35.[32]

Despite the lackluster early results, former governor Cornell made a bold proposal and set a goal of one million dollars. While it seemed ridiculously ambitious to some, especially in light of Burdette's public support of a Washington memorial, donations for the base of the Statue of Liberty had only recently reached about $250,000. Surely, Cornell surmised, people would be more generous for the man who fought to preserve the Union and bestow liberty upon four million enslaved. Other association members eagerly seconded his motion.[33] Indeed, the financial outlook did appear to be taking a favorable turn. The day after Cornell's announcement, the donor list stretched down to the bottom of the page of the *New York Times*. The one-day Grant Monument Association tally of $7,328.30 brought the total to $59,311.65, prompting the promising headline SUBSCRIPTIONS POURING IN.[34] Perhaps Cornell's proposal was not so outlandish after all.

But when it comes to raising money, one must strike while the iron is hot, and soon after the pomp of Grant's obsequies, the nation's collective attention began to turn to other things.

In Saratoga, people who a month earlier had been consumed with Grant's vital signs now studied the racing forms for the annual Thoroughbred horse races at Saratoga Race Course in early August.[35] In New York City, mourning drapery was removed from City Hall within three weeks after the funeral.[36] Evidence of waning enthusiasm could be observed at the tomb, too. In the first few weeks after the funeral, thousands of people visited the temporary tomb, making it one of the most popular tourist destinations in the city. On Sunday, August 16 alone, some 30,000 to 40,000 visited. (There may have been more, but a park policeman stopped counting at 22,000 because "his eyes ached."[37]) But after that, visitation dropped precipitously. Some blamed the weather but could not agree if it was too hot or too cold. On August 25, the *New York Times* reported, "The intense heat caused a marked decrease in the number of visitors."[38] Four days later, the same newspaper claimed, "Since the cold weather has set in, very few people visit Gen. Grant's tomb after sunset."[39] A reporter astutely observed, "The number of people that visit the tomb is daily growing smaller," before grimly adding, "and so are the chances of making money."[40] As feared, donations took a nosedive. Only two days after boasting of Subscriptions Pouring In, the newspaper lamented "a big falling off" after a sickly one-day tally of only $571.[41]

Though the association should have seized upon the public's sympathy in the wake of the funeral, in large part members were complacent when they should have been aggressive, despite the existence of multiple committees and some fundraising efforts that gave the illusion of getting things done. One critic from the *New York Times* complained of the association's "seeming supineness at a time when the nation was overflowing with sympathy." The association members conceded the soft spell but believed that once wealthy New Yorkers returned from their summer vacations (including many of their number, such as Chester Arthur, who was in Newport, Rhode Island, by August 22), the checks would start coming in.[42] As an example of their complacency, D. N. Carvalho from the United States Instantaneous Photographic Company, who later was named the official photographer of the association, had taken photos of the tomb on behalf of the Grant Monument Association, which owned the rights to images. Carvalho set up a "rustic table" at the tomb, but the plan was to erect a small building to serve as a shop from which to sell the photographs. In mid-August, the Parks Department had issued a permit, but two weeks later, the association still had not acted. Pressed on the issue, Cornell promised on August 28, "to attend to the matter to-day." He didn't.[43] The next day, a *New York Times* reporter complained, "Almost a month after the appointment of the General Committee—it was impossible to gather more than 10 percent of the membership at a meeting."[44]

Only a week after the funeral, Rutherford B. Hayes, deeply concerned about the prospects for the monument fund, wrote General Samuel S. Burdette—who had already gone on record supporting a burial site in Washington—that "All experience shows that funds, if raised by public subscription, must be obtained *at once*." Hayes added ominously, "The golden moment has already passed. Further delay imperils us all."[45]

Another significant challenge to the fundraising was direct competition. A few days after the Grant Monument Association was founded in New York, another organization of the same name formed in Illinois to erect a monument in Chicago and quickly raised $30,000.[46] People in Kansas made donations toward a more modest Grant monument at Fort Leavenworth; it quickly reached $3,000 and received an offer from a sculptor in Texas to "furnish gratis a design," leading the *New York Times* to declare that "Gen. Miles [who led the effort] is sanguine about the success of the monument."[47] Similar efforts for Grant monuments in San Francisco, Ocean Grove (New Jersey), and Philadelphia may have diverted donors from the New York fundraising efforts as well. At Mount McGregor, where the owners of the cottage where Grant had stayed expected to turn the home into a national shrine, a bold plan was proposed to cut "in the granite face of the hill a colossal profile of the General finishing his book." It was estimated that the cost for a thirty-foot memorial would be $100,000, but fundraising never got off the ground.[48] Yet another competing fundraising effort was to erect a memorial tomb for James Garfield, like Grant a Civil War hero who had been elected president, and who had been assassinated in 1881. In Cleveland, fundraising efforts were being led by the more efficient and participatory Garfield National Monument Association.

Yet another monument was also proposed in St. Louis, where Grant had lived. General Sherman was invited to serve as president of the St. Louis Grant Monument Association but declined. As a counter to the Grand Army of the Republic commander in chief, Sherman stated, "Grant was worthy of every monument that can be raised to his memory, but I think that the one over his grave should be finished before the others are begun."[49]

Potential donors had good reason to be confused about the situation and concerned about the prospects for the tomb in Riverside Park being built at all. In light of the competing memorials, the editors of the *American Architect and Building News* suggested to their readers: "We advise all people outside of New York who desire to contribute to the Nation's monument to General Grant to wait until Congress meets, for it is only probable that steps will be taken at once to erect a national monument in the Nation's capital."[50]

The fund limped through the rest of the month. When August ended, donations stood at $69,339.05.[51]

Shortly after the funeral, workers completed the temporary tomb: they resurfaced the walls with blue stone and covered the tarpaper roof in brick. Immediately after the funeral, the War Department deployed a battery of soldiers from the Fifth Artillery under Captain Joshua A. Feessenden to stand guard at the tomb. The site became known as "Camp Grant," and soldiers were assigned watch in two-hour shifts.[52] Soon a sentry building was built to shelter the guards from the elements.[53] Even as the association was lax in arranging to sell photographs of the tomb in their gift shop, the military was tasked with stopping members of the public from taking their own pictures.[54] They also guarded against the pervasive relic hunters, who tried to grab items from the tomb and now set their eyes on Camp Grant. Sometimes their desired keepsakes were almost laughable, such as chunks of spent coal from the furnace used by the workers. A reporter noted, "Their eagerness at times carries them close to the borderline of actual theft."[55] Some people even chipped pieces off the nearby grave of St. Claire Pollock, a young child who died on July 15, 1797, forcing the city to place a policeman to guard the site.[56]

Some took a more customary—and legal—route to obtain a souvenir. One hopeful individual offered $5,000 for the catafalque that held Grant's coffin. The United States government declined.[57] Another tried to hand a guard a silver dollar, asking only that the guard place the coin on the tomb and then hand it back to him. The guard refused.[58] But some were more fortunate. Guards regularly doled out flowers from inside the tomb that had withered and rotted.[59]

On August 12, a gilded lock was fastened to the oak door. Only four days after the funeral, Grant's memory remained strong in New Yorkers' minds, and even a minor fixture like a lock drew attention. A crowd of fifty gathered for an impromptu ceremony, and an armed guard stood nearby to keep the people at a distance. When some asked for the oak slivers to take as a souvenir, the soldiers obliged. But even those who did not obtain a special souvenir from the tomb did not necessarily depart empty-handed. The oak tree that was struck by lightning around the time that Grant breathed his last bore plenty of leaves to satisfy all relic hunters.[60] Requests also poured in to Stephen Merritt and the Grant Monument Association for scraps of cloth used in the service or anything else they could part with. The inquiries, some published in the newspapers, came from as far as Ohio, Michigan, and Iowa.[61]

The soldiers at Camp Grant charged with guarding the tomb numbered thirty men. They had hastily erected seventeen white canvas tents and a kitchen that lacked a roof. A dining area was set beneath a grove of trees but proved an irritant for the soldiers. "We aren't machinelike enough to enjoy our meals with hundreds staring at us," one soldier complained, pleading for "anything to prevent a lot of ignorant people from staring at us while we eat."[62] While they were not at war, the assignment did have its hazards. During a sudden storm in August, a mammoth fifteen-foot floral display was destroyed and lightning struck a nearby tree, causing one woman, frightened by the violent thunder, to faint.[63] A week later, the *New*

York Times reported that the soldiers were attacked by "an invading army of Jersey mosquitoes" that had crossed the Hudson and were "enormously large and ferociously hungry."[64]

Camp life occasionally afforded simple pleasures, such as sugar doughnuts brought by a Civil War widow. Within a few weeks of the funeral, the class of visitors changed noticeably. As wealthy New Yorkers returned from their summer retreats, one newspaper noted, "The lunch-basket families, who came to stay, have been succeeded by a constant stream of quiet, decorous men and women, while the loud, grating laugh of the excursionist is no longer heard."[65] A month after Grant's funeral, on September 10, 1885, the Battery K Fifth Artillery took over at Camp Grant. They stood guard until October 11, when they were relieved by Battery I.

The area around the tomb took on a parklike appearance. Benches were erected for visitors shortly after the funeral. Later on, some New Yorkers, eager to showcase their new and popular attraction to out-of-town visitors, proudly dedicated time and resources to make the tomb a more beautiful space. Some planted flowers. One woman asked for permission to plant ivy taken from Napoleon's tomb (this would not be the first time a connection was drawn between the two generals). While the tomb was democratic in that people from all levels of society could mourn Grant's death there, a class distinction still manifested itself, as some of the wealthy did not care to mourn Grant *simultaneously* with the poor. The well-to-do tended to visit early in the morning on carriage rides past the tomb before the day's barrage of "common" tourists arrived. Youth groups also visited, including African American children from a nearby orphan asylum, who stood at the gate, "their little eyes wide open in awe and astonishment."[66] For a dime, one could purchase *The Guide for Strangers: General Grant's Tomb in Riverside Park*, an eight-page guide that boasted containing "the exact information desired by every man, woman, and child." It included directions to the tomb from various locations: visitors could take a horse-car or the elevated railroad ("fare five cents") to the nearby 125th Street Station, which had been erected in 1874.[67]

Even after the funeral and the placement of Grant's casket in the temporary tomb, not all New Yorkers were thrilled with the selection of the site. A common complaint was that the choice of Riverside was purely to boost real estate values and attract tourists. A reverend from nearby Poughkeepsie asserted, "I am reliably informed that the Grant Monument proposition is a speculation gotten up for money, money, money and for enhancing the value of New York property."[68] Others, such as a reporter from the *Mechanicville Mercury*, continued to argue that Central Park was more appropriate.[69]

Fundraising began to evolve. In addition to direct solicitations of monetary donations, efforts took varied and sometime creative forms. Letters were sent to banks requesting "some energetic person connected with your institution . . . [to] solicit contributions from its customers." The request came directly from association chairman and former president Chester Arthur, which made it tough to refuse.[70] A baseball game in Albany on September 26, 1885, pitting

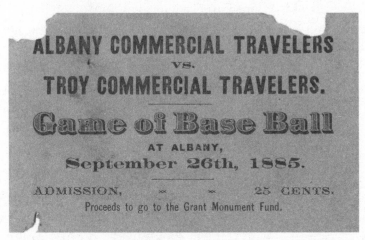

In the first months after Grant's death, there were all types of schemes to raise money for a permanent tomb, including a baseball game between the Albany Commercial Travelers and the Troy Commercial Travelers, with proceeds going to the Grant Monument Fund. (Courtesy of the National Park Service, Manhattan Historic Sites Archive)

the Albany Commercial Travelers against the Troy Commercial Travelers, netted a quarter toward the tomb for each attendee.[71] To appeal to Civil War veterans, the association deployed General George A. Sheridan on a speaking tour to drum up donations. Sheridan, who had served in the House of Representatives from Louisiana during Reconstruction, kept 25 percent of the donations for himself.[72]

Private interests and individuals also looked for ways to associate their products with customers' patriotic urges while boosting sales in the process. For instance, the Consumers Coal Company offered to donate seventy-five cents for every two tons it sold.[73] There were international donations as well, including $500 from Chinese Viceroy Li Hung-Chang, whom Grant had befriended on his world tour, and $15 raised in Chile by the United States consul, J. W. Merriam, who organized a drive.[74] Some sent gifts that were not monetary, such as the ten-year-old girl who identified herself as "Little Carrie" and recalled how she once met Grant and he tousled her hair. Offering a gift more precious than coins, she clipped a lock and sent it to Mayor Grace to place in the tomb.[75]

Suggestions for donation schemes poured in, some too peculiar to accept. S. Vos had invented a puzzle that he wanted the association to endorse (presumably he would have paid them a fee to do so). Another endorsement request came from Jacob Studer for his book *The Birds of North America*. If there was some sort of link to Grant for either of these proposals, it was difficult to ascertain. D. F. Adams proposed cutting the catafalque into slivers and affixing them to souvenir buttons. For those who might doubt the authenticity of the shard of wood, he suggested that the carving up be done in public at City Hall. There was also an idea for a fair to be held at Madison Square Garden, sponsored by the association. The event, which would have featured an electric fountain and music by Gilmore's Famous Band, was not pursued.[76] Most prominently, former Brooklyn mayor Seth Low opposed many of these ad hoc ventures. He deemed them too commercial, while on the other hand, baseball games were perfectly acceptable to the association. The truth was that the association lacked a fundraising strategy and coherent criteria by which such proposals could be evaluated.

Like the grifters and cheats of present times who exploit public sympathy and generosity for their personal benefit, there were charlatans then who sought to deceive the public and fraudulently collect donations in the name of the Grant Monument Fund. Perhaps the most unique scheme took place two days after the funeral at a meeting at the Theodore Parker Spiritualist Fraternity. A Mrs. Myra Hall was introduced to the crowd and informed them she was in touch with Grant from beyond the grave. At the time, many people believed in spiritualism, so surely some in attendance hoped to genuinely hear from Grant. The audience was astonished when Mrs. Hall told them that Grant "fully appreciated the splendid funeral," but grew skeptical as she conveyed his thoughts on current affairs, saying they were "quite coincident with published views by Gen. Grant in life." When an audience member pressed for more authentic proof of her spiritual connection, Hall quickly collected payment and departed, leaving others to argue the veracity of her talents after she left.[77] On September 4, 1885, the *Miamisburg Bulletin* from Ohio published a stern warning: "All persons that use the name of the [Grant] association for fraudulent purpose will be punished to the full extent of the law."[78]

Not everyone was supportive of the idea of public fundraising for the tomb. From Manchester, Michigan, a donation log was returned with no monies listed. Instead, the official donor sheet included a note from a Mr. Watkins, cashier at the People's Bank of Manchester, stating that "The universal sentiment here is that the country has done enough for Gen. Grant," and instead suggesting a fund for the sitting president Grover Cleveland.[79]

As the association struggled to gain fundraising momentum in the months after Grant's death, there were continued calls for locating the tomb at an alternative site and unrelenting efforts to sabotage New York's campaign. Many newspapers outside of the Empire State came out strongly against the New York burial location, and while news from New York was dutifully reported in many papers across the country, editorials called upon readers to resist donating toward the tomb. While surely an exaggeration, tomb historian David M. Kahn claimed, "Only two papers outside of New York State approved of the Association's objectives."[80] There had certainly been debate about where previous presidents including George Washington, James Monroe, and Abraham Lincoln would be buried, but never had there been such vitriol and sabotage—some of it perhaps owing to resentment of the city itself and the commercial preeminence of the state. "If the billions of New York are not sufficient," wrote Lew Morrill, publisher of the *Weekly Enterprise* of Michigan City, Indiana, "let the remains be placed in Washington or some other American city." Morrill pulled no punches, reporting, "The feeling is pretty general in the West that as the Empire City secured the remains of General Grant over the protests of 9/10th of the citizens of the United States she is in duty bound to place a monument over the grave of the grand old commander at her own expense second to no other monument in the country, but superior." The publisher continued, "I was one of General Grant's soldiers, and love him as no one but a soldier can, and I shall never get over the disappointment I felt when it was decided that his remains were to be deposited outside of Washington."[81]

A conflicted Daniel W. Eidier from South Carolina mailed a dollar contribution but did so reluctantly. In his enclosed note he complained, "I hope gentlemen it is not out of place for one to express my deepest regret that any place has been selected . . . save 'Arlington' or 'Soldier's House.'"[82] From faraway Nebraska, the *Weekly Schuyler Sun* may shed light on Eidier's rationale: "The fact that the Soldiers' Home is on the border line between north and south gives it a peculiar fitness as a place of interment."[83]

On August 24, the *Critic* from Washington, DC, purported to quote Julia Grant's brother Fred T. Dent, speaking about his nephew, "I know it was Fred Grant's wish that his father should be buried at the Soldiers' Home in this city. I am satisfied that the entire family would have liked him to be there; but who was there that could guarantee that Mrs. Grant could rest beside him?"[84]

On August 31, the *Oshkosh Northwestern* of Wisconsin predicted that the government would soon step in to settle the issue. "An effort will be made at the approaching session of congress to set apart a portion of the Soldier's Home grounds for the permanent burial of Gen. Grant's body with permission for Mrs. Grant to be by her husband after death and there is no doubt the necessary legislation will be enacted." Once this is done, the newspaper added, "Then it will remain with the family to decide where the tomb will be."[85]As the controversy reached a fever pitch in the fall of 1885, donations subsided. Potential donors became concerned that Grant's family might yield to the cacophony of calls for another location. In an effort to allay such fears, Mayor Grace wrote to Julia on October 16, 1885, while she was at their vacation home in Long Branch:

My Dear Mrs. Grant: The Executive Committee of the Grant Monument Association, to whom was intrusted the honored and patriotic task of collecting funds for a suitable national memorial to the memory of your distinguished husband, finds itself seriously hampered in its work, and to a great extent embarrassed, by utterances which appear from time to time in the daily press, and often purporting to come from your family. Our Executive Committee is much concerned in the reports quite industriously spread abroad and persistently reiterated, that on the reassembling of Congress a preconcerted effort, with the consent and approval of your family, would be begun to have the body of General Grant removed to Washington for final sepulture. Our fund has already reached a generous sum—nearly $90,000—it will be $100,000 soon; but it must be obvious that any doubt which the public may have as to the desire of the family in regard to the Riverside Park as a permanent tomb and the site of the proposed national memorial acts as a deterrent to those who would otherwise freely give. May I ask from your family a clear and emphatic expression of your wish and preference—may I add, determination—for the use of our Executive Committee.

Very respectfully,
W. R. GRACE.
Vice-President Grant Monument Association.[86]

When she returned from vacation, she found the letter waiting for her and responded on October 29:

Dear Sir: Your letter of the 16th came during my absence, and was received on my return from Long Branch. Riverside was selected by *myself* and *my family* as the burial place of my husband, Gen. Grant.
First—Because I believed New York was h*is* preference.
Second—It is near the residence that I hope to occupy as long as I live, and where I will be able to visit his resting place often.
Third—I have believed, and am now convinced, that the tomb will be visited by as many of his countrymen here as it would be at any other place.
Fourth—The offer of a park in New York was the first which observed and unreservedly assented to the only condition imposed by Gen. Grant himself namely, that I should have a place by his side.

I am, Sir, very sincerely.
JULIA D. GRANT.[87]

Julia Grant's affirmation that New York would remain Grant's burial place was duly published in the newspapers, but it had little effect on the ledger.

The association's problems ran deeper than lackluster fundraising owing the lack of a strategic vision and the divided public response. New York was led by the Democrat party under Governor Hill and Mayor Grace, and memorializing one of the nation's most popular Republicans required a delicate touch that would not allow the opposition party to gain political points in the process. Governor Hill, who on January 1, 1885, had assumed the office that had been vacated by Grover Cleveland after he was elected president, was facing an election challenge on November 3, 1885. He would barely squeak out a victory, winning by less than 1 percent of the vote. He could not afford to appear to support a Republican—even a deceased one—to the detriment of the Democratic machine. Horace L. Hotchkiss, an association treasurer after Greener, later revealed, "The organization was largely under the local influence of Tammany Hall—W. R. Grace was president, and the board of trustees was dominated by that faction. There was no particular friction, simply we were not functioning—there was quite evident a feeling that the Republicans might gain national and local influence. This thought was in the air."[88]

Even at the outset, the private interests of association members drew their attention away from the Grant memorial efforts. Perhaps it had been too much to expect anything beyond token participation from some of the Gilded Age titans who dominated the association leadership, given their other responsibilities. For instance, only two weeks before Grant died, J. P. Morgan had negotiated an agreement between two major railroad companies aboard his yacht.[89] During his tenure with the Grant Memorial Association, Morgan was simultaneously consolidating and reorganizing the nation's railroads while becoming one of America's wealthiest men. Meanwhile, Richard Greener was hired as the chief examiner of the City Civil

Service Board. While Greener remained in the Grant Monument Association, his new position kept him away from his fundraising responsibilities. Some hoped that after the political distraction of the upcoming election abated, members would be able to refocus on the task at hand. On November 1, the *New York Times* lamented that the association "has done little more than invite the community to contribute," but half-heartedly added, "When the election returns have been printed . . . the Grant Monument Association will begin its campaign."[90] Two days later, only $1.50 was reported in contributions—an indication of the ennui that had set in within the association.[91]

From October 1885 to February 1886, ten executive committee meetings were canceled due to lack of a quorum (the records of how many meetings were scheduled is unknown). Less than six months into their responsibilities, the group had lost interest in what some had labeled "a sacred duty."[92] In addition, despite the wealthy cadre that made up their ranks, few had led by example and donated to the monument fund. There were a few modest exceptions, such as $500 from Mayor Grace and $1,000 each from George Ehret, John Jacob Astor, and railroad executive Sidney Dillon.[93] The *Rutland Daily Herald* from Vermont complained, "Popular interest has largely passed and only a minority of the committeemen themselves are among the subscribers. The enterprise has been mismanaged from the start and is in danger of ending in a way creditable to no one concerned."[94] This was in stark contrast to the Garfield National Monument Association, which led the effort to build James Garfield's memorial tomb. John D. Rockefeller and other wealthy friends of Garfield had combined to donate about $75,000 toward the project, an amount that covered half of the eventual cost.

The Garfield National Monument Association's simultaneous effort highlights another deficiency in the campaign to finance Grant's tomb. In Cleveland, a competition to design Garfield's tomb was held in June 1882, less than a year after Garfield's death. In New

York, the Grant Monument Association's failure to begin discussing and planning the memorial tomb's design added to the uncertainty. What was the vision for the design? Would it be comparable to Lincoln's and Garfield's? Grant's memorial was planned for a city park and had no precedent. Grant was the eighteenth president but the nineteenth to die, and most of his predecessors had been buried in cemeteries (Garfield, Johnson, Lincoln, Buchanan, Pierce, Taylor, Tyler, Van Buren, Monroe) or on their family estates (Jackson at the Hermitage, Madison at Montpelier, Jefferson at Monticello, Washington at Mount Vernon). Others were buried in a cemetery first but later moved to a church or public space (Polk, William Henry Harrison, John Quincy Adams, John Adams). Never had anything like Grant's Tomb—whatever form it might take—been attempted: a grand memorial planned in a public park in America's largest city.

If Americans were looking to the Grant Monument Association for leadership, the association was abdicating its responsibility. A telling letter was sent to Chester Arthur by furniture manufacturer William D. Sloane, who warned, "The majority will hesitate sending in their subscriptions until they know what the monument or memorial is to be—its style as well as the actual cost."[95] New York, a city seen by many as underserving of the honor in the first place, was widely believed to be falling down on the job.

On November 27, 1885, the fund finally topped $100,000, providing a rare reason to celebrate. It was a symbolic milestone; in a not-so-subtle article beneath the headline SEND IN YOUR MONEY!, a hopeful New York Times chided its readers: "The second one hundred thousand dollars should be given more quicker than the first."[96] As 1885 came to a close, the Grant Monument Association had raised $111,006.17, despite its failings and flaws, but in reality they were no closer to building a memorial then they had been when the first gathered in Mayor Grace's office five days after Grant's death.[97]

At Camp Grant, meanwhile, in anticipation of the colder weather ahead, the soldiers had constructed more permanent sixty-by-twenty-five-foot living quarters, double-boarded and lined with paper, which were completed on November 9, 1885.[98] The rotations continued. On November 16, Battery E moved in and was replaced on December 16 by Battery M, which encamped for two months. They were relieved by Battery L on February 15, 1886. With little to do besides watch crowds, some soldiers grew restless and got themselves into trouble. In February, one Frank Kavanagh got into a brawl at a nearby saloon and was stabbed six times in the head and back.[99] Battery I took one more turn and would remain at the site until June 30, 1886. Finally, as its one-year anniversary approached, the War Department would officially close Camp Grant. Responsibility to guard the tomb would now belong to the gray-uniformed New York park police.[100]

The year 1886 had started off on an encouraging note for the Grant Monument Association when it was officially incorporated on February 3, with a stated mission "to erect a suitable monument or other memorial over the remains of the late Gen. Ulysses S. Grant, in Riverside Park in the City of New York."[101] The association's bylaws named thirty-three trustees (twenty-nine trustees and four ex-officio) "for the purpose of procuring and receiving by voluntary contributions, donations and bequests, such a sum of money as may be proper for the purpose of erecting a suitable Monument or other Memorial, to the memory of the illustrious Gen. Grant . . . and of keeping the same in repair, and of maintaining the same, and for these purposes to make and enforce such rules and regulations." The group included New York aristocrats Hamilton Fish, J. P. Morgan, and Cornelius Vanderbilt; newspaper magnates James Gordon Bennett (*Herald*), Joseph Pulitzer (*World*), Oswald Ottendorfer (*Staats-Zeitung*, New York's leading German-language newspaper), and Charles A. Dana (*Tribune*); and a ceremonial position for President Grover Cleveland.[102] Chester Arthur, who had served as chairman since the association's inception, was elected the first president of the incorporated association. But he was in poor health and suffered from Bright's disease, a degenerative kidney condition. A month later, Arthur wrote Richard Greener to respectfully decline the honor. (He did not live to see the completion of the monument and died on November 18, 1886.[103]) Sidney Dillon was elected to replace Arthur.[104]

Having proven unable to mount an effective fundraising strategy and raise the money themselves, the association pursued federal funds in Congress. In January 1886, a bill was proposed by the House Committee of Military Affairs to allocate $500,000 to the tomb, but only after the association raised $250,000. A month later, Representative Abraham Dowdney of New York introduced House Bill 1600, which reduced the allocation to $250,000 but kept the association's obligations the same. The proposals were met with strong opposition. Throughout the debate, Dowdney and Greener stayed in touch. Initially, the letters were optimistic about swift passage, but they became decidedly less so over time. On July 28, 1886, Dowdney delivered the somber news: "It appears to be the opinion that nothing can be done . . . this session as we require unanimous consent to get the Bill considered," before concluding, "and this we can not get."[105]

With no help from the federal government, the association was on its own. To add further insult, the Mutual Life Insurance Company no longer allowed the association to use their office rent-free; starting June 1, 1886, they were charged $250 per year for the space. Despite the flagging monument efforts, public enthusiasm for Grant himself continued to run high as evidenced by patriotic remembrances at the tomb. In late May 1886, in the midst of the federal fundraising appeal, the members of U. S. Grant Post 327 held a ceremony at the temporary tomb on Decoration Day (which would later become known as Memorial Day). Twenty thousand people were in attendance; the tomb was literally buried in floral arrangements, with none of the bricks visible in a photograph taken that day.[106]

The temporary tomb drowns in a sea of flowers on Decoration Day (later Memorial Day), 1886. (Courtesy of the National Park Service, Manhattan Historic Sites Archive)

On October 28, 1886, the Statue of Liberty was dedicated. The two monuments sat at the opposite extremes of the city and the fundraising spectrum. The Statue of Liberty stood on an island off the southern tip of New York City upon a pedestal funded by a generous public; Grant lay to the north, in a remote and unsightly temporary crypt that served as a grim reminder of the fading hopes of a permanent tomb.

Donations continued to trickle in from peculiar sources. *The Hermit of Cashel* was staged at the Metropolitan Opera House to raise money on October 4, 1886. Despite being billed as "A spectacular opera in IV acts with Great Chorus and Eminent Soloists" and a planned run of ten shows, it closed after a single performance and added only $35 to the coffers.[107] A Nickel Fund Association sponsored in Montclair, New Jersey, lived up to its name and netted only a handful of nickels.

When Julia Grant received her husband's back pay for service in

An opera, The Hermit of Cashel, *was staged to raise money for the tomb. Despite a planned run of ten shows, it closed after a single performance and only added $35 to the Grant Monument Fund.* (Courtesy of the National Park Service, Manhattan Historic Sites Archive)

the Mexican–American War, she forwarded the check to the monument fund in January 1887, along with a letter from Fred: "My mother feels that this money is too sacred to be used in any other way than as an offering towards the building of a monument to the memory of her husband."[108] While not significant in dollars, the $987.50 showed she had not lost faith in the association or New York City as a location. Julia could afford the expense. Grant's memoirs were published posthumously in two volumes, the first in December 1885 and the second in May 1886. They were an immediate, wild success, as evidenced by a headline in the *Boston Globe* that exclaimed, GENERAL GRANT'S MEMOIRS SELLING LIKE HOT CAKES.[109] On February 27, 1886, Mark Twain gave Julia a check for $200,000 and promised, "More is due her and will be paid as soon as collected."[110] By May 1887 her royalties had grown to $394,459.53, the largest amount ever earned by an author at the time. "The financial success of Grant's book is unprecedented in the history of literature," declared the *Indianapolis Journal*. In addition to being the victorious commanding general in the Civil War, Grant was now in the history books for another accomplishment.[111] Julia would eventually amass between $420,000 and $450,000 in royalties (about twelve to thirteen million dollars today). It was another reminder that Grant had dramatically and decisively won his final battle, achieving financial security for his beloved wife through his completed memoirs.

The book won great acclaim. The *Brooklyn Daily Eagle* praised Grant's "straightforward, plain speaking narrative" and his "modesty and strict adherence to truth."[112] The *Wichita Beacon* claimed, "The Memoirs will please every intelligent reader, and the entire work will prove a valuable addition to our historical literature."[113] Even today, a *New York Times* critic heralds its "authenticity" and adds, "Grant's voice is never confessional, it almost never rings false."[114] In a 2003 interview with presidential historian Michael Beschloss, former president Bill Clinton was asked, "What do you think is the best presidential memoir thus far published?" He responded without hesitation, "Oh, Grant's, no question."[115]

David W. Blight writes in *Race and Reunion: The Civil War in American Memory*: "During the late nineteenth century, literature was a powerful means of reuniting the interests of America both North and South."[116] From beyond the grave, Grant's own words in his memoirs helped further the spirit of reconciliation evidenced in the national mourning following his death. He became the embodiment of reunification, sparing criticism of Confederate generals such as Buckner, who visited him in his dying days, and holding no grudge against the Southern soldiers. In recounting Lee's surrender at Appomattox, Grant mused, "I felt like anything rather than rejoicing at the downfall of a foe who had fought so long and valiantly and had suffered so much for a cause." While Grant abhors their cause in the defense of slavery, he concludes, "I do not question, however, the sincerity of the great mass of those who were opposed to us."[117]

The fiscal year 1886–87 went from bad to abysmal when only an anemic $10,000 was added to the coffers after expenses, bringing the total to about $120,000. If there was discussion about the dilemma at the annual meeting in February 1887, the records could not be found. But obviously members were aware of the situation, because at this meeting Greener voluntarily reduced his monthly salary from $200 to $100 to save expenses.[118] Sensing that the Grant Monument Association had become a sinking ship, several trustees including Cornelius Vanderbilt chose to resign rather than continue to have their names attached to the bleak effort. In a sign of how dysfunctional the association had become, on April 7, 1887, three days *after* Vanderbilt sent his letter to the association to tender his resignation, he was elected its president. He refused the position.[119]

While the association's fundraising collapsed in 1887, local newspapers besides the *New York Times* pitched in with efforts of their own. A puzzle contest was held by the weekly periodical *Judge*. Entrants were instructed to send fifty cents and a list of the "eleven most popular living men in America." A quarter went to the Grant Monument Fund for each entry and the remainder to expenses and prizes. The contest netted $1,000 for the association.[120] That same year, the New York *Star* (oddly, not one of the dailies represented on the trustee roster) ran its own ambitious drive to raise $125,000 to match the amount already in the monument fund. Its most prominent donation came from President Grover Cleveland. While he may have hoped his modest $10 contribution would set an example for others to follow, instead it backfired. Noting his $25,000 presidential salary, one reader contrasted Cleveland's meager donation with how much he made per diem, "including the days he attempts to fish and holidays in which he is loafing from business."[121] Despite its valiant effort, the *Star* only raised about $10,000, far less than its goal.

Little fundraising was done in 1887–88, and for that fiscal year only an additional $10,000 was added to the fund after expenses. At the annual meeting in February 1888, now former mayor Grace was elected association president.[122] After three years and only about $130,000 in funds raised, it appeared likely that Grant's temporary tomb might become his permanent resting place. Three years after Grant had died, General Sherman rode past his good friend's temporary resting place and lamented, "Thousands visit it and gaze [at the] casket visible through the grated door," but added regretfully, "as to a monument not a thing has been done."[123]

Meanwhile, the Grant family was growing frustrated. On September 13, 1889, the New York *World* published Fred's account of his final discussion with his father about the burial location, mentioning St. Louis, Galena, and Washington, DC, as potential locations, but no mention was made of New York City. Fred was increasingly annoyed at New York's failure to erect a monument, and he was considering moving his father's remains to a more hospitable location. No doubt, he also sought to apply pressure to the Grant Monument Association to get their act together and start showing some progress.[124]

6

"An American Pantheon"

CALLS FOR A plan for the tomb—or at least a semblance of a plan—started as a low rumble shortly after Riverside Park was chosen and steadily increased as confidence in association members plummeted and the flow of donations dried up. Only three weeks after the funeral, the *New York Times* claimed pointedly, "The public would put forth greater efforts to raise the necessary money if it knew exactly how it was to be expended."[1] William Lummis conveyed a similar warning on behalf of wealthy members of the New York Stock Exchange who "wish some definite plan proposed before they feel much interest in the work."[2]

There was immediate public debate about the type of memorial, with some calling for a "characteristically American" monument. But what did that mean? A contributor for the *American Review* chided in response, "The only 'strictly American' monuments are Indian earth mounds and Central American buildings."[3]

There was also a compelling simultaneous push toward modernity. Mrs. Clarry A. Sheafor, a citizen architect, wrote to the association, warning that the memorial must be "decidedly modern or it will fail," because Grant was "a modern man of modern ideas." But was this true? While Sheafor offered no evidence to support her assertion, one can surmise her intent. Surely Grant's championing of equality among races and peaceable relations with Native Americans was enlightened compared to most of his predecessors. He was also the president most associated with the expansion of American economic strength and its rise on the global stage, which had occurred during the Gilded Age. The Transcontinental Railroad was completed and major advances were made in harnessing electricity by Thomas Edison, who opened his Menlo Park laboratory during Grant's last year in office. That same year, Grant officially opened America's first World's Fair in Philadelphia in 1876 to celebrate the nation's centennial, an event where American progress, industrialization, agriculture, and achievements in the arts were showcased for all to see, including Alexander Graham Bell's telephone (the Emperor of Brazil exclaimed, "My God, it talks!"), the first Remington typewriter (then known as a "typographic machine"), and a Women's Pavilion featuring more than eighty inventions patented by women.

To fit the monument to the man, Shaeffer suggested employing "modern materials"—glass and iron, and curiously, paper too—as well as bright colors, arches, and a "triangular edifice."[4] During the Gilded Age, great technological advancements allowed architects to design taller buildings with steam-powered elevators, making increased use of glass and cast iron and incorporating features such as electric lighting. But the notion of modern architecture for Grant's Tomb also had its critics. The editor of the *North American Review* warned, "Of modern architects only the French can be said to have devised style, and their charming creations are too gay and bright with Gallic levity to be applicable to mortuary purposes. It is the style in which to house a pretty and witty woman, not to cover in the ashes of a hero."[5]

The editor also pondered the suitability of Gothic style, which had partially influenced George Keller's design of James Garfield's memorial tomb, which was yet to be built. The Gothic style, which originated in the late Middle Ages, features towering heights and intricate designs predominant in churches and cathedrals. The Palace of Westminster in London, completed a decade earlier, was a modern interpretation of the Gothic style criticized by the author for its "vain repetition," "long drawn-monotony," and "un-Gothic sameness." To put the matter to rest, the editorial concluded, "this is neither the age nor people to meddle with Gothic art. To do Gothic work requires a Gothic heart, a Gothic head, and a Gothic hand."

Finally, a more traditional option was the neoclassical style, which had always held an allure for Americans. The constitutional government framed by the Founding Fathers drew inspiration from the Roman republics, and military heroes who returned to civilian life were compared to the Roman general Lucius Quinctius Cincinnatus. The editor observed, "Grant himself was not far removed from the type of the great Roman captain."[6] Neoclassic architecture was predominant in Washington, DC, and was used in the foremost democratic American institutions: the United States Capitol Building and the White House. Thus, the neoclassical would also link Grant to the Founding Fathers.

There were also precedents in American statuary. In the first half of the nineteenth century, sculptors often portrayed Washington in toga, sandals, and with the hairstyle of Caesar, to sometimes ludicrous effect, such as Horatio Greenough's bare-chested, muscle-bound rendition that more resembled a seated deity (it can now be seen on the second floor of the Smithsonian's National Museum of American History in Washington, DC). But such depictions had fallen out of favor more than a generation earlier. On January 17, 1853, Representative John C. Breckenridge of Kentucky threw down the gauntlet when he asserted, "The American people never will consent to have another statue of Gen. Washington erected in the Roman costume or in any other than the Continental costume."[7] While few sculptures of heroic Americans in Roman dress could be found after Breckenridge's declaration, the appeal of classical architecture remained strong in America, heightened by the opulence of the Gilded Age.

Suitable precedents in mortuary construction in the United

States were also debated. While memorial tombs date back thousands of years, they were a recent phenomenon in the United States, and architects had yet to find their footing with them. Lincoln's tomb in Springfield, dedicated in 1874, had yet to be embraced by the public—and never really was. The Gothic-influenced memorial tomb for Garfield would be more successful, but ground had yet to be broken at the time of Grant's death, and the dedication would not occur until 1890. As for monuments, Washington now had his in the nation's capital, statues and monuments in Lincoln's honor quickly proliferated across the country after his death, and a statue of Garfield had been dedicated in San Francisco on July 4, 1885. But there existed no such tribute to Grant yet. While there was precedent for a monumental tomb, a much deeper meaning was ascribed to Grant's final resting place from the outset. It was to be both his tomb *and* his monument.

It seemed almost everyone had an opinion on the matter, enlightened or otherwise. George F. Ditson, a doctor from Cleveland, proposed a modern yet idiosyncratic monument made entirely of red, white, and blue glass, with colored columns and a statue of Grant within the patriotic (and fragile) structure. The doctor concluded his letter by reminding the association that he was "not an architect."[8] This amateur's suggestion highlights the single group that was more eager than any other for a fitting tribute to Grant: the professional architectural community. Professional architects had a strong vested interest in an extraordinary design and sought to involve their best and brightest in a project that would reflect well upon their community. In April 1886, *Century Magazine* proclaimed, "Seldom indeed does any work of art bring with it responsibilities so grave as those which are involved in our contemplated memorial to General Grant. Not only for the sake of the monument itself, but for the sake of American art and the American people, is it peculiarly necessary that we should move warily in deciding who shall create it for us, and what he shall create, and how."[9] Accepting the weighty responsibility, the group took the lead. Only eight days after Grant died, two architects wrote to Chester Arthur in his capacity as the chairman of the Grant Monument Association to make a case for a professional design competition: "You are no doubt familiar with the custom in vogue in France in the matter of securing appropriate and meritorious designs for such memorials."[10] But "America," the architects argued, had "failed in her greatest ventures of this sort," although they offered no examples.[11] Unlike Lincoln's sudden death, Grant's long, public terminal illness had provided American architects many months to consider the inevitable grandiose memorial that would be erected in his honor.

In the August 1, 1885, issue of *American Architect and Building News* magazine, published in Boston, editors invited their readers to "lay aside their prejudices against competitions; forget that the ideas they evolve may be pilfered from them so that they may lose both glory and profit; disregard for the moment that a more legitimate and authorized competition may soon be announced; overlook the fact that the reward we may be able to offer is wholly incommensurate with the task," and "to show the world what the American architect can accomplish when such a theme is placed in its hands." The magazine laid out plans for its own design contest. The rules were simple: "A monument to General Grant, to be erected in a large city, at a cost of not more than $100,000."[12] The informal proposal was formalized in the following week's issue, with an end date for submissions set at September 19, 1885. Three token prizes of $50 would be awarded to the three best designs.[13] While the editors made clear that the competition was not for Grant's permanent tomb, the similarities—New York was the largest city, and their proposed cost was a reasonable expectation of how much the Grant Monument Association would raise—were unmistakable. Indeed, some of the architects who submitted designs would do so again when the design competition for the actual tomb was held, but that would be some years away.

When the competition concluded, the top prizewinner was Harvey Ellis from Utica, New York. The architect had recently returned from a trip to France, and his design was in the classical style of Roman antiquity. He drew his monument atop a hill beside a body of water, suggesting he had considered Riverside Park, and it "had a decidedly military character to it."[14] Daily newspapers with a much wider circulation than *American Architect and Building News* reported on the contest and announced the winner, which surely left more than a few readers confused and believing that a design competition for Grant's actual tomb had taken place. Clearly, though, this hastily put-together but well-executed design competition set an example for the Grant Monument Association to emulate and encouraged the American public to expect them to do so. In themselves, however, the proposed designs were unspectacular, and one fellow entrant lambasted the winner's design as "a preposterous piece of nonsense."[15]

Architects didn't hesitate to criticize Grant Monument Association's members, motivations, and the choice of location. On August 1, the editors of *American Architect and Building News* declared, incorrectly, that Grant's dying wish, to be buried in Washington, DC, was "summarily swept aside by the enterprise of the great City of New York, which immediately appointed a huge committee of its most eminent beer-sellers, brokers, politicians and Railroad men to 'take charge' of a 'memorial' of some unexplained sort." The writers had no issue with Riverside Park as "a resting-place for the bodies of weary mortals," but they strongly objected to the "neglected and remote strip of unimproved land, adjoining the Hudson River Railroad tracks" to "stow away a costly monument, to the most distinguished person of the age, in an uncultivated and uninhabitable strip of land."[16] The grounds were "almost inaccessible, as well as impassable, for anything except goats." The editors echoed criticisms of the day when they accused the planners of a swindle, as the only people who would benefit were the "owners of the cheap and neglected lots fronting the Park."[17]

Two months after Grant's death, the American Institute of Architects (AIA), sensing that the Grant Monument Association was struggling, wrote to offer advice. The AIA, formed in 1857 by Richard Upjohn to promote architectural excellence, urged that a design competition be held and offered specific rules to consider, such as the number of entrants and amount of the prize. What rules were needed to attract America's best architects was also debated on the pages of *American Architect and Building News*. Inexplicably, such advice from professional architects was ignored by the association. Nor, it appears, did any of its members contact anyone in the National Lincoln Monument Association or the Garfield National Monument Association to seek advice on how to proceed.

In early September 1885, Alonzo B. Cornell offered a hint as to the nature of the memorial that the association may have been discussing privately when he told a reporter from *Brooklyn Magazine* that "in his opinion, the memorial should consist of a monument, a library, and a mausoleum all connected and embracing within one edifice." In the same article, he made clear that the final decision depended on how much money was raised and hinted at his ambitious goal when he said, "a million is not too much, provided the people get their million's worth." Cornell assured the public that more information would be forthcoming.[18]

Rather than establish guidelines and specific instructions for submitting proposals in order to obtain the best design, association members were improvising and seemed simply to hope that things would fall into place. However, as donations tapered off, there was growing awareness that those who had contributed as well as those considering doing so "were desirous of knowing something about the manner in which the fund was to be expended." At an executive committee on November 9, 1885, it was suggested "that it might be as well for the committee to take some steps regarding a design." A Committee on Design was established, initially consisting of only three members, railroad executive Sidney Dillon, former mayor of

Brooklyn Seth Low, and lawyer and politician Adolph L. Sanger, "with power to review plans." The next day, their call for ideas was published in the *New York Times*. However, no formal rules or guidance were offered in the notice, only a vague request that "Designs for the national memorial may be sent to the committee or Secretary Greener."[19] The *New York Times* was quick to term this vague solicitation "ridiculous."[20] Perhaps realizing that Cornell's million-dollar target was unlikely and formalized rules were a necessity, as the end of the year approached, Secretary Greener drafted rules for a design competition with a $400,000 budget. Greener's rules, however, remained in draft form and inexplicably were never published.

Nonetheless, by the winter, designs from hopeful artists and architects were arriving at Grant Memorial Association headquarters. With pressure mounting to show progress, the association announced in January 1886 that they would "make a selection at once" from the entries received.[21] Unfortunately, all the designs that had been submitted turned out to be subpar. A National Park Service historian would comment years later that "most of them were dreadful." One in particular was so awful that a reporter from the *New York Times* feared it "could frighten people . . . completely away from the fund."[22] No selection was made, and an unfortunate consequence of this fiasco was that the deflated association made no further attempt to obtain a design for the rest of the year.

In the spring of 1887, almost two years after Grant's death, the association finally did what it should have done as soon as it was established. Greener sent letters to other monument committees, most notably the Garfield National Monument Association, to solicit advice, and they engaged Napoleon LeBrun, an accomplished architect originally from Philadelphia and with more than forty years of experience, to write up the rules for a competition. It appeared at long last that the association was taking their "sacred duty" seriously.

On June 10, 1887, the association announced a design competition. But rather than providing than a list of rules, their vague request for "sketches or designs for a monument or memorial" specified little more than that the structure could be of "granite, marble, bronze, or other appropriate material."[23] LeBrun had not yet produced his guidelines, and evidently, rather than wait for him, the association had decided to open the competition. National Park Service historian David M. Kahn later ridiculed the announcement, remarking that "the only solid piece of information" was that submissions must be received by October 31.[24] It was absurd, and criticism arrived in heaps as the public waited for more information. While Grant's remains moldered in the temporary tomb, the summer heat abated and autumn leaves began to fall. No additional details were provided as the submission date approached. Several days after the October 31 submission deadline, Greener was asked if an extension had been granted. Contrary to the June announcement, Greener incredulously responded that "no time frame had ever been fixed, and if there had been, the Executive Committee could not have granted an extension, as they have not met for some months past."[25] As the year ended and 1887 turned into 1888, there was no further announcement.[26]

That winter, LeBrun at long last provided a draft of rules for the design competition for the association to consider. A circular consisting of eighteen rules was drawn up on January 26, 1888, and released to the press a week later. On February 5, 1888, the *New York Times* announced, "The Grant Monument Association . . . has issued a circular to artists, architects, and sculptors inviting them to submit . . . designs for the monument of memorial building to be erected over the tomb in Riverside Park," followed by a detailed list of rules.[27] At long last, a competition was underway! The rules were published in European newspapers as well, as the competition went global. The contest was blind, with candidates requested to remain anonymous and mark their design with only a "motto or cipher." Entrants would not be paid for their submissions, but prizes ranging from $200 to $1,500 would be awarded (between $5,500 and

$41,000 today). Candidates were instructed to consider a budget of $500,000, but, "Should a larger sum be hereafter contributed, the surplus may be expended in additional ornamentation and decoration and suggestions embodying such a possibility should accompany the design." Buried toward the bottom of the list was Rule 14: "If the Committee do not consider any of the designs submitted and appropriate to the purpose of the monument, they may institute a second competition which may, at their option, be limited to five accepted competitors."[28] In short, the association had given themselves an escape clause.

Not surprisingly, architects vigorously protested some of the rules, particularly regarding payment. In the late 1880s, architects were organizing for the recognition afforded other professions along with standardized fees. Conventions and professional periodicals, some cited above, had roots in this period. What the architectural community might have tolerated a generation earlier was no longer acceptable. The clause that caused the most distress was that "Each competitor shall state . . . what further remuneration he would expect for furnishing all details."[29] At a time when the standard fee was 5 percent of construction, architects were instead being told to name their price.

On March 15, 1888, the American Institute of Architects wrote the association "to respectfully protest against the terms of the competition," listing the particular sections with which they took umbrage.[30] The Architectural League of New York also wrote to object to the "indefiniteness and ill-judged nature" of the rules.[31] Both organizations offered suggestions for improving the competition. A prominent American artist, Frederic Crowninshield, summed up the architects' position: "A good design implies thought and labor, neither of which an artist of repute can afford to squander."[32]

Indifferent to the objections of professionals as well as their suggestions, the association made no changes to the rules. The title of the circular announcing the contest should have been a telltale sign that the association was still fishing for ideas: "To Artists, Architects and Sculptors." The deadline for submissions was set for November 1, 1888, which was much more time than had been allotted a year earlier but still not enough, as evidenced by numerous complaints from architects. In response, the association made their one concession and moved the deadline to January 2, 1889. And then moved it again to January 10.[33]

Shortly after Grant's death, several newspapers, including the *Philadelphia Times*, had challenged the architectural community with a clarion call for "An American Pantheon." The origins of the term "American Pantheon" are credited to William Fearing Gill, the author of several books, including a biography of Edgar Allan Poe. Gill first mooted the concept in 1881, the year James Garfield was assassinated, and the idea of a grand neoclassical structure inspired by the classic architecture of Rome or its revival in Paris (there is a Pantheon in each city) took hold after Grant died. The translation of the Greek *panthéon* is "temple to all the gods," suggesting in Gill's concept a single structure to honor many of America's illustrious deceased, such as with England's Westminster Abbey or Germany's Walhalla.[34] While designs for the competition would focus on a burial place for Grant alone, many included classical inspiration in an attempt to fulfill the vision of "an American Pantheon."

Although the term "American Pantheon" was new, the concept of honoring America's greatest presidents with monuments was not. In the earliest years of the republic, Americans chose to look forward to a promising future rather than memorialize or preserve the past. As with so many things, one man alone proved the exception to the rule: George Washington, first in war, first in peace, first in the hearts of his countrymen, and also first to be memorialized in stone on a grand scale. The Washington Monument was the single outlier, but even that was not without its troubles. Following a design competition, Robert Mills's concept was selected in 1845. It included the iconic towering obelisk but also a substantial platform incorporating thirty hundred-foot tall columns. Construction started in 1848, but persistent fundraising problems meant that it would span two generations. During the Civil War, the incomplete stump was often used as an analogy for the fractured Union. The monument was finally completed in 1884 and dedicated by President Chester Arthur just five months before Grant died, on February 21, 1885.[35]

When the Washington Monument was slowly rising in the skies, America's citizens still did not embrace grand sculptures as a way to recognize other famous Americans. While Washington was universally loved, the 1840s and 1850s were a time of sectionalism and division between North and South, with neither side able to agree on much beyond an admiration for the nation's first president. Northerners held up this Founding Father as their champion of liberty and independence, while Southerners lionized him as a slaveholder who owned more than three hundred human beings at the time of his death. But then came the election of Abraham Lincoln, the secession of the Southern states, and over four years of lives lost and brothers' blood spilled on battlefields across the country. So much changed with the Civil War that, as a later historian observed, "The aversion to impressive monuments, to pomp, and to militarism, came to an abrupt end."[36]

The first monument to foreshadow Grant's Tomb memorialized the man who stood beside him as the savior of the Union. Since the death of George Washington in 1799, presidents were placed in humble crypts or buried in simple graves. The final resting places of Thomas Jefferson, James Madison, James Monroe, Martin Van Buren, John Tyler, and Zachary Taylor would hardly warrant a second look. The modest funerals and nondescript graves were consistent with the republican virtues of the founding era, which distinguished a democratic America from the monarchies and tyrannies of Europe. But all that changed in 1865 when Abraham Lincoln was murdered. The outpouring of grief was staggering. For twenty days, his embalmed remains traversed the country and were displayed at public viewings in major cities along the way to his final resting place in Springfield, Illinois. There his coffin was placed in a temporary vault while a more appropriate tomb could be erected. For the first time, a design contest was held to allow the public to participate. Construction started on Lincoln's tomb in 1868, three years after he died, and it was dedicated in 1874.

Lincoln's tomb was appropriate for the ostentation of the Gilded Age. It was an impressive memorial, partially in the Egyptian style epitomized by the Washington Monument, with an obelisk towering eighty-seven feet in the air and in each corner a twenty-five-foot

Abraham Lincoln's tomb in Springfield, Illinois, was the first colossal memorial tomb erected for a deceased president at the dawn of the Gilded Age. (Courtesy of the Library of Congress)

circular pedestal, with statues adorning the exterior. (During a 1901 reconstruction, an additional fifteen feet was added to the obelisk to increase the memorial's majesty.) The tomb was funded through popular subscription, the same approach the Grant Monument Association would take almost twenty years later. Not only did it memorialize a heroic American in stone, it also offered citizens a way to demonstrate their patriotism through their donation. As the *City News* from Muscatine, Iowa, suggested, Lincoln was "worthy of commemoration by the American people and everybody should embrace this opportunity to participate in the work."[37] Though Grant normally shunned such ceremonies during his presidency, he insisted upon traveling to Springfield to speak on behalf of his good friend and former commander in chief for the dedication on October 15, 1874. In his speech, he offered unequivocal praise: "To know him personally was to love and respect him for his great qualities of heart and head, and for his patience and patriotism." Grant closed with a lamentation for lost possibilities: "In his death the nation lost its greatest hero. In his death the South lost its most just friend."[38]

With the Civil War, the aversion to monuments evaporated, and across the landscape smaller memorials to battles, soldiers, and regiments popped up like dandelions. Not everyone was enamored with this trend. A reporter for the *Deseret News* in Utah lamented the "Mania for Monuments," blasting the fad as "among the most prominent follies of the times." While ancients erected monuments to their "gods and oracles," Americans, according to the reporter, had been recognizing ordinary people whose only achievement has been *to die*. Additionally, the monuments were not even "high art" and possessed "little or no beauty." The "waste of means" served "no earthly benefit save to the sculptor."[39] In light of such criticism, it is unsurprising that the Lincoln tomb was neither a critical nor a sentimental success and was lambasted as "an awkward obelisk [that] never became an effective symbol for the War President."[40] That honor would have to wait a half century for the completion of the Lincoln Memorial.

At the time of Grant's death there was a backlash to what was seen by some as the proliferation of unattractive monuments erected to unworthy individuals. Grant, argued the critics, deserved better. Puck, August 19, 1885, "No More of Those Hideous Monuments, Let Us Have a Memorial of General Grant that will be Worthy of a Great Nation." (Courtesy of the Library of Congress)

But the dam had broken, and the public was undeterred. Seven years after Lincoln's tomb was erected, Americans were again called upon to recognize another murdered Civil War figure and United States president. After James Garfield was shot in 1881, the second president to be assassinated was memorialized with another ostentatious tomb projected to be double the height of Lincoln's. The impressive 180-foot-tall Gothic tomb that would be erected in Cleveland's Lake View Cemetery in 1889 was praised as "America's first great mausoleum." But while the mausoleum was great, the man inside was not widely considered so. Garfield was not a military hero and had served only six and a half months in office. His memory quickly faded from the American consciousness, and his monument became devoid of meaning.

The colossal architecture of the period highlights another hallmark of the Gilded Age, which was massive inequality. A few basked in opulence while many suffered abject poverty. New York encapsulated these extremes better than any city in America. Uptown areas such as Millionaires' Row on upper Fifth Avenue and along the Hudson River were filled with mansions and palaces, while downtown tenements sagged under the weight of newly arrived immigrants crammed into dank, dark rooms. Unfortunately, the tenants were often as filthy as their housing. An 1894 report claimed, "Several hundred thousand people in the City have no proper facilities to keep their bodies clean."[41] Given the extremes of the times, people looked for an individual of character and integrity to make sense of it all. In other words, as David W. Blight states, "Gilded Age Americans desperately needed a hero." They needed to look no further than the tragic and triumphant Ulysses S. Grant.[42]

For Grant, the public overwhelmingly supported a final resting place at least as grand of that of his assassinated predecessors. Many more felt he deserved even better.[43] But not all were optimistic that American architects could rise to the challenge. The satirical American periodical *Puck* warned an overeager public to "try to resist the temptation to make further fools of ourselves" and avoid "another sculptural monstrosity."[44]

Of the sixty-five entries received for the 1888 competition, only twenty-three were from Americans. Several entrants had participated in the unofficial competition held by *American Architect and Building News* three years earlier. A surviving list of the submissions perhaps illustrates the association's preoccupation with finances, as each typed entry has a handwritten cost scribbled beside it. With so little money in the Grant Monument Fund in November 1888 and the price tag of some submissions exceeding $500,000, association members must have been unnerved.[45] But regardless of cost, the entries were disappointing. A National Park historian judged years later that "the designs, with rare exception, were quixotic."[46] This is not surprising. Given the association's tarnished reputation, dismal fundraising, and record of ambivalence and ineptitude, the best and brightest had decided to sit on the sidelines. An editorial in the *New York Times* lamented, "An open competition does not attract men whose reputation is established and who have a more trustworthy occupation than engaging in what must be a lottery. The competitors are for the most part either unsuccessful or novices."[47]

A committee of six experts was established to judge the designs, chaired by Napoleon LeBrun and including architects and professors of architecture.[48] They reviewed the entrants over the course of five meetings and, on April 23, 1889, formalized their opinions in a letter to Greener. They had chosen the top five, but each had its flaws. The design submitted by Adolf Cluss and Paul Schulze, titled "Sword and Laurel," was considered the best. It featured a 240-foot shaft topped by a statue of Grant on horseback. It resembled Lincoln's tomb but would cost a million dollars to construct. *Harper's Weekly*, which had reviewed the entrants and chosen their own winners (only four aligned with the committee's choices), was not impressed. The periodical criticized the design as "a light-house decorated in the worst of taste."[49] Second prize went to John Phillip Rinn of Boston, designer of the Bennington Battle Monument in Vermont. While that structure towered 306 feet in the air, Rinn's design, titled "Pro Patria," would have bested it at a staggering height of 518 feet. It also featured the world's largest light atop the structure, harnessing the novel energy source of the age, electricity. The committee liked the obelisk but observed, "The entire base below the shaft is bad."[50] Third place was awarded to "1822" by Hartel and Neckleman, a German firm from Leipzig, despite the fact their submission proposed a monument for "General *Grand*."[51] Again the committee found fault and noted, "the side is better than the front." Fourth prize went to another Boston architect, Julius A. Schweinfurth, whose design, "Let Us Have Peace," suspiciously resembled the original renderings of the still-incomplete James Garfield memorial. Not surprisingly, Schweinfurth had been in Cleveland several years earlier when the Garfield monument was undergoing final design revisions.[52] Lastly, in fifth place was Herbert A. Gribble from England, whose design "D. O. M." was inspired by the architecture of ancient Mexico, Greece, and Egypt. While noting the plan's "generally inferior details," the committee surely was intrigued by its bargain $81,000 price tag.[53] Interestingly, while only a third of the entrants in the anonymous competition were American, three of five winners were from the United States. Regardless, none of the five prize-winning designs were chosen to become Grant's Tomb, as none were deemed worthy, and the association strongly considered a second competition.

John Hemenway Duncan was one of the novices the *New York Times* bemoaned in its editorial, but he would not remain so for much longer. For the competition, the unknown Duncan had partnered with another architect, perhaps Jonathan Harder, about whom little is known now. Duncan's design, with four domes and an equestrian statue, did not earn a prize, but it did garner praise from the *Boston Globe*, whose critic called it "unmistakably a tomb of military character."[54]

The competition, like the association's fundraising, was an unmitigated disaster. Instead of announcing a decision based on the committee of experts' findings, the association held its tongue and said nothing through the spring and into the summer. They slowly evaluated their options while the public and the press could only speculate on their deliberations. The executive committee delegated a "board of experts" to review the predicament, but with none of the submissions "satisfactory and acceptable," the board responded on June 10, 1889, with a recommendation to hold a second competition.[55] However, the association was not ready to give up and instead designated another special committee to review their options. In December 1889, the special committee confirmed the board of experts' opinion and recommended "a second design competition when the committee have decided whether to build a Monument or Memorial Building or both." The report continued, "We recommend that only such competitors deemed worthy, and meritorious by the association be invited to compete."[56] In other words, the association should figure out what it wanted and refrain from unrestricted calls for artists, architects, and sculptors. No more game of chance in which any enthusiast with a pencil and paper could pull a chair up to the table.

Finally, after its 1890 annual meeting in February, the association announced the prize-winning entries. The next day, the *New York Times* seconded the association's judgment: "None is worthy of execution in the form it is submitted," concluding, "the competition must therefore be pronounced a failure."[57] A month later the association confirmed the inevitable: "Neither of the plans for the memorial which were awarded prizes will be adopted as practicable, nor will any of them be used as a source of suggestions for the design which is finally adopted."[58]

With the failure of the competition, another year was gone, with prize money wasted, expenses accrued, and the Grant Monument Association's reputation in tatters. Donations barely met operating costs. Four and a half years after Grant's death, they were no closer to selecting a design than they had been the day they were formed. The association was also no longer speaking in concert to the press. After the February announcement, Adolph L. Sanger gave an interview to a reporter from the *New York Times* to clarify the association's next step. Sanger stated that the association would send out letters to "six or a dozen artists and architects." He added, "Of course, the gentlemen who shall be picked out by the committee as the most famous in their professions will be paid for their trouble," before clarifying, "It will be in no sense a competition." He also addressed how they would seek to respond to the public's lack of faith in the project: "Upon arriving at a decision as to the general scheme of the memorial the committee will, I think, start right out and begin building. The people like to see something tangible, and when the memorial is begun it will not be long before the contributions will be coming in." He went on to list who might be contacted, though some of the names he cited were incorrect: "I think, Hartel & Berkelman [the actual name was Neckleman], who won the third prize and H. A. Gribble of South Kensington, London who won the fifth prize, in the recent competition."[59] Amazingly, Sanger's freewheeling interview seems to have preceded any communication with the five winners of the previous contest. It was not until six weeks later that the fourth-place winner, Julius A. Schweinfurth, who was hoping to participate in a second competition, discovered that not only was it already underway, but also that he had been excluded.

On April 1, 1890, the *New York Times* conveyed more definitive information from the association: "A resolution was adopted that the structure ought to be of such altitude and capacity as to present an attractive elevation, and to afford ample room within it, not only for a sepulchre for General Grant and his wife, but also for a memorial hall."[60] National Park Service historian David M. Kahn comments, "If these requirements had only been stated years earlier, how simple things would have been!"[61] Editors of *Architecture and Building* were satisfied but skeptical: "It is hoped that the Committee have learned a lesson from their last experience . . . and will avail themselves of professional advice and draw up conditions of competition with such inducements as to call forth the best architectural talent in the country."[62]

On April 7, letters were sent out to a number of potential candidates to ask if they might be interested in participating in another, more exclusive competition. (It is unknown how many letters were sent out or if the list included the two previous winners named by Sanger, as many Grant Monument Association records were lost over the years.) Only five days later, on April 12, Greener sent another letter to five of the architects who had expressed interest in participating in another competition, to inform them that they had been selected by the executive committee to do so. The letters went to Carrere & Hastings from New York; Charles W. Clinton from New York; Napoleon LeBrun and Sons from New York (recall that LeBrun had drafted the rules for the previous failed competition);

John Ord from Philadelphia; and John Hemenway Duncan from New York.[63] Why Duncan was chosen, though he was not one of the five winners in the earlier competition, is unknown. However, the architect had recently made a name for himself by designing the triumphant Soldiers' and Sailors' Arch in Prospect Park, Brooklyn, and it seems likely this brought him to the attention of the Grant Memorial Association.

The group was provided specifications for submission, including approval to submit multiple designs. There was a hard $500,000 cap on the cost, with no liberty to run over on the assumption additional funds might be donated. At this point, Cornell's million-dollar goal had long since been abandoned, and it was increasingly a long shot that they would even succeed in collecting $500,000. A deadline of July 1, 1890, was set for submissions, almost five years after Grant's death.[64] In contrast, a design for Abraham Lincoln's tomb had been selected just over three years after his assassination in 1865, while the design for James Garfield's was selected two years after his 1881 assassination.

Charles Clinton responded by suggesting that he convene with the other four contenders to draw up, and agree upon, the rules of the competition, and Greener concurred. The negotiations were done and the rules established in secret, rather than formulated off the cuff for the press, as Sanger appears to have done. At a meeting held a few days later, the competitors agreed on two entries per architect, detailed minutiae such as the color and scale of the designs and whether people and trees would be allowed in the drawings (people were allowed, but trees were not), and settled on a $500 payment to each entrant, win or lose.

With the rules set, the group came back to the association with five requests. First, they wanted a commitment for their designs to be put on display for public review before a winner was selected. The executive committee rejected this request, perhaps out of concerns that public opinion could differ from their own selection.[65] The second request was to augment the executive committee, who were to serve as judges, with three experts in the field, since the association simply did not have the professional expertise to critically judge architectural work. This had been a point of contention since the start of the process of commissioning a design. Again, the executive committee denied their request. The decision would be theirs alone. Third, the architects wanted an assurance that the winner would be employed to build the monument. The executive committee refused to provide such an assurance, claiming that they could not commit to building one of the designs sight unseen. This was perhaps understandable, since only several months earlier they had received sixty-five entries to the previous competition and none of the five winning designs they selected was deemed worthy of being realized. The executive committee did approve two less-controversial requests. The design submissions would be returned after the competition, and the competitors were granted a two-week extension for submissions until July 15. With the rules agreed upon, the architects went about their designs.

Meanwhile, the association continued to pursue the means to pay for the tomb. While years ago there were reservations about which fundraising efforts were appropriate, such concern seemed to have dissipated as the association proved they were no longer above "nickel and dime schemes."[66] One scheme was proposed by composer Silas G. Pratt, who wrote Greener, "I wish to offer a production of my Lecture-Concert the 'Musical Metempsychosis' for the Grant Monument Fund." Pratt, whose proclaimed specialty was reincarnation of a human's soul into an animal, or vice versa, claimed that his peculiar belief was "not an experiment, but a recognized success."[67] By May 1890, a small gift shop had finally been built near the tomb. Only the association had permission to sell images of the tomb, and prints of its commissioned photographs could be purchased there along with other Grant souvenirs.[68] The relatively simple gift shop project, first proposed a month after the funeral, had taken almost five years to complete.

Ulysses S. Grant photograph taken by Matthew Brady while Grant was serving as President of the United States. (Courtesy of the Library of Congress)

Ulysses S. Grant reading a newspaper on the porch at Mount McGregor. This is the last photograph of Grant and was taken on July 19, 1885, four days before he died. (Courtesy of the Library of Congress)

Grant's funeral procession in New York City on August 8, 1885. A crowd of one and a half million saw the event. Note the audacious men who climbed telephone poles for a bird's-eye view. (Courtesy of National Park Service, Manhattan Historic Sites Archive)

A lone soldier stands guard at Grant's temporary tomb. The picture was taken by D. N. Carvalho, official photographer of the Grant Monument Association. (Courtesy of the Library of Congress)

A lithograph featured the temporary tomb. Note the surrounding landscape. While the lack of other buildings was authentic, the lush plantings and full-growth trees were largely a figment of the artist's imagination. (Courtesy of the Library of Congress)

An early drawing of John Hemenway Duncan's design featuring a broad base, adorning statuary, and a prominent staircase to the Hudson River to allow visitors easy access by boat. (Courtesy of the National Park Service, Manhattan Historic Sites Archive)

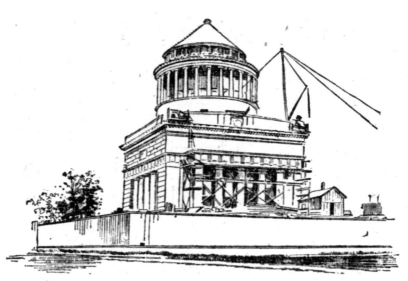

During the years when construction of Grant's Tomb was underway, newspapers kept the public apprised of the progress and often included sketches in their articles. These two drawings were from the summers of 1895 (top) and 1896 (bottom) and show the tomb before and after the dome was completed. (From New-York Tribune, July 28, 1895 and New York Times, August 2, 1896)

Construction on Grant's Tomb nears completion in 1896. In this extraordinary photograph, one can see supply shacks, scaffolding, cables suspended above, and dozens of workers. Among the four people standing are (second from the left) architect John Hemenway Duncan and (to the right) Superintendent of Construction George D. Burnside. (Courtesy of the National Park Service, Manhattan Historic Sites Archive)

Program from the Dedication of Grant's Tomb on April 27, 1897. Twelve years after his death, public affection for Grant was still strong as 53,000 people marched in a six-mile parade. (Courtesy of the National Park Service, Manhattan Historic Sites Archive)

Grant's Tomb had become an altar of reunification as evidenced by this Puck cartoon from April 28, 1897, depicting an aged Confederate and Union soldier mourning together at Grant's final resting place. (Courtesy of the Library of Congress)

"Obituary of Graffiti—Grant's Tomb being treated with Hydron 300 [. . .] Renee Weiss is shown in the process of wiping off the problem," August 4, 1972. *Despite the optimistic legend, declaring an obituary for graffiti at Grant's Tomb in 1972 was a quarter century premature. Note the missing beak on the eagle: The appendage was broken by vandals so frequently the Park Service had a cache of replacements* (Sanford Teller Communications, PR 068, ID 90483d. Collection of the New York Historical Society)

Frank Scaturro, a student who enrolled at Columbia University in 1990, took a special interest in Grant's Tomb. He raised awareness of the deplorable conditions and crusaded for much-needed repairs and security. No single person deserves more credit than Frank for the restoration and resurgence of Grant's Tomb. (Courtesy of Frank Scaturro, Grant Monument Association)

Grant's Tomb in 2020. (Author's collection)

Meanwhile, the architects busied themselves with their designs. As the deadline approached, the five asked for a further extension, this time to October. The association resisted initially to avoid further public embarrassment, but eventually they compromised and granted an extension to September 1, 1890. They had a larger concern. A year earlier, General Charles H. T. Collis from the Grand Army of the Republic had begun lobbying again to have Grant's remains moved to Washington, DC. In response, the association had decided to ask Collis to join, and they later designated him chairman of the executive committee. The co-option worked, but the federal government could not be swayed so easily.[69]

In August 1890, Kansas senator and former Union officer Preston Bierce Plumb proposed a resolution to move Grant's remains to Arlington National Cemetery in Virginia. In Plumb's own state, money had been raised and a memorial to Grant already built in Leavenworth, Kansas. At the dedication a year earlier, a *Kansas City Times* reporter noted, "Those who sympathized with the South are not less glad to view a perpetuation of the memory of a brave Northern soldier than those who followed him."[70] Plumb's resolution passed the Senate with no protest from New York on August 8, five years to the day after Grant's funeral, when his remains were first placed in the temporary tomb.[71] The next day, the resolution was sent to the House of Representatives. Pressure was ratcheting up to approve a design and show that progress was being made.

On September 1, the designs arrived at association headquarters on the fifth floor of 146 Broadway. In some ways, they were all quite similar. Every one of them featured the classical inspiration so popular in the Gilded Age, and each included observatories and space for exhibitions. They were also considerably more inspired than earlier submissions. John Ord's design towered 201 feet high, was influenced by Napoleon's tomb at Hôtel des Invalides in Paris, and included conical structures reminiscent of Islamic architecture from antiquity. Ord provided five drawings, boasting that "The design speaks for itself and requires no special description."[72] Perhaps Ord allowed the design to speak for itself because it did not have much to say. A later historian bemoaned that it "had the sad distinction of being the least interesting."[73]

Napoleon LeBrun presented a design with a gilded, domed roof topped by a statue of Victory, which was well received by newspaper critics.[74] Carrere & Hastings submitted the most complex entry, which included a large tower and three main sections: the tomb, a memorial hall, and a "Hexadra or Peristyle" (columns surrounding an open space) to tell the history of the Civil War.[75] While some saw elaborate beauty, others were disappointed. The *Brooklyn Daily Eagle*

A losing design for the Grant Monument Association competition submitted by Carrere & Hastings. It was criticized as "meaningless and expensive" by the Brooklyn Daily Eagle. *(Courtesy of the National Park Service, Manhattan Historic Sites Archive)*

reported that the Carrere & Hastings design was "a very ambitious one, but [it] was regarded as meaningless and expensive by some of the committee."[76] Charles Clinton, who had coordinated the architects at the outset of the competition, submitted a simple circular design borrowed from John Phillip Rinn's second-place entry in the previous contest. It featured columns at the lower and upper levels and, adding a unique twist, combined classic with modernity by including the world's largest electric light to illuminate a statue atop the structure.[77]

John Duncan's design was "a monumental tomb, no matter from what point of view it may be seen." His six-page proposal was meticulous and prefaced by humility: "In modern times no greater task, nor greater honor could be given or desired than to construct a proper mausoleum to the general who led the Union forces to victory in the war of the rebellion." Duncan's use of the term "war of the rebellion" is perhaps worthy of note. In the years after the war, multiple terms were used to name the conflict depending on the perspective. While the term "Civil War" had been used from the outset, some in the North also called it the "war of the rebellion," the "war of secession," or simply the "insurrection." Southerners, on the other hand, were more likely to call it the "war for southern independence," placing the North as aggressors. As the country moved more toward reunification, the less accusatory "Civil War" became predominant.[78]

In his proposal, Duncan strove to include "the expression of repose and dignity in architecture, conforming to the character of the hero we intend to honor." But his design was also emblematic of the age he lived in. He acknowledged borrowing from "the best Greek Precedents in Architecture" as well as "Classical Roman Work," referring in particular to the Pantheon in Rome for the interior vault and arch. The interior was adorned with full relief panels depicting how Grant saved the Union in the Civil War. Recognizing that the tomb must "tie requirements of our day and times," Duncan explained that his design was also practical, for the cavernous hall beneath the dome could be a meeting place for patriotic organizations such as the Grand Army of the Republic and Society of the Cincinnati. Perhaps unnecessarily, he added that the tomb would "avoid all resemblance of a Habitable Dwelling." To ensure that the structure would last through the ages, and demonstrating an aversion to modernism, Duncan proposed that "all glass be avoided." Within a sunken chamber would rest Grant's sarcophagus, which, Duncan acknowledged, "recalls the tomb of NAPOLEON in the Hotel des Invalides."[79] Visitors would view the tomb from above, in effect forcing them to bow their heads in order to see the final resting place. The exterior included a statue on top of a stepped pyramidal roof (as opposed to a traditional dome), which reached 160 feet skyward. The tomb was flanked by multiple equestrian statues. At least eight were visible from the front.[80]

Not only striking in concept and appearance, Duncan's design was also practical, for it had "the advantage of flexibility, as the structure itself could be built for under one million dollars, then decorative embellishments could be added later when the money was raised."[81] One of the most valuable features, according to the public and the judges, was that it looked impressive from any vantage point. The tomb would be the crown on the highest part of Riverside Park, about 130 feet above sea level, and Duncan proposed steps ascending from the banks of the Hudson River to accommodate visitors who arrived by ship. At the time of the competition, the Egyptian and Gothic styles, as deployed in Garfield's tomb, had fallen from architectural favor, but the neoclassical retained its allure, and for many thought leaders and members of the public, "Grant himself was a great captain of the Roman mold."[82]

On September 9, 1890, the executive committee met at 240 Fifth Avenue, the home of Edward M. Knox, committee member and Medal of Honor recipient for his heroism at Gettysburg. In attendance were Greener, Grace, Collis, and several others. After careful consideration of the five entries, they unanimously selected their winner, John Hemenway Duncan.[83] The press was notified right away of the choice, and the executive committee presented their decision to association trustees two days later on September 11.

The relief must have been palpable. After more than five years and numerous failed attempts, false promises, and plenty of public shaming, they had finally chosen a design. On September 12, Greener sent Duncan a letter, apprising him of the association's decision: "Sir, I have the honor to inform you that at a meeting of the Grant Monument Association held Sept. 11, 1890, the recommendation of the Executive Committee relative to your design . . . was unanimously adopted."[84] In a prepared statement presented by the executive committee, it was noted that Duncan's design presented "the features of treatment found in the Pantheon at Rome."[85] Years

John Hemenway Duncan's winning design. Note the stepped roof and statues that adorned the top, face, and front of the tomb. Over time these features would be eliminated due to financial challenges. (Courtesy of the National Park Service, Manhattan Historic Sites Archive)

earlier, the call was issued for Grant's Tomb to be an "American Pantheon," and Duncan's bold design had answered that call.

The next day, the *New York Times* announced that the selection of a design had saved the association "the reproach of failing to provide a dignified tomb for the body of Gen. Grant."[86] To coincide with the announcement, the designs were put on display for the public to review at Ortgies Gallery at 366 Fifth Avenue, who provided their space free of charge (the press had been given an earlier view when Duncan was selected on September 9).

John Duncan went from being a little-known architect to one of the most notable people in New York City, sitting atop the architectural world. Duncan was born in New Orleans eleven years before the end of the Civil War, on January 22, 1854. Before the war began, the Duncan family moved north, to Binghamton, New York. He left Binghamton around 1874 and made his first documented appearance in New York City around 1879.[87] Four years later, he was working in an architect's office on 19 Park Place. He left the city for a short time and returned around 1885 to work at 237 Broadway. His first notable entry on the scene was as an "artist and architect" for a monument to honor another president, when Duncan helped design the Washington Monument at Newburgh, New York, which was dedicated in 1887.[88]

As mentioned, his design for the Soldiers' and Sailors' Arch at Prospect Park in Brooklyn was probably what brought him to the attention of the Grant Monument Association. Duncan was one of thirty-six people to submit a design. On August 6, 1889, the organizers announced that they had "no hesitation in selecting [Duncan's] design . . . as the best among them. Indeed, it is, in our judgement, the only design of all those submitted which is at the same time suitable, in its general conception and character, to the position and purpose in view, and also shows such technical and artistic merit as to redeem it from the commonplace."[89]

While some of the architects he was competing against believed that Duncan should not have been invited to participate in the first place, the accolades he received so soon before the final Grant competition provided ample evidence of his qualifications. Additional credentials would come in May 1891, when Duncan was also awarded the top design for the Trenton Battle Monument, a competition in which, somewhat surprisingly, he was also a judge. His winning entry was a granite triumphal column that towered 148 feet in the air, topped by a platform with thirteen electric lights, once for each colony.[90]

Not all were enamored with Duncan's design for Grant's Tomb, however. Words like "cheap" and "flimsy" (*World*), "squat" and "ugly"

JOHN H. DUNCAN
ARCHITECT

John Hemenway Duncan, the architect who designed Grant's Tomb. (From Notable New Yorkers of 1896–1899: A Companion Volume to King's Handbook of New York City *by Moses King, 1899)*

(*Herald*), "clumsy" (*Nation*), and "heavy" and "awkward" (*Sun*) were used by New York critics.[91] But the *New York Times*, long critical of the Grant Monument Association, approved of their selection and conceded that both "disinterested and competent observers must agree that the choice was well made." Duncan's winning design, the reporter continued, "has been more successfully studied with reference to the site," and added the tomb is "impressive alike in the view from the river and in the view from the shore."[92] The *Brooklyn Citizen* added, "The famous soldier's tomb will be worthy of the man and a credit to the great metropolis."[93] Respected architectural critic Montgomery Schuyler concurred with the association's selection: "There was no question among those who saw the designs submitted for the Grant Monument, that the accepted design was by far the best of them. . . . The others were either unduly wild or unduly tame."[94]

The design was lauded as original, as in a *New York Times* editorial that noted, "so far as novelty is a merit, this design has it in greater degree than any of the others." The feature praised as most original was its stepped roof.[95] Some astutely claimed that Duncan had not invented that feature from whole cloth, but in fact one had to go back a long time to find his inspiration—more than two millennia, to the tomb that introduced the word *mausoleum* into the lexicon.

The Mausoleum at Halicarnassus, in what is now southwest Turkey, was completed in approximately 353 BC. The 135-foot-high tomb was constructed for Mausolus, a provincial Persian king. The structure was so original and influential that the very name of the man it was built for became synonymous with all tombs, which is why a freestanding building constructed to store human remains is now called a *mausoleum*. But to add mystery to the architectural inspiration, the Mausoleum at Halicarnassus no longer existed. It was destroyed in the Middle Ages by an earthquake, so by the time Grant died, only the foundation remained as well as a few pieces of stone.[96] Over the years, artists have attempted to determine what the tomb looked like based on historical description. Those renderings featured the stepped roof that so intrigued the critics of the late nineteenth century.

The *New York Times* claimed that Duncan's design "had no precedents, exact or approximate,"[97] but in fact it showed similarities to several submissions from the earlier competition, raising the question: While Duncan himself could not claim to have invented the stepped roof, did he purloin the idea from a contemporary? Several architects who had recently designed their own interpretation of the tomb of Mausolus may have crossed paths with Duncan, including Henry O. Avery, who had studied at the École des Beaux-Arts in Paris, where he designed a structure in the spring of 1878 that included the peculiar stepped roof. Avery, who was the same age as Duncan, later moved to New York and submitted a design for the unofficial Grant's Memorial competition sponsored by the *American Architect and Building News* shortly after Grant's death. Among Avery's drawings was later found a similar undated and unsubmitted design annotated "for Grant's Tomb," with even more similarities to Duncan's winning submission, including in dimensions (100-foot-square base and 153-foot height) and the river approach. Avery's death in April 1890 made suspicions of a pilfered design unpursued and unprovable.[98]

Although a design had finally been selected and association members were exultant, the federal government did not share their enthusiasm. On December 9, 1890, a heated debate over Senator Plumb's resolution to remove Grant's remains to the capital was held on the House floor. Supporting removal was Michigan representative Byron M. Cutcheon, who speculated that the temporary tomb sat beside "a roadside inn, erected and kept, as I was informed for the benefit of the sporting community, with its horse sheds and other surroundings."[99] The strong opposition to the resolution was voiced most vociferously by representatives from New York. Democrat Roswell P. Flower, from New York's twelfth district, responded that

"The resolution shocks our sense of decency, as it reminds us of the line 'Rattle his bones over the stones.' It is a revolting precedent!" After Pennsylvania representative Charles O'Neill spoke in favor of moving the remains, Republican John Raines from New York's twenty-ninth district pounced on him and attacked Pennsylvania's courage during the Civil War. "Why Sir," he postured, "when that state was shivering with fear, so that you could hear her teeth rattle almost to the Canadian border . . . the citizen soldiers of New York were hurrying to her defense."[100] He concluded with an emphatic declaration that "New York will erect a monument to the memory of Ulysses S. Grant" that was met with thunderous applause throughout the chamber.

This was one of the rare resolutions that the New York delegation stood in solidarity to defeat from both sides of the political aisle. After Raines's triumphant speech, Democratic representative and Medal of Honor recipient Amos Jay Cummings spoke at length. The bill, he said, was "abnormal and monstrous," and he complained, "The cogging spirit that degrades patriotism to the office of a dark lantern to break open the tombs is little better than a crafty evasion of the statute against body snatching." His characterization was met with both laughter and rousing applause. Cummings summed up his argument: "You can not break into a graveyard with a joint resolution of Congress." Once again, a combination of laughter and applause helped convince his colleagues.[101] After the rhetoric came to an end, a vote was taken. The bill to remove the body of Grant was soundly defeated, 154 to 92. Needless to say, the New York press was elated.[102]

With a design secured and the movement to relocate the remains defeated, the association still faced a lack of sufficient funds. They had raised $111,006.17 by the end of 1885, but afterward donations had been atrocious. By the beginning of 1891, the coffers held only $150,000.

Nonetheless, the association members determined it was time to use the money to start construction while they continued with their fundraising efforts. It was estimated they had enough to complete the base of the tomb. Some criticized the strategy, such as a reporter for the *Brooklyn Daily Eagle* who warned of the "unpleasant possibility that the fragment may remain, without addition, for twenty years."[103] Others were even less optimistic and feared that Grant would forever "be entombed, essentially, in a massive square."[104] Any nonessentials were cut. For instance, Duncan's design had included a river approach to the tomb for an estimated $54,000, but the feature was scratched when the New York Parks Department instead calculated the cost at five times the amount.[105]

On April 27, 1891, on what would have been Grant's sixty-ninth birthday, a small groundbreaking ceremony was held. Up until the last minute, there was discussion as to the exact location for the tomb, and because the location was not settled, the association had not yet obtained a building permit, which made the ceremony truly ceremonial.[106]

Gathered at the tomb were members of the Grant Memorial Association and Grand Army of the Republic posts from New York and neighboring New Jersey, Pennsylvania, and Connecticut. The GAR commander for the State of New York, Charles H. Freeman, was the host and organizer for the festivities. To avoid the appearance of endorsing a Republican, New York's Democratic governor, David B. Hill, and mayor Hugh J. Grant, who were both association ex-officio trustees, did not attend, highlighting a growing political divide within the organization.

Commander Freeman introduced General Horace Porter. Nine years junior to Grant, Porter graduated third in his class at West Point in 1860 and joined Grant's staff as aide-de-camp in Chattanooga. At their first meeting in 1863, Porter was taken aback by the great general's small physical presence but struck by his intellectual curiosity, later commenting, "So intelligent were his inquiries, and so pertinent his suggestions, that he made a profound impression upon everyone by the quickness of his perception."[107] Porter rose to the rank of brigadier general and served as Grant's personal secretary in the White House, where they occasionally played croquet together.[108] Porter resigned in 1873 to accept the position of vice president of the Pullman Palace Car Company in Chicago, but after Grant's presidency, he resumed his role as a personal aide. Throughout Grant's final illness, reported the *New York Times*, "One of the most frequent callers at General Grant's is General Horace Porter."[109] He remained a family friend after Grant's death and was with Fred as he reviewed several locations for the tomb, including Riverside Park.

Calling upon his intimate familiarity with his former commander and friend, Porter spoke eloquently at the ceremony about Grant's life and recounted firsthand experiences in witness of his character. When Porter finished, the crowd sang "America" as the warship USS *Yantic*, anchored in the Hudson River, fired a twenty-one-gun salute. Commander Freeman addressed the crowd: "Now in the presence of Almighty God and these witnesses, we, the representatives of the Grand Army of the Republic, break the sod preparatory to laying the foundation of the monument that shall stand as a slight expression of the love of the nation for its chieftain, and shall tell to all the world that the United States of America does not forget her heroic dead." Freemen held up the ceremonial spade and praised it as "a superb specimen of American handicraft, bearing an inscription containing the chief events of General Grant's life."[110] He then stuck the shovel into the ground and placed the dirt into an ornately decorated ceremonial wheelbarrow. To conclude the ceremony, a Marine band played as three hundred children from the Sheltering Arms Asylum slowly walked past the tomb and each placed bouquets of forget-me-nots upon it. The children were closely trailed by tactless relic hunters, who snatched up the flowers moments after they were set down.

After the ceremony, the association members and other guests made their way to Delmonico's for dinner. The restaurant had become the jewel of Gilded Age New York, as well as one of the first in the city to welcome women—assuming, of course, that they were accompanied by a man.[111] At long last, with a design selected, the association had something to celebrate.

7

"THE HUMILIATING SPECTACLE"

PRIOR TO THE ceremonial groundbreaking in late April 1891, the association had not settled on the exact site of the tomb, nor obtained a permit from the city, nor selected a contractor, but it did solicit bids to build the foundation. Ten bids were received, and on May 4, a week after the groundbreaking, the association awarded the job to John Thomas Brady, an Irish-born forty-two-year-old residential contractor. While the contract was being formalized, the small wooden shack used to sell photographs and a flagpole were moved to make way for construction. On June 10, Brady signed an $18,875 contract that covered the foundation for the northern end of the tomb. The southern portion, where the temporary tomb stood, would be addressed later. Shortly thereafter, the site was finalized on the highest part of Riverside Park, as expected.

By the end of June, a true ground-breaking occurred without ceremony. While Brady excavated sixteen feet of earth over the summer of 1891, Duncan went back to his drawing board. He created a more detailed architectural plan because, "in case of delays or death, I wish to leave a record of the entire scheme as projected."[1] Not only was Duncan providing more substance, he also made changes to his original proposal. In the interior, he reduced the size of the opening to the subterranean crypt. From the exterior, he eliminated two Doric columns and also eliminated windows toward the roof of the tomb.

Excavations continued into late August, when the workers began to lay concrete. Brady's crew was now working twenty hours a day in shifts, using lamps at night in order to finish before the colder weather set in. To oversee the project, George D. Burnside, a relative of Civil War general Ambrose Burnside, was hired as superintendent of construction. He would go on to work at the tomb for forty-nine years.[2] By the beginning of October, the northern portion of the tomb's foundation was complete, fulfilling the initial contract obligations.

Brady was next contracted for the southern portion of the foundation. Before he could start digging, he needed to move the temporary tomb. Timber and jackscrews were placed under the hundred-ton tomb, which was raised using hydraulic pumps. Once it was fifteen feet in the air, it was slowly made to traverse approximately thirty feet over three greased beams and was gently placed down at the center of where the new tomb would be constructed. In *Stone*, an Indianapolis periodical that billed itself as "A Journal for Producers, Workers and Users of Stone, Marble and Granite," a reporter hailed the relocation as a "A Monumental Engineering Feat."[3] A reporter for *American Architect and Building News* saw the move through a different lens and lamented, "With more sentimental people, this transfer of the tomb would have been marked by some ceremony, but the New Yorkers appear to have looked upon it simply as an engineering feat, and no one but the workmen and a few reporters seemed to have witnessed it."[4] Although the delicate transferral took a month, only one photograph is known to exist.[5]

With the temporary tomb in its new location, the plan was to build the permanent tomb around it like a Russian *matryoshka* doll. As the days grew shorter, Brady's team raced to complete the southwestern and southeastern piers and the foundations for the front steps. By November the entire foundation was done. For his work through the end of 1891, Brady was paid a total of $47,286.80, or almost a third of what was raised by this time. At this pace, the

Grant Monument Association would run out of funds long before the tomb was completed. In January 1892, Brady signed another contract with the association for $17,000 to construct a six-inch granite base. This was as far as the association was prepared to proceed until more money could be raised.

As always with the Grant Monument Association, lackluster finances betrayed deeper problems. In the middle of 1891, as Brady began work on the tomb, Secretary Richard Greener, whose fundraising efforts had sputtered after a promising start, proposed to restore his own salary to $200 a month (recall that his salary started at $200, but he had reduced it to only $100 a month to save money). With construction finally underway, he felt a restoration was justified. Association president William Grace supported Greener, but other board members, notably General Charles H. T. Collis, disagreed. In October, an executive committee meeting was planned to elect new trustees, including to a seat vacated by Frederick Kuehne, who had died. Grace, who was in Washington, DC, when he learned of the meeting, "protested against it by letter, but during his absence, the committee, acted as it proposed to do."[6] The "Collis faction" went ahead with the meeting and Collis successfully added two allies to the board of trustees: Horace Porter, Grant's good friend for almost a quarter century, and James C. Reed, who had served as private secretary to Chester Arthur.

These changes tipped the political balance within the association from Democrat to Republican, sending shockwaves throughout the old guard. The press closely followed the discord, as evidenced by a provocative headline in the Chicago *Inter Ocean*: TRUSTEES IN TURMOIL.[7] The New York *Sun* lamented, "The association is divided into two factions now."[8] But there were also expectations that the changes would finally get the tomb on track. Beneath a headline that read PUGNACIOUS PORTER, the hopeful reporter for the *Chicago Evening Post* found his elevation to the board of trustees to be "encouraging. Porter is very strengthening."[9]

Greener was "very much alarmed," while Grace, who had been involved literally since the day Grant died, now felt his authority usurped by the "Collis faction." A furious Grace resigned in protest, while Greener took a less drastic approach but to the same effect and declined reelection as secretary. More members followed their lead. Resignations were tendered by Seth Low, who was now president of Columbia University, and New York governor Roswell P. Flower, who as a Democrat member of the House of Representatives had argued a year earlier to keep the tomb in New York. In addition, Vice President Hamilton Fish resigned due to, as the *Manhattan Nationalist* from Kansas reported, "the result of a strife among the

Horace Porter, Grant's good friend and aide-de-camp in the Civil War. Porter became the president of the Grant Monument Association in 1892 and is the man most responsible for completing Grant's Tomb. (Courtesy of the Library of Congress)

members regarding the power of the executive to fill vacancies in the board of trustees."[10] With both Grace and Fish having resigned, the presidency was temporarily filled by Elliot F. Sheppard, who was a member of the "Collis faction."

At the annual meeting on February 18, 1892, the new Republican majority elected Porter as president, Major General Grenville Mellen Dodge as vice president, Reed as secretary in the position vacated by Greener, and Horace L. Hotchkiss as treasurer. Porter had been upset at the lackluster efforts to date and dismayed at the political infighting he had witnessed in the four months since he joined the association. Grant deserved better, he felt. While past presidents had made only disappointingly slow progress under their tenure, Porter understood that dramatic change was required and vowed to be different. He accepted the position "with the understanding that there would be a re-organization of [the association] and a vigorous prosecution of the work of constructing Grant's tomb."[11] In addition to his allegiance to Grant, Porter brought military, professional, and patriotic credentials, and he certainly did not lack ambition and energy.

Porter wasted no time implementing money-saving changes. He moved the headquarters to the fifth floor in the Mills Building at 15 Broad Street. The small room was offered rent-free by its owner, Darius Ogden Mills, a banker and philanthropist who had made his riches by providing financial services in California during the Gold Rush.[12] To ensure nobody else got the same idea as Greener, Porter added a bylaw that "no officer or member of the Association should receive any compensation for his services."[13]

Porter tripled the number of trustees from thirty-three to one hundred "to infuse more new blood into the operations."[14] To do so, he leveraged some of the many connections he had made in the military, as vice president for the Pullman Company, president-general of the Sons of the American Revolution (formed in 1889), and a member of the Union League Club of New York (of which he became president the following year). Porter boasted, "Every one is an intimate friend or personal acquaintance of mine."[15]

Porter's coup d'état was complete, and some in the Gilded Age elite were thrilled. Andrew Carnegie, who had watched from the sidelines, wrote Porter, "It is a great relief to me to hear that you are the head of the hitherto unfortunate Grant Monument movement."[16] From Vienna, where he was serving as American ambassador to Austria, Fred Grant wrote Porter and vented his frustrations dating back to the first overtures from Mayor Grace to bury Grant in New York [underline his]: "Of course it was mentioned that a Grand Tomb would be built to my father when the ground was offered." A now optimistic Fred added, "I feel assured that the matter [of the tomb] will reach a successful end soon now with you in charge."[17] The press, which for almost seven years had chronicled the disappointing progress, was more hesitant. A reporter from the *Illustrated American* wrote, "Presumably new blood has been infused into what seemed very like a mummified body."[18]

Ten days after assuming the office of president, on February 28, 1892, Porter met with Duncan for the first time. While no record was kept of the discussion, at around the same time Duncan was asked officially by the association to rework his design. In a resolution passed on March 4, the association granted authority for the executive committee "to modify the plan and general design for the tomb," including the direction that "the apse [a semicircular recess covered with a half-dome, a common feature in churches] may be dispensed with and the sarcophagus located beneath the center of the dome."[19] In other words, the design should be simplified so the tomb could be constructed for less money.

On March 14, Duncan presented two revised plans at a committee meeting: one retained the apse the architect preferred, and the other eliminated it. At first, the executive committee heeded his wishes and the apse remained, but two weeks later they reversed course and eliminated it. Another cost-saving change was to reduce the size of the monument. The tomb was originally designed with a one-hundred-foot-square base and a height of 160 feet but was now reduced to a ninety-foot-square-base and a height of 150 feet, making it one foot shorter than the Statue of Liberty. The inside height of the dome from the main floor was reduced to a still-cavernous 105 feet. Duncan's changes were finalized before Brady began his work for the season, but it is unclear if they required Brady to make any revisions to his plans.

While these reductions may have seemed minor, the savings, estimated in the tens of thousands of dollars, were significant.[20] Over the next few years of construction, there would be additional cost-saving measures. For instance, a statue of Grant on horseback, part of Duncan's original design, was eliminated, though only after the pedestal had already been built.[21] (While the cost was not finalized, one can surmise the estimated savings, as a similar equestrian statue of Grant was dedicated in 1899 in Philadelphia at a cost of $32,675.35. What is known is that the cost to remove the pedestal was $684.45.)[22] Other interior and exterior sculptures and ornamental accoutrements in the original design, such as bronze candelabras, were also eliminated, saving thousands more.[23]

But Porter knew that reductions in cost alone were not sufficient to bring the monument to completion. He needed to revive the other side of the ledger. For that, he reinvigorated the fundraising efforts and did so with gusto. Like the previous administration, Porter sought the endorsement of, and coordination with, the Grand Army of the Republic. He set an ambitious goal of $250,000. Given the association's dismal track record so far, this target was conceivably bolder than Governor Cornell's original goal of a million dollars. Years earlier, the leadership of the Grand Army of the Republic had objected to the New York tomb and discouraged their members from donating, but now, to encourage their goodwill and loosen their purse strings, Porter proposed that the name of members who donated be listed on an "Autographic Roll of Honor to be placed at Grant's Tomb."[24] He personally invited various New York chapters to attend the cornerstone ceremony on April 27, 1892. In the invitation to Colonel Michael Cummings, chairman of the New York Grand Army of the Republic memorial committee, published in the *Brooklyn Daily Eagle*, Porter warmly welcomed "the comrades of all the posts in Kings County." To demonstrate that under Porter the veterans would receive VIP treatment from here on in, he added, "there will be reserved immediately in front of the speakers' platform sufficient space to accommodate" them.[25]

Porter also sought government funding, despite the failure of previous efforts by the association. For this, he collaborated with New York Assemblyman George L. Weed, who introduced a funding bill on March 7, 1892. On the surface, the bill would have given the association $500,000, 10 percent of which would be the commission for the contractors. But the deal also included a share of Tammany Hall graft. In exchange for the money, Brady and the Union Granite Company were expected to kick up a significant portion to legislators in Albany. Fortunately, the deal was never completed and the bill never passed. The public had been following the changes in the Grant Monument Association as reported in the press. For years, people had felt they were donating to a lost cause, but now, with the ousting of the old leadership, hopes were high for newly inspired New Yorkers to get behind the tomb and see it completed once and for all. Had the bill passed, the new leadership might have been branded as corrupt, and as ineffective as its predecessors.

While the effort to secure government funding was still pending, Porter turned his gaze to the people. The public's disposition may have changed, but the amount of money the association needed to complete the monument was more than double what they had obtained in almost seven years. By 1892, the amount collected stood at a mere $155,000. They needed to raise the rest of the estimated half-million-dollar cost quickly so construction could continue. This was a tall order, and Porter realized he needed professional help to tap into the public's goodwill. Enter Edward F. Cragin, who was one of the most important, if least known, power brokers associated with Grant's Tomb.

Cragin is as mysterious as he was integral to the completion of Grant's Tomb. Little is known of his personal life besides that he was from Evanston, Illinois, a suburb north of Chicago, and he was praised as "a rigorous religionist." (His namesake "Edward F. Cragin Bible Class Choir" performed at a temperance meeting in Chicago in 1889.[26]) What is better known is his business and organizing experience. He was a member of the Union League Club, had served on the board of directors of the St. Paul Carriage and Sleigh Company, and organized a statewide event to celebrate George Washington's birthday. His main credentials when it came to Grant's Tomb were his role in raising money for the World's Columbian Exposition, which would prove wildly successful when it opened in Chicago in 1893. His shrewdness in negotiation is suggested by one event that occurred during the planning, when it was proposed that the fair should close on the Sabbath. Cragin, surely concerned about the loss of revenue, argued that "a closed fair would throw thousands of visitors into saloons or brothels." Instead, he offered to hold religious services at the fair so the devout could attend services without affecting revenue. His compromise was accepted.[27] A reporter would later praise Cragin's role in the World's Columbian Exposition wholeheartedly: "Ed Cragin was the energy, if not the brains, of the enterprise."[28] In short, Cragin was a "wheeler-dealer," as Scott Martelle calls him in *The Admiral and the Ambassador: One Man's Obsessive Search for the Body of John Paul Jones.*[29]

It is unclear exactly how Porter and Cragin first came in contact. David M. Kahn relates that Porter's friend James W. Cott wrote him to suggest Cragin might be able to help. However, an account in the *Chicago Tribune* claims a more dramatic first contact: "Just at a time when the New York committee was at wit's end, Gen. Horace Porter received a letter from Cragin."[30]

Using his Pullman Palace Car Company connections, Porter investigated Cragin and determined that while he was "full of push, enthusiasm, etc.," he was legitimate and not a con man.[31] Porter and Cragin then engaged in several direct exchanges, with Cragin offering to travel to New York City at his own expense so they could continue the discussion in person. The two men met on March 14, as the bill introduced by Assemblyman Weed was falling apart. What Cragin thought about Grant is unclear. He was a Republican who had opposed Grant in 1880, but for him this was strictly about making money. Cragin told Porter he could raise the rest of the funds for a fee and was so sure of his prowess, he pledged that if he failed, Porter would owe him nothing. Porter reportedly was impressed and told General Collis, "This is one of the most remarkable men I have ever met, I should not be surprised if he raised the whole amount before Grant's birthday."[32] Porter accepted the proposal.

Despite the fact that donations had stalled at $155,000 after seven years, Cragin proposed the ridiculously aggressive target of raising $350,000 by April 27, 1892, only thirty days hence! He chose the date because it was Grant's birthday, as well to coincide with a cornerstone ceremony to be held at the tomb on that day. A skeptical reporter from the *Illustrated American* scoffed that the American public outside of New York was "inclined to admit that the prospects [for raising the money] are not very bright."[33] But without realizing it, these naysayers played right into Cragin's plan. Seven years earlier, the announcement that the tomb would be built in New York City was met with hostility from other parts of the country. Now, with the tomb still not built, sentiment outside of New York City had only grown more negative. While most saw this as a problem, Cragin understood that he could use it to his advantage by associating Grant's Tomb with New York pride. In other words, *If the rest of the country believed New York should not—and could not—provide a proper tomb for Grant, let's prove them wrong!* Fully aware that a carpetbagger from Chicago was not the right person to drum up local pride and patriotism, Cragin knew that his role must be kept secret and Porter should be the front man, presented to the public as driving the fund-raising strategy. The plan was quickly put into execution. Following Cragin's guidance, Porter published an open letter in the *New York Times*, chiding the public to rectify "the humiliating spectacle of the remains of the most illustrious soldier of his age . . . lying in a temporary vault in an open city park."[34]

To the members of the association, Porter argued that the money could "not be obtained by piecemeal methods" but instead must be "practical and comprehensive."[35] Cragin and Porter decided they needed to get more people with a vested interest in raising money, so they organized 185 fundraising committees (the number eventually grew to 300) representing local trade and business organizations to canvass their respective communities. The committees, which comprehensively represented covered New York business interests, included the Hotels Committee; Publishers of Books and Periodicals and Importers and Dealers in Books Committee (headed by W. W. Appleton of D. Appleton & Co. and George Haven Putman of GP Putman and Sons); Restaurants Committee (led by Charles Delmonico); Piano Manufacturers Committee (led by William Steinway); Decorators Committee (led by Louis C. Tiffany); Jewelers Committee (led by Charles S. Tiffany); as well as Educational and Scientific Papers Committee; Religious Papers Committee; Trade Papers Committee; News Companies Committee; Paintings Committee, Engravings and Frames Committee; Trunks and Travelling Bags Committee; Manufacturers and Wholesale Retailers and Dealers in Boots and Shoes Committee; Manufacturers and Dealers in Rubber Goods Committee; and the Retail Grocers' Association Committee.[36] With these committees, Kahn later recalled, there were now "scores of fundraising committees instead of just one."[37] To any businesses not directly contacted, Porter made a public plea for support and promised to submit their names and contributions to the press for public recognition.

HE RAISED THE MONEY.

The Man Who Made Collections For the Grant Monument.

There has been much talk of late about the Grant mausoleum, which has just been dedicated in New York, and the credit for

EDWARD F. CRAGIN.

A rare image of Edward F. Cragin from Chicago, the mastermind behind the 1892 fundraising blitz that successfully raised the money needed to complete Grant's Tomb. While few were aware of his critical role, a few newspapers did highlight his contribution after his snub at the dedication. (Atchison Daily from Kansas, May 3, 1897)

In an astounding letter to the citizens of New York City, Porter informed the public that completing the tomb was the responsibility not of the association but rather of *all* New Yorkers, to fulfill the "sacred trust" that the city had entered into when *their* elected officials invited the family to bury Grant in New York. Porter appealed directly and in blunt terms to their sense of patriotism, honor, and obligation to future generations: "It is a duty we owe to our children," he wrote. If they did not succeed, the "unfinished, exposed structure" would serve as a reminder for their collective failure. "We have contracted a debt, and like honest men, we must pay it," he sternly reminded them. With thousands of foreigners expected to attend the World's Columbian Exposition in Chicago the following year, Porter warned, "If the funds required for the promised tomb should not be supplied promptly and the structure be well under way before that time, the name of America should suffer a lasting reproach in the eyes of all the world."[38]

Thousands of flyers were distributed to notify the public where they could donate. Porter personally attended many of the business committee fund drive meetings, where he delivered a prepared speech showcasing the businesslike approach that was now being taken by the association. New York Mayor Hugh J. Grant declared April 8 as a day to donate to Grant's Tomb, and the message was relayed in the city's newspapers.[39] For people not in one of the targeted trade organizations, wooden donation boxes were placed all around the city. A proprietor from the Union Hotel enthusiastically pledged to "do all we can to push on the good work."[40] No tactic was left untried, including an art sale, which netted $3,500.[41] The association was transformed from a charitable pariah to a cause célèbre. The *New York Times* proclaimed, "It actually became a fad to raise money for the Grant Monument Fund."[42]

April 27, 1892, was a beautiful day for the cornerstone ceremony: clear, "with balmy breezes and a genial sun."[43] The ceremony, which was traditional to celebrate the first stone laid for an important building, had Masonic origins. George Washington, a Freemason, laid the cornerstone for the United States Capitol on September 18, 1793, with much fanfare. While the Grant Memorial was not a Masonic affair, it did include much pomp and ceremony to mark the long-awaited milestone. Commemorative medals had been minted to mark the occasion. On one side was stamped an image of the tomb, on the reverse the visages of Washington, Lincoln, and Grant beneath the legend FATHER, SAVIOR, DEFENDER.[44] Many buildings in the city were decorated in patriotic bunting. The New York legislature had declared the day a state holiday, and federal employees in the city were given time off to attend, with government offices in New York City closing at noon. The stock market and exchanges followed suit. Among the 60,000 spectators were, as the *Brooklyn Daily Eagle* reported, "the gray heads of most of the still living heroes of the great war. . . . [T]here are fewer of them at every meeting now."[45] Grant's widow, Julia, was also in attendance, dressed in black and accompanied by her sons and grandchildren and seated among the honored guests on the grandstand. Additional seating had been erected for the general public. Farther afield were spectators who had arrived by foot and carriage as well as "a few hearty wheelman on bicycles."[46] Vice President Levi P. Morton and members of the cabinet were there, but the most esteemed guest, replete in top hat and tails, was President Benjamin Harrison. Harrison had stayed at the Fifth Avenue Hotel, and upon arrival at the tomb, the crowd, which had started gathering early in the morning, broke out in wild applause. According to the *Brooklyn Daily Eagle*, Harrison "acknowledged the crowd with the gracious dignity which, [was] the most striking feature of his public appearances."[47]

At around 3:00 p.m., after the Fort Hamilton marine band played "Hail to the Chief," the ceremony began with a prayer by Reverend John Hall. Next, Porter took to the dais to update the crowd on the results of the fundraising blitz. Despite herculean efforts, only $202,890.50 had been raised in the past thirty days—more than in the previous seven years, but still short of the goal. He commented on the future meaning of the tomb: "When the structure shall have reached completion, the dome will point out the path of loyalty to unborn children. Hallowed memories which cluster around it will remind us of his heroic aid to the republic."[48] Those who could hear him cheered, while those who could not, according to the *New York Times*, also applauded, being "quite willing to take it for granted that he must be saying something that deserved a cheer."[49] Porter next detailed the contents of a copper box that would serve as a time capsule, never to be opened, within the foundation of the tomb: the Bible; a silk American flag; newspapers; several of Grant's letters; his memoirs; commemorative medals and coins from the US Mint; and a copy of the Articles of Confederation, the

Harper's Weekly, *May 7, 1892. President Benjamin Harrison lays the cornerstone at Grant's Tomb before a crowd of 60,000 on April 27, 1892.* (Courtesy of the National Park Service, Manhattan Historic Sites Archive)

Declaration of Independence, and the United States Constitution.[50] After Porter finished, the box was placed in a cavity beneath and then the twelve-ton square granite cornerstone was gently lowered on top of it. Using a ceremonial, ivory-handled golden trowel specially designed for the occasion, President Harrison spread mortar upon the stone as the crowd cheered their approval. Harrison then stepped to the podium to deliver a brief speech, which was punctuated by cheers. "No orator, however gifted, can overpraise General Grant," he declared before praising the recent progress on the tomb: "I am glad to see here what seems to me to be positive assurance that this work, so nobly started upon, will be speedily consummated."[51]

Following Harrison came an address by Chauncey M. Depew from Peekskill, who worked for Cornelius Vanderbilt. Depew's official role was as an attorney, but he was so indispensable he was called "the prime minister to the Vanderbilt family."[52] Typical of the period, his speech was ridiculously long and laborious. Depew began by recounting the decision to place the remains of Grant at Riverside Park, a justification that was still required almost seven years after his death. Recalling ex-president Grant's world tour, he observed:

While visiting the capitals of the Old World, [Grant] had seen the stately mausoleums of their great soldiers or statesmen resting in the gloom of cathedral crypts, or the solitude of public places, far from the simpler graves of their kindred. Under St. Paul's he saw the massive tomb which encloses the remains of the Iron Duke. He was impressed by the grandeur of the Temple of the Invalides, the superb monument which France erected with so much pride and tenderness over the resting place of Napoleon. The perpetual ceremonial, the inhuman coldness, of these splendid tributes chilled and repelled him. He had shrunk all his life from display, and he desired to escape it after death. To lie in the churchyard where slept his father and mother would have been more in accord with his mind. But he appreciated that his countrymen had a claim upon his memory and the lessons of his life and fame. He knew that where he was buried, there they would build a shrine for the study and inspiration of coming generations.[53]

After Depew's oration, Reverend Hall delivered the benediction, and then children lined up to throw flowers on the tomb. Concluding the ceremony, the USS *Miantonomoh*, polished and decorated in bunting in the Hudson River, fired a twenty-one-gun salute. Afterward, the association members headed south to Delmonico's with Julia Grant and their special guests, but not President Harrison. While eager to attend the cornerstone ceremony, he wasn't interested in lingering, and in his acceptance letter to Porter had written that he would depart immediately after the ceremony so he could arrive at the White House, "if possible, by bed time." So, while revelers ate their steaks and toasted Grant, a sleepy Harrison was on a train bound for Washington, DC.[54]

With the ceremony completed, the focus returned, as always, to fundraising. Despite a congratulatory note from Vice President Levi Morton, Porter still had work to do.[55] Although the goal had not been met for the cornerstone ceremony, public enthusiasm was still strong, and the association was open once again to "nickel and dime" schemes. Handsome certificates were distributed for any contribution of fifty cents or more. An essay contest was held for school students to generate interest—an impressive eight thousand entries competed for the twenty-dollar award.[56] Larger donations arrived from the elites, who now proudly attached their names to the newly popular cause, including $5,000 checks from Andrew Carnegie and John D. Rockefeller.[57] Four weeks after the cornerstone ceremony, $100,000 had been added to the fund, which brought the total to approximately $454,000, but it still left Porter $46,000 short of his goal.

On May 23, Porter, presumably with guidance from Cragin, set a new goal for Decoration Day, which was only a week away. Porter challenged association members to increase their efforts, urging each to (emphasis his) "make *personal visits this week* [to trade organizations] and appeal to the people's pride and public spirit."[58] He continued to work all angles, including attempting to revive House Bill 1600 to obtain $250,000 of federal funding that had first been introduced six years earlier. He worked with Montana senator Wilbur F. Sanders, who urged Porter to get New York congressmen to exert their influence. But Sanders also warned the "cheap clamor of provincialism may have some influence upon thoughtless people" who believed New York should pay to finish the job. Once again, the hope of federal support faded.[59]

The day after Decoration Day, a total of $350,700 had been raised. The campaign had succeeded. Together, the former staff officer and the organizational wizard had pushed the citizenry and the Gilded Age elites into action. An additional point of pride was that only $22,000 had come from outside New York.[60] The *Buffalo Enquirer* declared, "New York City has at last redeemed its reputation in the Grant monument matter."[61]

Even after victory was declared, donations continued to pour in. Among them were dozens of small contributions from the New York Institution for the Instruction of the Deaf and Dumb, including sixty-five cents from "Third class boys."[62] At a dinner at the Waldorf Hotel to celebrate Grant's birthday the following year, Porter announced the fund drive started a year earlier had topped $400,000 (bringing the total in the fund to approximately $550,000) before asking the guests to stand, raise their glass, and drink "to the memory of Ulysses S. Grant."[63] On the expense side of the ledger, a mere $17,960.26 had been spent to raise the money, including Cragin's $4,000 commission. In total, adding in the money collected under Greener, more than 90,000 people (either individually or through organized drives) had combined to raise $600,000 toward the memorial.[64] It was at the time the largest public fundraising effort in history.

Now all that was left to do was to build Grant's Memorial Tomb. Unfortunately, at the time of the cornerstone ceremony in late April 1892, a rash of stoneworkers' strikes had occurred in New England. While one financial newspaper noted that the "Accounts of New England strikes of granite cutters and polishers, quarrymen and stonecutters . . . have been generally exaggerated," the effects were real.[65] Brady was able to accomplish little construction for the rest of 1892. But there was still work that could be done. With the removal of the apse, which was to have been the location of the crypt in the original plans for Grant's monument, the temporary tomb had to be relocated once again. Seven months earlier, it had been moved thirty feet from its location on what would become the southern portion of the foundation. On May 25, 1892, it was once again lifted off the ground and slowly transported seventy-five feet north, outside of the permanent tomb's footprint. Brady's workers built a set of wooden steps to allow visitors to climb the small hill to view the coffin inside. While the original two locations had the door to the temporary tomb facing south, this time, inexplicably, the entrance was facing west, toward New Jersey.[66]

Despite the New England quarrymen's strikes, granite needed to be obtained, and a lot of it: sixteen million pounds, to be exact. Duncan and Porter took a road trip through several states to personally review stone, monuments, and suppliers. Samples were submitted for chemical analysis at Harvard to determine strength and how many pounds of pressure the stone could endure before breaking. For six months they searched, and a weary Porter later recalled, "It seemed impossible for a time to find a stone that would fulfill all the exacting conditions opposed."[67] Finally, they decided on the Maine and New Hampshire Granite Company. According to the Harvard study, their stone would not break until it was under 15,720 pounds of pressure per square inch. Add another 590 pounds and the stone would pulverize. The company had been formed only six years earlier in 1887, and its first president, George Wagg, had died January 1, 1892, only months before his company would play a role in the greatest tomb in American history.[68] The company, now led by Tucker Payson and Ara Cushman, was deemed financially sound after an audit by R. G. Dun and Company (the firm that later evolved into Dun and Bradstreet). The $230,000 contract, which may not have been its largest in dollars billed but was certainly among its most prestigious, was signed in the spring of 1893. By the time they fulfilled their contractual obligations, they had removed 82,000 cubic feet of granite from their quarry in North Jay, Maine.[69]

In contrast to the association's earlier stumbles with design competitions and vague and open-ended instructions, the contract with Maine and New Hampshire Granite Company was meticulous, strict, and unequivocal. The costs were broken down by the square base ($131,000), tower ($84,000), and steps ($15,000) and delivery was to begin on June 1, 1893. The number of cuts to be applied to each stone were dictated by where it would be placed. The lower and more visible the stone, the more stringent the tolerance for blemishes and other imperfections. To assemble the monument, Brady was awarded his fourth and largest contract, worth $104,482.[70]

At the annual meeting in February 1893, Horace Porter was unanimously reelected president of the Grant Monument Association; Elihu Root (secretary of state under President Theodore Roosevelt) was named vice president. After a revolving door of presidents, Porter would introduce continuity and stability. He would go on to hold the post for twenty-seven years, until 1919.[71]

At the meeting, a target date to complete the monument was set for the fall of 1895, based on estimates that the project would take three working seasons.[72] But delays from the previous year's strike meant the 1893 schedule was set back even before construction resumed for the year. That spring, matters got worse. After a period of unprecedented growth during the Gilded Age, starting

around the time Grant was elected in 1868, the American economy began to show signs of weakness. As concerns grew, people
began to withdraw gold from the banks. In 1890, the United States
gold reserves stood at $190 million, but on April 22, 1893, they
dipped below $100 million. At the time, the country was on the
gold standard (meaning that treasury notes could be redeemed for
a fixed amount of gold), and $100 million was a symbolic bulwark
that had previously been approached but never breached. The event
triggered a crisis of confidence and a run on banks as concern grew
that the United States might cease converting notes for gold. Stock
prices fell, banks closed, and railroads filed for bankruptcy. The economic calamity that came to be known as the Panic of 1893 was
"one of the most severe financial crises in the history of the United
States."[73] Thousands of businesses were shuttered, and while Brady's
crew was secure, millions of others were left unemployed during the
depression.[74]

By June 1, 1893, the Maine and New Hampshire Granite Company
was prepared to deliver its first shipment on schedule, but Brady was
not yet ready to accept, as his crew was still working on the water table
(the feature near the base to deflect water running down the building
from the foundation). By the time winter began and construction
ended for the year, the foundation and water table had been completed, but work on the building itself had not yet begun. Meanwhile,
city residents struggled through the economic consequences of the
Panic, leading a reporter from the New York *World* to lament, "This
winter will go down in history as the blackest in the history of New
York."[75]

At the annual meeting in February 1894, the association acknowledged the delays and moved the target date for completion to
spring 1896. It was yet another setback, but the progress that had
been achieved was undeniable. The first stones arrived in May
1894, transported on flatbed cars along 370 miles of railroad tracks
from North Jay, Maine. Along the way, coal dust from the engine

accumulated on the exposed stones. An annoyed Duncan threatened to return shipments in the future if the stones were not covered properly in transit.[76] He reluctantly accepted the initial load but followed through on his threat during construction, rejecting $10,000 worth of stones during the project, or more than 4 percent of the contract.[77] As stones arrived at Riverside Park, Brady's team worked to quickly assemble them. Throughout the remainder of the year, the tomb perceptibly rose into the New York sky. By December 1, when both the quarry and the construction site ceased operation for the winter, it stood at forty-five feet. While still less than a third of its eventual height, for the first time in almost a decade since Grant's death, the public saw something tangible and substantial in return for their emotional and financial investment.

After the winter rest, work resumed in the spring of 1895. While Riverside Park had been criticized a decade earlier as being remote and undeveloped, New York's one constant throughout its history has been change. The area had transformed, and Brady's contractors saw many other workers in the area. The energetic construction of Grant's Tomb in the mid-1890s coincided with several important cultural, patriotic, and historic movements that underlay these changes. It was during this decade that the City Beautiful movement had taken hold. The vision that "cities should aspire to aesthetic value for their residents" had been inspired by the 1893 World's Columbian Exposition in Chicago. New York City, previously lambasted as a "ragged pin cushion of towers," was undergoing a transformation in the area of the tomb, known as Morningside Heights.[78]

Among the buildings that had recently been erected or were under construction was the Columbia University Library, designed by Charles Follen McKim of the famous architectural firm McKim, Mead & White. The neoclassical library was built in 1895, along with other new buildings also designed by McKim, Mead & White that were part of Columbia University's planned move from its site at Forty-Ninth Street and Madison Avenue to its present campus in

Morningside Heights. The library is known as the Low Memorial Library, named for the university president at the time of construction and former association trustee, Seth Low. In addition, St. Luke's Hospital was also under construction in the 1890s, as was the St. John the Divine Cathedral, with a spire that towered 232 feet in the air. The cathedral's cornerstone was laid on St. John's Day, December 27, 1892, exactly nine months to the day after the Grant Monument cornerstone was laid.[79]

Along with the City Beautiful movement, the Colonial Revival period spanned the 1890s. The revival aesthetic bound together groups with a stronger interest in and appreciation of the past, who sought to celebrate and preserve it, especially in architecture. Organizations such as the Association and Preservation of Virginia Antiquities, founded in 1889, concerned themselves with saving America's historic treasures, while the American Historical Association, incorporated that same year, was tasked with "the promotion of historical studies."[80] Patriotic organizations that formed during this period include the Sons of Revolutionary Sires, founded in 1876 and later renamed the National Society of the Sons of the American Revolution; the Massachusetts Society of Mayflower Descendants, founded in 1889; the Daughters of the American Revolution, founded in 1890; the National Society of the Colonial Dames of America, founded in 1891; and the Montana Society of Pioneers, founded in 1894.

Changes were also taking place in the South. During the years after Grant's death, there was a notable shift in Southern sentiment from the bitter defeatism after the Civil War to a nostalgia for the "Lost Cause." This sectional pride was fueled by a renewed adoration of Confederate soldiers, the enactment of Jim Crow laws to suppress the rights of African Americans, and a resurgent white supremacy movement. Amid this renewed Southern sentiment, parallel organizations cropped up in the former Confederate states, such as the United Daughters of the Confederacy in 1894 and the Sons of Confederate Veterans in 1896. Southern nationalism manifested itself in the building of Confederate monuments. The first monument to Grant's chief adversary, Robert E. Lee, was dedicated in Richmond, Virginia, on May 29, 1890. A massive crowd estimated at 140,000 attended the event, including 8,000 Confederate veterans who marched in a procession. After much pomp and ceremony during which "the 'rebel yell' was echoed and re-echoed," Grant's pallbearer Confederate General Joseph Johnston unveiled the twenty-one-foot-tall bronze equestrian statue of Lee astride his horse, Traveler. The sculpture is perched upon a granite base, which increases its height to sixty feet.[81]

While monuments to Confederates were few and far between before this period, in the 1890s they began to proliferate exponentially. This phenomenon was largely driven by the United Daughters of the Confederacy, who often paid for and dedicated the monuments. UDC ranks had grown to more than 100,000 by the 1920s, when they conceived the Confederate magnum opus, Stone Mountain, near Atlanta, Georgia, where Confederate heroes and leaders Stonewall Jackson, Lee, and Jefferson Davis are carved into the face of the mountain.[82]

This development was criticized particularly in African American newspapers in the South and the New England press in the North. A reporter for the African American *Richmond Planet* feared that "The South may revere the memory of its chieftains. It takes the wrong steps in doing so. . . . It serves to retard its progress in the country and forge heavier chains with which to be bound."[83] But it was also widely tolerated by many in the North, if it helped ensure the peace. While the South had a sixty-foot-tall monument to Lee in Richmond, Unionists could take solace in the progress being made on the 150-foot-tall memorial to Grant.

But progress was frustratingly slow that spring, and construction ceased when stones did not arrive on schedule. In addition, smoke that spewed from a steam hoist used at the site during construction had stained some of the stones that were already in place. Duncan held the Maine and New Hampshire Granite Company responsible.

A familiar nemesis also continued to plague the project, one that had existed since the earliest days after Grant's death—relic hunters. Overzealous people had commandeered oak leaves, flowers, and anything they could get their hands on from the funeral and the temporary tomb. Now they set their sights on the permanent tomb, carving slivers of granite from stones yet to be set in place, necessitating that a fence be built around the construction site.

By May 1895, the squared base of the structure was complete, and work was underway on the cornices. A reporter from the *Fayetteville Recorder* noted "the rapidly growing pile of rocks is gradually taking the shape of its final structure."[84] Another optimistic reporter from the *Daily Leader* of Gloversville, New York, predicted the tomb would be "the ninth wonder of the world."[85] At the close of the 1895 season, it stood at eighty-five feet.[86]

Work resumed in the spring of 1896, and there were no major delays for the first season since construction had started. The men focused on the drum and an iron skeleton for the dome. By the middle of the summer, the roof was finished. Before the public's eyes, the tomb had taken shape, and finally, passersby could easily envision what it would look like once completed. Duncan's 5 percent commission on the contracts (including material) had netted him $25,588.24. However, the architect had developed such a passion for his project and a vested interest in its successful completion that he donated $5,000 back to the association.[87]

By September 1896, Brady's crew completed the exterior stonework. The ninety-two-foot square base stood seventy-two feet high, and the entire monument towered 150 feet in the air. At the entrance were ten Doric fluted columns (six in a front row and four behind them), and above the doors, in a final nod to Duncan's neoclassical style, Grant's name and birth and death dates were inscribed in Roman fashion:

VLYSSES S. GRANT
BORN APRIL XXVII MDCCCXXII
DIED JVLY XXIII MDCCCLXXXV

While the tomb looked nearly complete from the outside, the interior stonework had yet to be started. Inside was a sunken chamber for the tomb, and in the rear corners were smaller "trophy rooms." The previous year, initial estimates on the interior work were undertaken and several materials, including various types of marble and polished granite, were evaluated. In the spring of 1896, Duncan decided that "The entire interior of TOMB should be near as white as possible."[88] Once again, the contract was awarded to

Construction of the dome in early 1896. (Courtesy of the National Park Service, Manhattan Historic Sites Archive)

Brady. Italian marble was used for the stark interior and was installed by Schneider-Birkenstock Marble Co., which had been subcontracted by Brady. Four allegorical pendentives (interior triangular structures that support a dome atop a square building) were sculpted by Scottish artist J. Massey Rhind. The accomplished sculptor symbolically depicted Grant's birth, military career, civilian life, and death. Rhind also carved two figures, appropriately representing war and peace, for the front exterior. They represent Grant's career

A view of both the temporary tomb and the permanent Grant's Tomb (from the rear). The image is from late 1896. Note the fence still surrounding the tomb as well as the bicycles. Cycling had become a popular activity in New York City when this photograph was taken in 1896. (Courtesy of the National Park Service, Manhattan Historic Sites Archive)

of military and public service, and between them were engraved the four words that had become his lasting epitaph: Let Us Have Peace.

After some discussion with his widow, two sarcophagi were included in the plan instead of one for the couple to share. (Julia complained that Duncan had only made the proposal to "save space.") But there was a problem—the monument fund was almost depleted. Porter wrote the Berlin and Montello Granite Company in Montello, Wisconsin: "We will have left in the treasury . . . $3,500.00, and this is the only amount which can be devoted to procuring the two sarcophagi."[89] The company, surely considering the honor of creating a sarcophagus for Grant, agreed to the price and a contract was signed. The company excavated a large piece of red granite from their quarry, chosen due to its resemblance to Napoleon's sarcophagus.[90] But as they worked the stone, it became marked with blemishes. As nothing less than perfection would be acceptable to Duncan, the stone was scrapped and another piece was excavated. The final product was immense: it weighed 17,000 pounds, stood twenty-seven inches tall, and was eight and a half feet long. As a final touch, Grant's name was cut into the lid. The sarcophagus arrived in New York City on March 15, 1897. After a brief stop at the Pennsylvania Railroad Yard on Thirty-Seventh Street, five teams of horses pulled it north to the tomb site. There it was placed on a square block of gray-blue Quincy granite that had been constructed by the New England Monument Company. Atop the stone platform, the sarcophagus stood at seven and a half feet in the subterranean crypt.[91]

One of the last features to be added were the massive wooden ash doors manufactured by Borkelt and Debevoise. They stood sixteen and a half feet tall, four feet wide, and together weighed three and a half tons. Like the other association contracts, the $1,900 agreement for the doors was precise. The manufacturers, however, chose to add a feature free of cost, albeit one that would be obscured from the public through the ages. Mr. Borkelt collected the "signatures of scores of people, many of them prominent" and placed them on the wooden doors.[92] He covered them, as specified in the contract, with bronze panels secured with 296 bronze rosettes, forever hiding the signatures. On April 12, 1897, the doors were hung. Grant's Tomb, at long last, was completed. At peak construction, six hundred people were working on the tomb, and one was reported to have died on the job.[93] At 8,100 square feet, it was, and remains to this day, the largest memorial tomb in America.[94]

Hundreds of people visited the tomb each day during its final days of construction. Even twelve years after Grant died, many still sought out the oak tree for a souvenir leaf.[95] Now the last thing to do was to move Grant's remains. On April 10, laborers entered the temporary tomb. Over three days they methodically removed the 165 bolts from the steel casing, completing their work on April 13 at 5:00 p.m. Duncan distributed the bolts to members of the Grant Monument Association.[96]

Fred had requested the transfer to be "quiet and simple," so the date for the reinterment was not made public.[97] But citizens were eager to witness the spectacle and stopped by each day, looking for an indication that the event was about to occur. When a dispatch of 130 police gathered at the tomb at ten in the morning on April 17, they had their signal. As word spread, people arrived and set up their blankets and picnic baskets. Soon there were thousands at the tomb. A carriage arrived at 2:25 p.m., and Fred, accompanied by his fifteen-year-old son, Ulysses S. Grant III, stepped out. A half hour later Grant's son and namesake Ulysses S. Jr. arrived along with Porter, signaling that the removal was ready to begin. A roofless enclosure had been erected by the entrance to shield the proceedings from the crowds.

An undertaker, James F. Quinn from J. Edward Winterbottom & Co., unlocked the gate. and the group, along with Duncan, stepped inside. The lid of the steel casing was raised, and the copper casket slowly removed. The coffin was in good shape, but in case it had deteriorated or did not fit in the sarcophagus, Duncan had another on hand. Several times Fred asked about the wreath of oak leaves that had been made by his daughter Julia at Mount McGregor. The workers found it where it was set twelve years earlier, atop the coffin and in "a remarkably good state of preservation." It was carefully wrapped for safekeeping. There were no ceremonial pallbearers, and at 3:55 p.m., six of Quinn's assistants, dressed in black, carried the casket the short distance between an honor guard consisting of members of the U. S. Grant Post 327 from Brooklyn, still on duty a dozen years after Grant's death. Inside the permanent tomb, they placed the coffin in the sarcophagus, and Fred unwrapped the wreath and placed it on top. The lead casing was soldered shut and a derrick lowered the lid of the sarcophagus. Eight policemen remained to stand guard over the tomb.[98]

After a dozen years, Grant was now in his final resting place. He was not the first or last president to have his body rest in a temporary tomb while a permanent memorial was under construction. George Washington, John Adams, John Quincy Adams, William Henry Harrison, James K. Polk, Zachary Taylor, Abraham Lincoln, and James Garfield, and later William McKinley, Woodrow Wilson, Warren G. Harding, and John F. Kennedy were all interred temporarily with the understanding that one day their remains would be moved.[99] Only Washington's thirty-one years in a temporary vault exceeded Grant's sojourn, but Washington's crypt at his Mount Vernon estate was a private matter handled by the family. The delay in building the permanent memorial to Grant was unprecedented.

Porter basked in the adulations of a generous city and a grateful country. Few knew of the crucial role Edward F. Cragin had played. While Porter's contributions were covered extensively in the press, if Cragin was mentioned, it was only in passing. In fact, most people didn't even know his name—he was not listed in the official dedication program and was not invited to the ceremony. While remaining inconspicuous had been Cragin's plan from the start, he was having second thoughts as the dedication approached. Frustrated that Porter was taking credit for his efforts, Cragin urged Porter to publicly acknowledge his role and sent him two telegrams to that effect. What he wrote is lost to history, but Porter's response survives: "Both telegrams received. . . . Please recall your first dispatch. It is not like you. My address contains full acknowledgments of your valuable services." A disappointed Porter added, "You should have trusted me."[100]

8

"Let Us Have Peace"

APRIL 27, 1897 was clear but unseasonably cold, with the temperature at forty-one degrees. Winds gusted up to fifty-seven miles per hour, blowing dust and dirt that pelted people in the streets. It was the day for the Grant Memorial to be dedicated, and Porter was juggling multiple responsibilities to the end. Only three weeks earlier, he had organized President William McKinley's inaugural parade in Washington, DC, and led the procession on horseback. While his energy was seemingly inexhaustible, he had recently celebrated his sixtieth birthday and looked his age, for his once jet-black hair had grown gray.[1] Preparations for the dedication had started a year earlier when the city allotted $50,000 for the event.

To manage the arrangements, Republican New York City mayor William Lafayette Strong, who had been elected two years before, created a "Grant Monument Municipal Inaugural Committee." Mayor Strong was chairman of the three-hundred-person committee, which included past and current association members, John Duncan, Andrew Carnegie, General Daniel Butterfield (who had written the haunting melody "Taps" during the Civil War), Charles Tiffany, and Theodore Roosevelt. The group was divided into sub-committees to handle all facets of the celebration, the largest being the reception committee. The committee on public safety and order was chaired by Theodore Roosevelt, who had resigned as New York City police commissioner just three days earlier to serve as assistant secretary of the navy under President McKinley.[2] The grand marshal was Major General Grenville Mellen Dodge. Dodge had served under Grant as intelligence chief in the western campaign and had later distinguished himself as chief engineer of the Union Pacific Railroad and as a Republican congressman from Iowa from 1867 to 1869.[3] Just as had been done at Grant's funeral, Dodge tried to showcase a spirit of reunification and asked Confederate cavalry leader John S. Mosby to serve as his aide-de-camp for the ceremony. For the few who were opposed to such an olive branch extended to a former enemy, Mosby was as uncontroversial a choice as could be made. While he was ruthless during the war, he had since become

Grant Memorial edition of Harper's Weekly, *May 1, 1897, featuring a stunning interior view of the tomb.*

a Republican, supported Grant's presidency, and served in several federal positions, including as a consul in Hong Kong.[4]

On March 13, Mayor Strong penned an open letter to President McKinley that was published in the *New York Times*. He formally requested McKinley, the last president to serve in the Civil War, to "officially bring to the attention of all other nations the notable character of the event . . . and that you invite all foreign governments to cause themselves to be represented in the naval part of the ceremonies . . . by sending a ship of war to attend and participate."[5] Two weeks later, Secretary of State John Sherman sent about thirty-five letters to "officially invite the maritime nations to send warships to participate in the ceremonies."[6] The celebration to dedicate Grant's Tomb was to take place both on land and at sea.

In the final days before the dedication, workers frantically completed the finishing touches. A flock of sparrows that had nested in the dome was removed, and during the hasty polishing of the interior marble, several workers found themselves inadvertently locked inside the tomb![7] The day before the dedication, the temporary tomb was torn down. Before relic hunters could abscond with the debris, the bricks were carted to City Hall and placed in a basement jail cell for safekeeping. Mayor Strong later distributed them as souvenirs to schools and Grand Army posts.[8] The steel case that had held the coffin was destroyed by a boilermaker. John T. Brady was awarded a final contract for $20,500 to construct bleachers and a temporary wooden memorial arch on the east side of the tomb.

Soldiers began to arrive in the city en masse several days early, and soon the boys in uniform flooded Manhattan. Some began the celebration early, alarming reporters from Philadelphia. New York, they warned, "is a wicked city, where the men will be exposed to temptations so strong that almost certainly, they will disgrace their State by yielding to them." Reporters from the *New York Times*, who could not resist a snarky retort, admitted, "New York may be wicked, according to Philadelphia standards," before adding, "it is certainly more exciting."[9]

Perhaps Philadelphians were right to be concerned. Reports abounded of soldiers, after having a few drinks too many, staggering around Central Park. When one such inebriated individual was found passed out in the Bowery, a good Samaritan helped him into a carriage and sent him back to his unit.[10] City police bolstered their patrols, and officers scanned crowds as they departed the trains and ferries. Any potential ne'er-do-wells were quickly carted off to the local jail, where they remained until the ceremony ended, their constitutional rights notwithstanding.

One sad note preceded the festivities. Only days before the ceremony, James C. Reed died at the age of fifty-eight. Reed had suffered from a nervous condition that his obituary listed as "structural decay of the brain."[11] According to doctors, the stress of the tomb literally killed him, as they blamed his condition on the "great strain to which he had been subjected in connection with this work" as secretary of the Grant Monument Association.[12] He was buried on April 26, a day before the dedication.

As it had for the cornerstone ceremony five years earlier, the New York legislature declared the day of the dedication a state holiday, billed as "Grant Day." Twelve years after Grant's passing, the day was to be a celebration of Grant's life rather than a mourning of his death. A reporter from the *Northern Observer* from Massena, New York, wrote that the ceremony "promises to be the grandest of its kind ever held in the country,"[13] and a reporter from the *Gouverneur Free Press* anticipated that "the parade . . . is to be a big and brilliant one."[14] The day even inspired sheet music, including "The Grant Memorial Day March and Two Step," composed by John J. McIntyre, and "Here Sleeps the Hero," composed by Robert F. Walsh with lyrics by Gerald Carlton.[15]

Early in the morning, two events highlighted the great irony of the reunification sentiment and the paradoxical meaning of Grant's

Tomb. Before crowds gathered, an elderly African American man walked toward the crypt with a handful of violets. The white-haired man approached the policemen on guard and asked him to lay the flowers by the tomb, saying, "He helped to make me a free man, boss."[16] Later that morning, a group from the Sons of Confederate Veterans placed an elaborate floral arrangement of crossed swords at the tomb. Only at the altar of Grant's Tomb could both oppressed and oppressor worship together.

Six miles to the south, at Madison Square Park on Madison Avenue and Twenty-Sixth Street, thousands of marchers had gathered. At 9:30 a.m., the procession began.[17] To help spectators follow along, businesses printed programs that included the full list of organizations participating in the parade. One was the typo-riddled "Souvinier Programme of the U. S. Grant Memorial Parade and Cerimony," produced by "Vogel's, Introducers of up-to-date novelties" and sold for a dime.

The parade was led by General Dodge, who rode with the Native American chief Joseph of the Nez Percé and Buffalo Bill. They were followed by the Platoon Mounted Police and the Governors Island Band. After a slew of distinguished guests, division after division of military units from all branches followed. All told, a staggering 53,000 military veterans, including Union and Confederate soldiers, paraded to the tomb. Once again, Grant's death was an opportunity to showcase that the country had moved on. Grant's words, LET US HAVE PEACE, were stitched on banners all over the city, as they had been at the funeral. The *Paterson Daily Press* proclaimed, "In that throng, there was no north, no south . . . the gray had blended with the blue."[18] Along with saving the Union, the press heralded the lasting peace as Grant's great achievement. "It is often said," *Harper's Weekly* enthused, "The real reunion of the United States is an achievement without precedent in the history of the world." To ensure there was no question about who deserved credit, they featured an illustration rich with meaning, of Grant dressed as a

Roman standing before his tomb and gazing upon a stone emblazoned with his inspirational words, LET US HAVE PEACE. The caption reads, "The stone that Grant himself selected."[19]

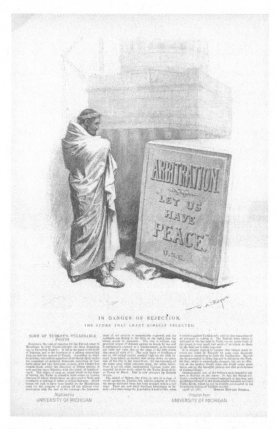

Harper's Weekly, *May 1, 1897. The theme of reunification permeated every aspect of the dedication of Grant's Tomb. This illustration places the credit for the reunification of the North and South squarely on Grant's broad shoulders.*

Not all participants were content, however. Notably, the governor of Illinois, John Riley Tanner, was upset that his state was last to march. Disregarding the fact that the order was established by the order in which states joined the Union, Governor Tanner complained to a reporter that the organizers "did not know that Grant came from Illinois."[20] Also toward the rear of the parade marched several civic, cultural, and fraternal organizations such as the Saloon Men's Protective Association; Knights of Sherwood Forest; Italian American Pioneer Corps; and Order of Scottish Clans. The parade was an opportunity for newly arrived immigrant communities to demonstrate their patriotism, just as it was a way for those who had donated toward the tomb's construction to display their generosity. Bringing up the rear were platoons of mounted police.[21]

Since 1885, the city had grown larger and taller—and to many, more intimidating. It was also more crowded, as the population of Manhattan had reached around 1.75 million people, compared to 1.4 million at the time of the funeral. (Brooklyn was not merged with Manhattan and other municipalities to form the City of New York until several months after the funeral, on January 1, 1898.) With the introduction of the electric passenger elevator and the steel-frame building in 1889, buildings quickly climbed skyward. In 1893, the new Manhattan Life Building on Broadway towered 313 feet in the air. Three years later, in 1896, it was joined on Broadway by the twenty-one-story, 312-foot-tall American Surety Building.[22] That same year, Siegel-Cooper's department store opened on Nineteenth Street as the largest store in the world. A trade magazine at the time claimed the new cityscape "evokes only one feeling, that of horror," and feared it would bring about "a dark, dank city with windy, cellar-like streets."[23]

The marchers proceeded north on Madison Avenue. At Fifty-Fifth Street, they turned left onto Fifth Avenue, where they passed more buildings adorned with opulent decorations. The procession headed north four blocks, and at Fifty-Ninth Street turned west and passed in front of the southern end of Central Park. They turned north at Columbus Circle onto the unpaved Boulevard (today known as Broadway). Spectators shielded their eyes from the relentless winds as they watched the parade pass by. Along Boulevard, various groups and entrepreneurs had erected bleachers in the days leading up to the dedication, covering them with patriotic bunting. The most eager among the spectators purchased individual seats for up to $10 each, and boxes sold for as high as $50 at a time when an average weekly salary was between $70 and $80.[24] The more industrious and patient noticed that many empty seats remained and were able to bargain down to prices as low as a quarter for an individual seat as the parade approached. All throughout the city souvenir sales were brisk, from the larger department stores like Bloomingdales to the opportunistic street salespeople whom the newspapers called *fakirs*. Their wares included buttons, programs, and badges. Some claimed to have chips from the marble tomb for a price. The most popular souvenir was a bronze medallion pressed by the American Numismatic and Archaeological Society that sold for $2.50 (a gold original was minted by Tiffany and Company and had been presented to Porter four days earlier). It depicted Grant on one side and the original design of the memorial tomb (featuring the stepped dome) on the other. Above the tomb read the words, DEDICATED IN NEW YORK, APRIL 27, 1897.[25]

At Seventy-Second Street the parade again turned west, and at Riverside Drive it made a final push north. Marchers passed opulent Beaux-Arts mansions overlooking the Hudson River. The extravagant homes of the wealthy along Riverside Drive rivaled those they had passed earlier on Fifth Avenue. Some spectators, who had climbed trees to get a good view of the parade, tossed food to appreciative soldiers. One visitor from France shouted, "Great are Grant and Napoleon! Honored only among all men in such a way!"[26] While Grant's tomb was modeled after Napoleon's and the comparisons between the two generals were profuse and inevitable, the irony is that Grant thought little of Napoleon—while he conceded Napoleon was a "military genius," his doctor later recalled that Grant felt Napoleon's "treatment of Josephine was abominable . . . and would be a blot on his character for all time."[27]

Grant's Tomb, at the highest part of the park, loomed in the

distance and steadily grew in the eyes of the marchers as they
approached. At 112th Street they passed the St. Christopher's Home
for Children and Young Girls, founded five years earlier as part
of the movement of benevolence societies that proliferated in the
Gilded Age. Riverside Park had been transformed in the twelve
years since Grant's passing. Brownstones and shops had replaced the
farms that still abounded in Harlem in 1885. One weekly newspaper geared toward younger readers, the *Great Round World and
What Is Going on in It*, now praised the neighborhood as "well worth
visiting not only on account of Grant's Tomb, but also to see the
many beautiful buildings erected here." The periodical continued
its exultations and declared the "beauty" of the neighborhood "has
gained for it the title of the 'American Acropolis.'"[28] In addition, an
area that was once criticized as "almost inaccessible . . . for anything
except goats" was now serviced by mass transit. Throughout the
day, crowds poured out of the elevated railway lines between 104th
and 125th Streets. Some passengers, frustrated by delays, got out and
walked or took a carriage to the tomb. Spectators filled the official
grandstands, which had been decorated in purple and black bunting.
Those without seats scaled walls or climbed trees to get a glimpse of
the ceremony.

In contrast to the gay atmosphere, the weather remained dismal.
One reporter wrote, "the sky became leaden and the wind rose until
it almost howled around the trees."[29] Dust clouds whipped through
the unpaved walkway, causing black overcoats to turn brown, and
soon the tomb was also covered in an ashen hue. An inventive and
persistent photographer by the name of William A. Eddy tried to
get an aerial shot by attaching a camera to a kite. Thirty-four times
he tried, and thirty-four times he failed, as each contraption met its
doom and crashed back to the ground.[30]

American battleships and seacraft from foreign countries who
had responded to Sherman's call filled the Hudson River. The *Daily-
News Democrat* of Huntington, Indiana, praised the "Civic, Military,

and Naval Pageants" as "Most Brilliant" as the impressive spectacle
of anchored ships decorated with patriotic bunting spanned from
Seventy-Second to 140th Street.[31] Included among them were the
USS *Maine* and the *Infanta Maria Theresa* from Spain. Within a year,
both would be destroyed in the Spanish American War.[32]

Harper's Weekly, *May 1, 1897. Cadets from West Point Military
Academy pass through the memorial arch to salute President William
McKinley seated in the reviewing stand.*

At 12:40 p.m., through a cloud of dust, General Dodge and his
lead entourage appeared and marched beneath the memorial arch.
Their arrival prompted a signal for the warships in the Hudson,
which responded with a twenty-one-gun salute. "A smoky mist
enshrouded the warships for a minute, but only a minute before
it was dispelled by the wind," recounted the *New York Times*.[33]
President McKinley, who was eating in a lunch tent set up behind
the tomb, emerged from the tent twenty minutes after Dodge
arrived and took a seat beside Grant's widow, Julia, on the reviewing stand. Seated nearby were former President Grover Cleveland,
dignitaries from twenty-six countries, and fifteen state governors

(only Virginia Governor Charles Triplett O'Ferrall was from a former Confederate state).[34]

Thousands continued to arrive beneath the memorial arch. As each soldier passed the tomb, he removed his hat as "a touching tribute to the memory of General Grant."[35] The marchers continued around the tomb before reaching the end of the parade route at 117th Street and Boulevard. The lines included Union and Confederate veterans, prompting one reporter to boast he had witnessed "the grandest military pageant ever seen in the city."[36] Reunification hung thick in the air, as it did at the funeral. In the crowd that day was Varina Howell Davis, wife of Confederate president Jefferson Davis. Years earlier, Varina had met Julia at a resort in New York's Hudson Valley, and the two kindred spirits had developed a fast friendship. In 1893, Jefferson Davis, who had died and been buried in New Orleans in 1889, was reinterred in Richmond, Virginia, amid grand festivities, although it was a strictly Southern affair.[37]

Finally, the ceremony began. A band played "America, My Country 'Tis of Thee" as guests looked upon the largest flag flown in the country (thirty-five by fifty feet) from the tallest flagpole (a 150-foot-tall pine) in the city.[38]

Grandest, largest, tallest, and *most brilliant*—indeed, it was a day for superlatives.

Reverend John P. Newman delivered a prayer that was followed by a rendition of the "Hymn of Thanks" (otherwise known as the "Old Netherland Folk-Song"). The main event was an address by President McKinley. He began: "A great life, dedicated to the welfare of the nation, here finds its earthly coronation. Even if this day lacked the impressiveness of ceremony and was devoid of pageantry, it would still be memorable because it is the anniversary of the birth of the most famous and beloved of American soldiers." McKinley acknowledged "the veteran leaders of the Blue and the Gray," and also reminded the crowd, "Let us not forget the glorious distinction with which the metropolis among the fair sisterhood of American cities has honored his life and memory." This triumphal moment for New York was also one for the new president, as his speech was widely praised. The *Sacramento Daily Union* called it "an impressive address," and his biographer praised it as "one of the finest speeches of his life."[39] The crowd at the tomb agreed and welcomed it with enthusiastic applause, including from those too far afield to hear a word he was saying.

After the band played "The Star-Spangled Banner," Horace Porter stepped up to speak. It was an emotional moment as he looked at the thousands in the crowd there to celebrate the completed tomb. "It is all like a dream," he began. He may have been in the shadow of the president, but it was he who was most responsible for the completed tomb and the day's celebration. Porter acknowledged McKinley: "It is peculiarly fitting that this memorial should be dedicated in the presence of the distinguished soldier who marched in the victorious columns of his illustrious chief, and who now so worthily occupies the chair of state in which he sat."

Porter went on to praise Grant's character and note how his reputation had risen in recent years: "Now that more than a decade has passed since he stood among us we can form a better estimate of his character than when he was close by. Time has shed a clearer light upon his acts. He has reached a higher altitude." After a lengthy oration, Porter closed: "In this tomb, which generosity has created and which his services have sanctified, his ashes will henceforth rest, but his true sepulcher will be in the hearts of his countrymen."[40]

He did not mention Cragin.

On behalf of the Grant Memorial Association, Porter then ceremoniously turned the tomb over to the city of New York, and Mayor Strong accepted. Finally, closing the ceremony, Handel's *Messiah* was performed, followed by the doxology sung by a chorus led by Frank Damrosch.[41]

President McKinley raced to the luncheon tent to escape the treacherous weather as spectators swiftly scattered. Most left the grounds, while some sought shelter behind the tomb's Doric columns. But only the family of Grant were permitted to enter. For ten minutes they remained inside, alone with their husband and father. Later, President McKinley, accompanied by Porter, boarded the small boat *Daisy*, which transported him to the presidential yacht USS *Dolphin* so he could review the aquatic parade on the river.

The colossal structure, which had taken twelve years to complete, was now dedicated. Over the years, it would come to embody much more than one man. The National Park Service has observed that the tomb "in a very real sense symbolizes an entire generation's feelings not just about Grant, but about the Civil War and the role every foot soldier played in it."[42]

The *Kansas City Journal* summed up the magnitude of the day: "Never before in the history of the United States has such a tribute been paid to the noble dead."[43]

"Long-Range Good Hands"

Immediately following the dedication ceremony, a twenty-four-hour police guard was stationed at Grant's Tomb, with one officer inside and another outside. While the grandstands were disassembled shortly after the ceremony (the *New York Times* noted the "big heaps of lumber with signs reading 'Grand Stand Seats, $1' and 'Let Us Have Peace' scattered among them"), the memorial arch stayed in place another month until Decoration Day.[1] Less than two weeks later, on May 7, a tree was planted and a plaque erected near the site of the temporary tomb, both gifts from Chinese Viceroy Li Hung-Chang. The plaque reads in both English and Chinese:

> THIS TREE IS PLANTED AT THE SIDE OF THE TOMB OF GENERAL U. S. GRANT, EX-PRESIDENT OF THE UNITED STATES OF AMERICA, FOR THE PURPOSE OF COMMEMORATING HIS GREATNESS BY LI HUNG-CHANG, GUARDIAN OF THE PRINCE, GRAND SECRETARY OF STATE EARL OF THE FIRST ORDER, YANG YU ENVOY EXTRAORDINARY AND MINISTER PLENIPOTENTIARY OF CHINA, VICE PRESIDENT OF THE BOARD OF CENSORS' KWANG HSU 23RD YEAR, 4TH MOON, MAY 1897.

A year earlier, on August 30, 1896, Chinese ambassador Li Hung-Chang had visited the temporary tomb of "his old friend." The two had met while Grant was on his world tour almost a decade earlier, and Li had enlisted Grant to help China negotiate a treaty with Japan over the disputed Ryukyu Islands. Li arrived in a carriage and stepped into a ceremonial "chair of state." Four "husky, blushing," and very unhappy Irish policemen then hoisted the sedan chair and carried the Chinese dignitary on their shoulders up about a dozen steps.[2] At the tomb entrance, the burly officers set down the chair. Slowly, Li stepped out and bowed his head in reverence. Horace Porter stood waiting at the tomb to greet him. The Chinese statesman told Porter that Grant's Tomb was one of the foremost places he hoped to visit while in America. Li stepped inside and was pleased to see the garland of bay leaves and orchids he had sent as a gift in advance of his arrival. Li was very curious about the temporary tomb and the permanent one that was nearing completion nearby. *How was it paid for? Who guarded it? How would it be maintained?* asked the inquisitive guest. After several minutes, Li exited and bowed deeply before the hushed crowd of twenty thousand.[3]

The tomb won critical accolades for its architectural prowess. It became a point of pride for New Yorkers and created a powerful sense of place for the Civil War generation. Three decades since the end of hostilities, during which time many other memorials to the Civil War had been erected, Grant's Tomb held a special place in the American consciousness. A reporter for the *Critic* claimed, "It is to be our one great memorial of the struggle for union; a monument not only to the foremost of our generals, but to the cause of 'liberty and union' and, in a sense, to all who fought and died for that sentiment."[4] For many Americans, particularly Civil War veterans, a visit to Grant's Tomb came to resemble a religious pilgrimage.

While much was made of the Grant Monument Association turning the tomb over to the city of New York at the dedication ceremony on April 27, the truth was that nothing had changed. It remained under the auspices of the association, and for the next few months they continued to pay for maintenance. In November, a legislative act passed with the lengthy title of "An act to authorize the board of commissioners of the Department of Public Parks of the City of New York to Enter into a Contract with the Grant Monument Association for the care and preservation of the tomb of General Grant at Riverside Park." The bill allocated $7,000 annually, for eleven years, to the Grant Monument Association to cover maintenance costs. Shortly after the dedication, the building began to leak, and the problem continued to get worse over the years. Each storm seemed to bring new streams raining down from the dome above. The leaks were left unattended for so long that minute stalactites began to form, similar to those that develop, like stone icicles, over thousands of years in subterranean spaces. Fears arose that the ornamental plasterwork would one day break loose and crash to the ground. In early 1905, the granite was sealed with wax and the tomb was optimistically declared "waterproof."[5] The maintenance contract was renewed in 1908, this time for twenty-one years. However, though costs continued to rise, the allocation did not. In fact, the $7,000 per year allocation remained in effect until the 1950s.[6]

With the tomb now open to the public, George D. Burnside was retained on staff as the first curator, a position he held until 1940. He took the role seriously, dressing in a Civil War uniform that had been provided by Brooks Brothers. Another long-timer, John Buckner, who was hired in 1897 to keep the tomb clean, remained on the job as janitor for the next twenty-five years.[7] The workers maintained a strict decorum at the sacred location. A sign reading REMOVE YOUR HAT was posted during the peak years, and most guests adhered to the request and spoke only in a hushed whisper. Buckner even suggested that the tomb held a redeeming power, recalling that one visitor who had been drinking and had staggered up the steps "straightened up like a man" and removed his hat as soon as he entered the sacred space.[8]

The area that was once seen as a no-man's-land had become a bustling tourist attraction. Visitors arrived in droves by elevated train cars, carriages, boat, bicycle, and on foot. The day after the 1897 dedication, about 13,000 people visited the tomb, many undoubtedly picking up souvenirs left by the previous day's raucous crowd.[9] By the time the year drew to a close, 560,000 people had stopped by the tomb since its dedication just over eight months earlier. Its only rival was the Statue of Liberty; the two sites emerged as top attractions in the city, vying for tourists' attention and their patriotic affection. But in the battle of the attendance counts, Grant was once again victorious. Sundays were the busiest day. Grant's Tomb was also a popular destination for bicycle riders, known as "wheelmen." The sport had taken off in New York in the late 1800s, and one newspaper reported, "Young people made up parties, properly chaperoned, to ride up through the park and along Riverside Drive to Grant's Tomb."[10] While attempts were made to prohibit riders from Riverside Park, champions of the sport prevailed, and eventually bicycle racks were built near the tomb.[11] For the remainder of the century attendance remained strong, averaging about a half million visitors a year.

Into the early years of the new century, the site was generally tranquil and the crowd law-abiding. Of course, there were exceptions, and Porter complained that "an unruly class sometimes enter who refuse to remove their hats, insist upon smoking their cigars and using offensive language."[12] In addition, occasionally loiterers gathered by the entrance in the summer, and the more indolent among them were brazen enough to lie down on the front steps. At night, children roller-skated on the monument grounds, and some young vandals marked the tomb in charcoal. Clearly, some of the reverent luster of the earliest years had dulled, and the tomb's meaning was becoming diluted to some. The twenty-four-hour guards who once protected the tomb were withdrawn shortly after the dedication. Yet the plague of relic hunters continued. They now set their sights—and chisels—on the monument itself, chipping slivers of stone as souvenirs. Eventually, in 1909, veterans from the Grand

Army of the Republic appealed to the New York police commissioner to express their concerns, and three guards were temporarily stationed at the tomb.[13]

But while there were few reports of actual vandalism or disturbances in these early years, traffic was the more prevalent danger. Automobiles debuted in New York a year before the tomb was completed, and on May 24, 1899, a parade of "eighty horseless conveyances" rode from Madison Square Garden to Grant's Tomb in an event sponsored by delegates of the National Electric Light Association.[14] By the early years of the new century, the proliferation of automobiles had outpaced traffic laws, proving a hazardous combination. The unlit area around the tomb was deemed "a veritable death trap."[15]

On December 14, 1902, at the age of seventy-six, Julia passed away in Washington, DC, from heart and kidney failure. Over the years, she had largely remained out of the affairs of the Grant Monument Association and the construction of Grant's—and her— tomb, interjecting her opinions only sparingly. A funeral was held on December 20 at the Metropolitan Methodist Episcopalian Church in Washington, DC, before "a notable assemblage," including President Theodore Roosevelt. After the ceremony, her remains were transported by funeral train to New York. The next day, December 21, as a cold rain fell, the coffin was transferred to Riverside Park. For the first time ever, electric lights brightened the inside as a derrick lifted the lid from the sarcophagus and her coffin was placed within. Members of the Grant Monument Association were joined by a detachment from the ever-loyal U. S. Grant Post from Brooklyn.[16] Julia's interment was a reminder to all as to why New York was selected in the first place. While some still grumbled that Grant should have been buried in Arlington National Cemetery or at West Point, New York City had been chosen so the two could rest side by side for all eternity. After her death, Fred donated thousands of letters to the association that had been sent to Grant when he was ill and to the family after he died. Many were put on display inside the tomb in the rear trophy rooms.

Grant's Tomb remained an important location to express the sentiment of reunification. The spirit of harmony that had prevailed during the funeral and dedication helped perpetuate comradery between the former enemies. At the 1885 funeral, members of the U. S. Grant Post from Brooklyn first fraternized with Confederate veterans. On Decoration Day in 1890, about fifty Confederate veterans who now resided in New York first joined Union soldiers at the Grant's Tomb remembrance. While some celebrated the spirit of unity, others criticized the U. S. Grant Post for having "a warm corner by its campfire for the old Johnny Rebs." General James McLear warned that "The danger is in overdoing the matter of brotherly love, as it is sometimes called. We must take care that we do not underestimate the services and sacrifices made to save the Union. There was a right and wrong side to the war." Put simply, McLear declared, "We of the North were right and the South wrong."[17]

But the desire for peace and forgiveness was strong, and Grant's Tomb retained its aura of reconciliation, especially on Decoration Day, when both sides remembered their fallen comrades. At the 1902 remembrance, Confederate veteran Judge Thomas Jones spoke before a crowd of five thousand:

> When but a beardless youth I drank, of the cup of defeat at Appomattox and was one of those who was "allowed to return to his home, not to be disturbed by the United States authorities, so long as they observed their parole and the laws in force where they resided." From that day to this there has never been an hour when I would willingly omit an opportunity to do honor to the memory of the immortal who forbore to add to the burden of our sorrows. No true soldier can deny to the illustrious man whose mortal remains lie here, the possession of all the qualities of a great commander.[18]

Three years later, members of the U. S. Grant Post from Brooklyn voted unanimously to invite Confederate veterans to the 1905 Memorial Day ceremony at Grant's Tomb. (There was no single moment when Decoration Day became known as Memorial Day, but the changes started to take place around the turn of the century.) Four hundred accepted, prompting a reporter for the *Morning Astorian* to cheer from faraway Oregon: "Confederates and Johnnies to join Memorial Day."[19] The ceremony included a brief parade, which was the first time since the dedication that the Blue and Gray veterans marched together in New York City.[20]

In addition to having become an obligatory tourist attraction and a place to express Civil War and patriotic sentiment, Grant's Tomb also became a pop cultural icon when, in the earliest days of the cinema, it was the focal point in two silent short romantic comedy films. In 1904, the Biograph Film Company produced *Personal*, a

A lovesick bachelor is chased by a bevy of available women in a scene from How a French Nobleman Got a Wife through the *New York* Herald Personal Column, *produced in 1905 by Thomas Edison's film company.* (Courtesy of the Library of Congress)

vignette about a lovesick Frenchman who posts a want ad in the *New York Herald*. The plot could be seen as a precursor to that of *Sleepless in Seattle*, but instead of the Empire State Building, the rendezvous point is the most iconic site in the city at the time, Grant's Tomb. The following year, in 1905, Thomas Edison's company produced the nearly identical *How a French Nobleman Got a Wife through the* New York Herald *Personal Column* with the same plot and same meeting place.[21]

In 1906, attendance soared as 607,584 people visited the tomb.[22] The iconic building in New York City had become one of the most recognizable structures in America. Aided by a newly popular postcard, the tomb achieved worldwide renown as well. The postcard was first introduced by the US government in 1872 at the cost of only a penny to mail. While privately produced postcards were permitted by the post office, they cost two cents to send and enjoyed only limited popularity. In 1898, Congress passed a law that allowed these cards to ship at the same penny rate, and their popularity surged, sparking the so-called "Golden Age of postcards."[23] Private companies created attractive postcards that featured photographs or lithographs of popular attractions. Unsurprisingly, Grant's Tomb appeared in many. These cards introduced the tomb to people around the globe, who added it to their must-see list when they visited America. Among their number were Belgium's King Albert and the Prince of Wales. Grant's Tomb was also a popular stop among American celebrities and politicians such as Buffalo Bill and his Wild West troupe, who visited in 1908, Theodore Roosevelt, and William Howard Taft.

When Ulysses S. Grant was born, in 1822, the fastest a man could travel was on horseback. By the time he died, the locomotive was the preferred mode of long-distance transportation. A year before his tomb was dedicated, the automobile was introduced in New York City, and in the early years of the new century, American inventors and daring aviators had turned science fiction into fact.

In 1909, the city was hosting the Hudson-Fulton Celebration to mark three hundred years since Henry Hudson had arrived in New York and approximately a century since Robert Fulton introduced the steamboat. As the main event of the commemoration, aviators Wilbur Wright and Glenn Curtiss participated in a flight competition. Both set out to fly from the southern tip of Manhattan to the greatest structure in the city, Grant's Tomb. Only one made it.[24] On Sunday, October 3, Custiss was the first to make the attempt when he took off at 5:30 p.m. However, he quickly landed his craft, telling reporters, "I did not like the wind I found up there. . . . I did not like the way the machine lurched and I came down."[25] It was still windy the following day, October 4. But Wilbur Wright was undeterred, and took off in his "aeroplane" from Governor's Island at 9:55 a.m. After passing the number two attraction, the Statue of Liberty, he headed north to number one. Wright arrived at Grant's Tomb at 10:17 a.m., where "crowds of people cheered the daring aviator." A million people witnessed the historic event, which the newspapers hailed as "the most spectacular airship flight the world has ever seen"[26]

Grant's Tomb became a popular location for staging other types of demonstrations, such as on Woman Suffrage Day, May 2, 1914, when hundreds gathered there.[27] When foreign delegations were in town, such as for the Italian, French, British, and Japanese War Commissions during the First World War, the tomb was decorated accordingly, similar to how the Empire State Building is lit today.

Despite the tomb's popularity, not everyone was enamored with the structure. One *New York Times* editorial from 1910 blasted the monument as a "mausoleum monstrosity."[28] Indeed, it looked so incongruous that some passersby were confused as to what it might be. Grant's Tomb was mistaken for a bank, a post office, a mansion, a library, a church, and a synagogue.[29] A troubled woman once entered and approached the curator. "Excuse me, sir," she asked, "which cell is my husband in?" Apparently, she had asked someone

On May 2, 1914, supporters of women's voting rights gather at Grant's Tomb on Woman Suffrage Day. (Courtesy of the Library of Congress)

for directions to the Tombs, a nickname for the city prison in Lower Manhattan, and was misdirected to Grant's Tomb instead.[30]

After the astronomical 1906 attendance, visitation tapered off steadily but remained at about 400,000 per year over the next decade. To accommodate the crowds, an impressive permanent bathroom building was erected in 1910 to the west of the tomb. The structure, made of Clemsford granite and designed in the same neo-classical style as the tomb, with Doric columns, was built at a cost of $45,000. Prior to that a temporary wooden structure had served the purpose.[31]

But by 1916, Grant's Tomb had slipped behind the Statue of Liberty as the most visited destination in New York City.[32] Not only were Civil War veterans, the youngest now in their late sixties, dying off, but in Europe the Great War was raging. With advanced weapons of war such as airplanes, the Browning machine gun, tanks, and chemical warfare, the death toll numbered in the millions. The Civil War seemed almost congenial by comparison. In addition, other destinations and forms of recreation vied for New Yorkers' attention. Seventy blocks north, on Amsterdam Avenue between

190th and 192nd Streets, Fort George Amusement Park, often called "Harlem's Coney Island," opened in 1895.[33] The Harlem River Speedway opened in 1898 and quickly became a popular attraction to watch horse racing and boat races.[34]

The period also saw the rising popularity of baseball in New York. Although the New York Giants, who played at the Polo Grounds fifty blocks north, had been perennial losers, in the early 1900s their new manager, John McGraw, transformed them into a pennant-winning machine that drew large crowds. In 1903, a new franchise was added to the American League, the New York Highlanders. The team included superstar pitcher Jack Chesbro and outfielder "Wee Willie" Keeler and finished their inaugural season at a respectable 72–62. Hundreds of thousands of fans attended Highlander games each year at Hilltop Park, located just forty blocks north of Grant's Tomb. In 1913, the team changed their home field to the Polo Grounds and their name to the New York Yankees, a tip of the cap to the Union soldiers Grant led in the Civil War.

In addition to sports, there was the increasing allure of the theater, which started to migrate north from Union Square. The first Broadway venue was Oscar Hammerstein's Victoria Theatre, which opened in March 1899 on Seventh Avenue and Forty-Second Street (which later became Times Square).[35] Within a few years, theaters were opening at a clip of one or two a year, and the Broadway Theater District was born.[36] Thomas Edison's first "Kinetoscope Parlor" also opened at 1155 Broadway (near Twenty-Seventh Street) in 1884. The theater featured twenty-second film clips that showed mundane events and exotic scenes like cockfights. It was later heralded by the *New York Times* as "The Birthplace of the Movies."[37] As if these other entertainment options were not enough, the employees at the tomb also blamed reduced interest on simpler distractions such as "boat excursions, low price music and dancing."[38]

Perhaps another reason for the reduced attention to the Civil War hero's final resting place was a disturbing change in sentiment about the war and race relations in the United States. In 1915, the film *The Birth of a Nation* was released. The three-hour epic takes the normal roles of Civil War heroes and flips them on their head. In D. W. Griffith's film, it is not the Union soldiers led by General Grant but rather the Ku Klux Klan who are the saviors in a war-ravaged South during Reconstruction. While the film undeniably contains elements of cinematic mastery, it is most significant for having revived the KKK and the "Lost Cause" myth of the Confederacy. The film coincided with a period when Jim Crow segregation laws were expanding under Woodrow Wilson and Confederate monuments were being erected at a steady pace throughout the South, as well as a few in the north, including an equestrian statue of Grant's adversary, General Robert E. Lee, in Gettysburg, dedicated in 1917.

At the end of the 1910s and into the 1920s, tomb attendance dipped to around 300,000 annually.[39] Though celebrities did not visit as often, a visit to Grant's Tomb would often remain long in the memories of less famous visitors. In the early 1920s, a six-year-old John F. Kennedy visited the tomb. Years later, the story would be recounted, with a touch of humor, that when the precocious future president was told that Grant was entombed inside, he innocently inquired, "Whiskers and all?"[40]

On April 27, 1922, a ceremony was held at the tomb to commemorate Grant's 100th birthday. The event was hosted by the Grand Army of the Republic, the Military Order of the Loyal Legion of the United States, and the Grant Monument Association. The day's events featured the planting of an oak tree relocated from Grant's farm in St. Louis and an olive wreath dropped in front of the tomb out of an airplane flying overhead. The *New-York Tribune* proclaimed that "Military history of past and present was linked at Grant's Tomb," for there were many young World War I veterans in the crowd mingling with the few aged Civil War veterans who attended. The featured speaker was French general Joseph Joffre, who praised Grant as the "one who made military history and whose soldierly life was admired in France and the United States."[41] But Grant's centennial celebration is most notable for how unnotable it was. His birthday was recognized at many locations across the country including St. Louis; his birthplace in Point Pleasant, Ohio; and Washington, DC, where the equestrian Ulysses S. Grant Memorial was dedicated. (It was sculpted by Henry Merwin Shrady, son of Dr. George Frederick Shrady, who cared for Grant in his final struggle.) While Presidents Hayes, Arthur, Cleveland, Harrison, and McKinley had attended events at the tomb years earlier, on this day President Warren G. Harding was in Ohio, and former president William Howard Taft was in Washington, DC. More surprising, however, was that neither the governor of New York, Nathan L. Miller, nor the city's mayor, John Francis Hylan, attended. Furthermore, coverage was sparse, even in the New York press. Reporters who did cover the event focused most of their attention on Joffre, with the *New-York Tribune* claiming that "The continual handshaking which he has undergone since his arrival has painfully affected his muscles of his right hand and the conventional welcome is taboo for the remainder of his visit." The event marks an important turning point from Grant's Tomb: from being *the* site at which to commemorate Grant's legacy to being one of many.

Modest celebrations continued to be held annually at the tomb on Grant's birthday and on Decoration Day, increasingly known as

Stereograph image of Grant's Tomb circa 1920. Note the development along Riverside Drive. (Courtesy of the Library of Congress)

Memorial Day since World War I. The Brooklyn U. S. Grant Post led the ceremonies until 1929. After that, with the Civil War veterans largely deceased, the torch was passed to the next generation, and the Sons of Union Veterans took over.

While the original plans for Grant's Tomb had included statuary and a staircase leading down to the river, the fact was that most of the public, and several people within the association, had considered the tomb completed back in 1897. In the initial design competition, architect John Duncan had a larger, more grandiose tomb in mind. Duncan felt sculptures outside the tomb were required.[42] The problem was always financial. In 1892, when Horace Porter took over as association president, Duncan reduced the scope of his design concept to meet the fundraising projections and timeline. But even after the memorial was constructed, some sought to have the initial vision fulfilled. Indeed, on the day of the dedication, Horace Porter optimistically declared, "The monument itself is now completed. Provision has been made for a colossal statue to surmount the dome of the monument, the work of which will begin without unreasonable delay."[43] But as the years went by with no progress, Porter's and Duncan's vision drifted farther and farther away. A later historian lamented, "The Association never seemed to have enough money, or willpower to do anything."[44]

In addition to ongoing maintenance, a few minor improvements were made over the years. In 1913, the association paid Louis Comfort Tiffany Studios $975 to create a set of nine stained-glass windows. They replaced the clear glass and curtains in the lower level that had grown ragged over the years. Porter declared the effect "vastly superior to the purple silk curtains."[45] A decade later, the gas jets that had illuminated the tomb since its inception were finally extinguished when it was wired with electricity. While the memorial never had an entrance fee (and still does not) to help augment its meager allotment from the city, souvenirs were sold inside. This commercialism prompted one outraged visitor to complain about the "venerable peddler shouting his wares in a raucous tone."[46]

Though Grant's Tomb remained largely unchanged, the surrounding neighborhood continued to transform over the following three decades. While at one time it stood out in a little-developed area, now it was in the shadow of newer and taller buildings.[47] In comparison to them, the tomb started to look old and dated. On February 17, 1929, a reporter for the *New York Times* complained, "Grant's Tomb occupies one of the most conspicuous sites on Riverside Drive. The lozenge-shaped strip of land on which it stands divides the heavy traffic sweeping north and south. . . . Everyone entering or leaving New York by motor along the Hudson River parkway must gaze at the granite pile with its unrelieved tall pillars and its unadorned front steps."[48]

In the 1920s, many in the association saw their primary responsibility as maintaining the structure, but Duncan was still making overtures about completing the tomb. He had envisioned it would be capped with a figure, but each time he was asked what it should be, it seemed he had a different opinion. Over the years his thoughts included the symbol of Victory, the symbol of Peace, and a bronze pine cone (which had also topped Julius A. Schweinfurth's design from the failed 1889 competition). In large part due to his indecisiveness, that project failed to gain traction.

The association soon realized they had bigger problems than missing statuary: In 1925, it was discovered that Grant's Tomb was sinking. Engineers noticed that a poor drainage design had caused the southwest corner to sag two inches into the earth. Fearing the tomb might eventually topple over if the situation remained unchecked, the city repaved the surrounding plaza.[49] Catastrophe averted, focus again returned to completing the structure, but as Duncan turned seventy-four in 1928, he was simply too old to take on the task alone. Thus, on February 27, 1928, a resolution was adopted by the association, which had met to form an exploratory committee to fulfill Duncan's vision. The respected architect William R. Mead of McKim, Mead & White recommended John Russell Pope.

His suggestion was quickly seconded by other leading architects. Pope had designed the neoclassical Abraham Lincoln Birthplace Memorial in Hodgenville, Kentucky and in later years would be best known for his designs of the National Archives Building, the National Gallery of Art, and the Jefferson Memorial. Pope worked with Duncan and produced a series of architectural drawings that included an ornamental structure over the entrance, landscaping, walkways, and retaining walls so the tomb would not appear as exposed. Perhaps most favored by the association was an equestrian statue in front of the tomb. Several years earlier an impressive memorial had been dedicated in Washington, DC, in front of the Capitol Building, featuring a statue of Grant on horseback. Another was erected in Fairmount Park in Philadelphia. Chicago also had its own Grant statue, and across the East River an equestrian statue of him had been erected in Brooklyn in 1896.

Association members were embarrassed that there was no statue of Grant at the tomb. Curiously, an unexpected obstacle emerged to creating a likeness of Grant on horseback. Despite being a gifted equestrian and something of a horse whisperer, and having spent uncountable hours in the saddle during his military career, no photograph of Grant on horseback was known to exist. Gurney C. Gue, writer for the *New York Herald Tribune*, took up the challenge to find one. Gue scoured the New York Historical Society, private dealers, and the New York Public Library with no success. But he was persistent. He called the editors of *Century Magazine*; Daniel Chester French, who had sculpted the likeness of Grant on horseback in Philadelphia; and the oldest living member of the Grant Monument Association, General Warren M. Healy. Healy did not know of a photograph, but offered a non sequitur: "I'm ninety-one now, with nine more to go!"[50]

Other accoutrements deemed necessary to complete the tomb included a portico and bas relief to replace the "grimly plain facade."[51] Pope presented his design to association board members on December 4, 1928. The estimated price tag of over $400,000, which included construction, Pope's commission, and the equestrian statue, was almost as much as the tomb itself had originally cost, but the association eagerly agreed to proceed with the project. A fundraising effort was kicked off two months later, but the group chosen to lead the new effort, the Special Committee to Complete the Monument, experienced many of the same fundraising woes that had beleaguered the original effort. Association members were as unenthusiastic about soliciting donations as they were about donating money themselves. Still, these were the Roaring Twenties, and by June, they had accumulated $106,375—a seemingly impressive sum, considering that many reckoned the tomb to have been finished in 1897, but far below the association's goal. It was enough, however, to have a $35,000 contract signed with Pope (10 percent of the $350,000 estimated cost) on June 11, 1929. Another contract was written for sculptor Paul Manship to create an equestrian statue for $75,000; it is unclear, however, if this contract was signed. The *New York Times* optimistically declared TOMB OF GENERAL GRANT TO BE FINISHED AT LAST with an illustration of what it would look like once completed.[52]

The optimism was short-lived. Just over four months later, on October 29, 1929, a stock market crash ushered in the Great Depression. Soon thousands of banks were shuttered and millions were unemployed. It is unsurprising that the effort collapsed. Fundraising ground to a halt, and many who had pledged donations balked on their commitments. On paper, though, the project was still moving forward. For the next year, the association reviewed progress reports in hopes that the economic calamity would end as quickly as it had started. But since June 1929, only $16,150 had been raised, and by 1932 the project was almost bankrupt. What had not been spent on contracts that would never be fulfilled was invested in stocks and bonds barely worth the paper they were printed on. Contracts were suspended, and in 1933 the project was shelved.

Perhaps it was for the best. Though plans were met with enthusiasm at a time when the tomb was criticized by some as "a good deal of an aesthetic eyesore that possess[ed] too cumbrous and gloomy an effect," years later the planned changes were less admired. National Park historian David M. Kahn considered the "sculptural pediment Pope posed . . . an absolute disaster . . . unnecessary and out of scale."[53] Even the long-awaited equestrian statue was disappointing, and Pope's choice of Paul Manship was "less than inspired." These changes were seen not as the completion of the tomb that Duncan envisioned, but rather a modernization. The Special Committee to Complete the Monument never officially disbanded, even though the efforts to complete the memorial had been abandoned. Now, instead of a reimagining or an ambitious enhancement, the committee focused on more mundane maintenance and required upkeep.

The Great Depression brought more problems than financial ones. Grant's place in the public consciousness was diminishing. Even before the economic crisis, sales of his *Personal Memoirs* had dropped off; now they fell "into obscurity."[54] Conditions at the tomb reflected Grant's diminishing popularity, as the minor grievances of loud visitors and roller-skating kids escalated into outright destruction. In 1932, vandals broke two glass doors and a police sentry box that had stood vacant since the twenty-four-hour guards had been removed and set it on fire. The most unsettling incident occurred on August 27, 1932, when Louis Gangl, an unemployed painter, desecrated the tomb. Gangl wrote a desperate poem in red paint on the granite: "The good but starve, The order of the day, Is Prey on others or become a prey." Before the days of surveillance cameras, Gangl might have gotten away with his crime if he had not done the same thing in the Bronx two months later.[55] He was sentenced to five days in jail for his crimes.

But while times had changed, there was also some continuity with the past: George G. Burnside was hired in 1933 as assistant curator, following in the footsteps of his father, George D. Burnside, who began as superintendent in 1891. George D. stayed on until 1940, the year George G. took over as head curator.[56]

Attendance plummeted during the Great Depression. New Yorkers rarely visited the site anymore; most of the guests were tourists from outside the city.[57] In 1933, only 95,584 visited, the first time attendance had dipped below 100,000.[58]

The economic calamity of the Depression also brought opportunity. Franklin Roosevelt's New Deal programs ignited a "new activism in Washington, reinforced by a sense that much of America's past was rapidly vanishing [that] encouraged the Federal Government to take a central role in preservation."[59] Under the federal Works Progress Administration (WPA, later renamed the Work Projects Administration), much-needed renovations were completed on Grant's Tomb, either directly by the WPA or by using their labor on projects initiated by the New York Department of Parks. In December 1935, the marble floor, which had cracked and stained over the years, was refurbished by the WPA. In 1937, WPA laborers cleaned the interior of the tomb, and the following fall they set their brushes on the outside granite using the "steam and acid method."[60] In addition, cables that had hung like vines throughout the interior ever since electricity was installed were now discreetly hidden within the walls. The tomb was fitted for heating at a cost of $1,000. To prevent birds from nesting in the dome, screens were installed for $150.[61]

In 1935, association president Herbert Satterlee had two suggestions for highlighting Grant's military service. His first initiative, to adorn the interior of the tomb with Civil War murals, was adopted two years later; much like the war itself, it became a competition of brother against brother. Lynn and William Dean Fausett, who had been born in Utah two decades apart (Lynn in 1894, William in 1913), moved to New York City to study at the Art Students League. Both submitted designs in June 1937, and William's was selected. He was awarded $3,000 to paint murals that included battle maps. By the fall of the following year, the paintings were completed and the proud artist claimed its effect was one of "calm dignity, simplicity, and general warmth to complement the general coolness of the marble."[62]

Satterlee's second suggestion in 1935 was to add bronze busts of Grant's fellow Civil War generals and military officials, including Generals William Tecumseh Sherman, Philip Henry Sheridan, George H. Thomas, Edward Ord, and James B. McPherson. Though never actually given the go-ahead by the Grant Monument Association, a Mr. Piccoli from the New Deal Federal Art Project assigned the busts to German sculptor William Mues and Hungarian sculptor Jeno Juszko. Piccoli determined that the busts could be donated to schools if not used in the tomb. Besides, he had plenty of sculptors on his staff who were already being paid, and this was something for them to do. Completed in the end of 1938, the busts cost the association only $350 for casting and materials. They are still placed around the sarcophagi today, and according to the National Park Service, "keep eternal vigil over the couple."[63]

Another addition was made to Grant's Tomb in 1938. When the City Hall Park Post Office was demolished, two eagle sculptures were relocated there and placed on either side of the staircase at the entrance.[64] While the eagles appear fitting for the site, the donation was an omen of things to come. Instead of a comprehensive "completion," the Grant Monument Association was now accepting discarded hand-me-downs from other structures.

Extensive changes were made to the grounds. Again using WPA labor, a $51,850 contract was signed with the H. E. Fletcher Company from West Chelmsford, Massachusetts, to add steps and retaining walls; $6,841.50 was allocated for landscaping.

The final project of the Great Depression years occurred in 1939 with the erection of two flags, one on either side of the entrance, to recognize former Grant Monument Association members. The flag to the left honors Fred Grant, who served from 1908 until his death in 1912. The other one is for Horace Porter and incorrectly reads "President Grant Monument Association 1891–1919." (He became a member in 1891 but was not elected president of the association until 1892.) While perhaps no man deserves more credit for the successful completion of Grant's Tomb, Porter became an absentee president shortly after its dedication. While many from the association were still celebrating after the 1897 ceremony, Porter was soon on an eastbound ship to assume his post as US ambassador to France. He stayed abroad for eight years, during which time he led the successful recovery of the remains of Revolutionary War hero John Paul Jones, who had been ignominiously buried in a long-lost Parisian cemetery.[65]

Despite reduced attendance during the Great Depression, Grant's Tomb had not lost its place in popular culture or its status as an iconic American site. In 1936, the romantic comedy *Mr. Deeds Goes to Town* was released, starring Gary Cooper as Longfellow Deeds. While in New York, Deeds expresses a desire to see Grant's Tomb but is warned of the diminishing meaning of the site: "To most people, it's an awful let-down. To most people, it's a washout." An undeterred Deeds replies, "Well, that depends on what they see. Me? Oh, I see a small Ohio farm boy becoming a great soldier. I see thousands of marching men. I see General Lee with a broken heart surrendering. And I can see the beginning of a new nation, like Abraham Lincoln said. And I can see that Ohio boy being inaugurated as president. Things like that can only happen in a country like America."[66] Just like in the Gilded Age, Depression-era Americans needed a hero. For Deeds, that hero was Grant.

A rededication ceremony was held at Grant's Tomb on April 27, 1939, to recognize the renovations of the previous decade. The tomb looked better than it had in many years. At the end of the decade, there was also one final attempt to obtain an equestrian statue of Grant. New York Parks Commissioner Robert Moses proposed that instead of building a new statue of Grant, why not just move the existing one in Brooklyn to the tomb? Moses suggested it would be "a very fine gesture on the part of Brooklyn," and his proposal was supported by Grant Monument Association president Herbert L. Satterlee. While it was surely a cheaper option than creating one from scratch, it was met with strong resistance from groups in Brooklyn, including 5,000 veterans.[67] Moses, who wielded extraordinary power as park commissioner, suffered a rare defeat, and his plan was shelved. Paul Manship's fee to sculpt Grant on horseback had been out of range a decade earlier, but now the association could look to the inexhaustible WPA labor force—they recruited a sculptor named Flinta. Though his price was right, he completed a disappointing model in the spring of 1939, leading Grant's grandson to decry the statue as "entirely unacceptable" and blast the likeness as "very stiff." The figure, he said, "expressed distress and sadness."[68]

Piccoli reassigned the project to William Mues, the German artist who had successfully sculpted the busts to the association's satisfaction. Piccoli, however, then left the WPA and was replaced by a Mr. Sobolski from Russia. It was the early 1940s by then, and with America on the brink of war, attitudes had changed. President Satterlee pulled no punches when he stated that "No one seems to want a statue of the General made by a German under the supervision of a Russian."[69]

After America entered the Second World War, the association leaders contemplated closing the tomb. President Satterlee feared sabotage or a takeover by a hostile group who could fire upon innocent bystanders from the roof.[70] Despite this imaginative doomsday scenario, the tomb remained open, but the war necessitated some changes. A Japanese embroidered silk, a gift from the citizens of Nagasaki that had hung in the tomb for years, was seen in a new light after Pearl Harbor, causing a stir among visitors. It was removed, along with photographs of Grant in Japan and "whatever else there is from Japan."[71] Precautions were also taken in the event of an air raid. Display cases were taped, sandbags were put in place, and a felt blanket and tarp were spread over the sarcophagi each evening.[72] Later, in more rational times, these actions were ridiculed, being seen in "some unfathomable way as protection."[73]

After World War II ended, life at Grant's Tomb returned to normal, with the only security provided by the New York policemen when they made their rounds. Annual attendance climbed to almost prewar levels, at a quarter million people. But with the tomb now fifty years old and in need of constant repairs, the Grant Monument Association found it increasingly difficult to pay for maintenance. In 1952, the association posted a meager profit of just $230.[74] At the spring 1953 meeting, it was suggested that they explore turning the tomb over to the federal government. No action was taken, but it came up again the following year. The federal government was not initially receptive; in a letter from President Dwight Eisenhower's personal secretary, the association was warned there was little "warmth on the part of the National Park Service towards the proposal."[75]

Despite the chilly response, the association had an advantage it had not had since the tomb was completed. President Eisenhower happened to be the only man since Grant who had served as a commanding general and then been elected president with no previous political experience. Despite his initial resistance, Eisenhower agreed to send a delegation to review the site on October 26, 1955. As head of the exploratory team, George A. Palmer expressed familiar reservations as to how to interpret the site: was it a tomb or a memorial museum? Regardless, he ended up supporting the transfer of Grant's Tomb to the National Park Service. By the following year, the annual maintenance cost had reached $11,635. Association members began the hard work of maneuvering through government bureaucracy to donate the tomb to the federal government.

This year was also significant for the death of Albert Henry Woolson on August 2, 1956. Born in Antwerp, New York, on February 11, 1850, Woolson had served in the Union Army and was wounded in the Battle of Shiloh while under the command of Grant. At 106 years old, Woolson was the last Union soldier—and the last verified Civil War veteran—to die.[76] With Woolson's death, Civil War historian Bruce Catton, writing for *Life* magazine, proclaimed, "This chapter of our history has been closed."[77]

The following year, Congress began to debate whether the federal government should accept the tomb. On March 21, 1957, House Resolution 6274 was introduced in the House of Representatives (by New York representative Herbert Zelenko) to transfer it to the Department of the Interior. The timing was fortuitous. That same year, Congress also established the United States Civil War Centennial Commission to plan for the hundredth anniversary. In December, the commission named its chairman: Major General Ulysses S. Grant III, grandson of the Civil War hero. Amid this nostalgia and patriotism, Zelenko's bill received swift Senate approval. On August 14, 1958, President Eisenhower signed the legislation.

Two months later, on October 23 at 4:00 p.m., the trustees of the Grant Monument Association held a special meeting, accepted the act of Congress, and designated a committee to make arrangements for the transfer.[78] They attempted to estimate the number of tourists from 1897 to date. While official numbers were inconsistent over the years, they somehow calculated that precisely 18,631,152 people had visited Grant's Tomb.[79]

The transfer of 0.76 acres was finalized on May 1, 1959, and the tomb was rechristened the General Grant National Memorial.[80] Plans were made for a grand ceremony. President Eisenhower, New York mayor Robert F. Wagner, Jr., and New York governor Nelson Rockefeller were all invited. But when none were available to attend, the plans were canceled and the transfer completed without fanfare.[81] While the National Park Service already had several Civil War sites under its domain, the General Grant National Memorial became the first burial site in the National Park System.

The new president of the Grant Monument Association, retired

Major General Edward J. McGrew, confidently proclaimed that the transfer ensured the monument was now in "long-range good hands so that we would not run the risk of the structure ever getting into a state of disrepair."[82] Less true words have rarely been spoken.

10

"We Have Fights Here Too"

THE POSTWAR AMERICA of the 1950s saw dramatic changes to society. After the defeat of Nazism and fascism in World War II, and with the United States now engaged in an existential contest with Communism, the Civil War had lost some of its relevance, seeming small and distant. Not only had the last Civil War veteran died, but there was a growing feeling of irreverence toward historical figures. Because of all this, the era represented a turning point for Grant in the national consciousness. Historian Joan Waugh notes: "Grant's star shine[d] so brightly for Americans in his own day" but "has been eclipsed so completely for Americans since at least the mid-twentieth century."[1]

Influential mainstream historians such as Douglas Southall Freeman of Virginia, who published a four-part biography of Robert E. Lee in the thirties that won the Pulitzer Prize, helped establish the negative view of Grant by elevating his Confederate adversary.[2] By the 1950s, most historians thought little of Ulysses S. Grant. For instance, in *The Pictorial History of the Presidents of the United States,* John and Alice Durant portrayed him as "a shy, stumpy little man" and reported that he "was called 'Grant the Butcher' during the war because of the way he drove his troops to wholesale slaughter."[3] The Durants subscribed to the "Lost Cause" mythology about the noble South; regarding Grant's presidency, they informed the reader that "Grant supported the radical Republicans with the result that northern political adventurers (carpetbaggers) rushed South and joined the white riffraff (scalawags) to exploit the Negro vote."4 Grant's diminished stature, his virtual eclipse by Robert E. Lee, was reinforced each day when Americans received their mail. In the 1950s the United States Post Office issued a "Liberty Series" of stamps. Along with denominations showing Washington, Jefferson, Lincoln, and Theodore Roosevelt, there was a thirty-cent stamp featuring the image of Lee. Absent was Ulysses S. Grant, though the post office found a place in the series for Benjamin Harrison (twelve cents). Disdain for Grant came right from the top, for Harry Truman once called him "the worst president in our history." In Truman's opinion, Grant was "a sleepwalker whose administration was even more crooked than Warren Harding's, if that's possible."5

Amid this zeitgeist of disdain and disregard, Grant's Tomb was thrust back into the national consciousness. In 1950, *You Bet Your Life* debuted on NBC, starring the legendary comedian Groucho Marx. The incredibly popular quiz show lasted ten seasons, in no small part due to Groucho's brand of improvisational humor. Contestants were there to serve as foils for his jokes; therefore, according to NPR, "the quiz would be the least important part of the show."6 It was on *You Bet Your Life* that the host uttered the most obvious question in history: "Who's buried in Grant's Tomb?" The line was an oft-used gag, meant as a softball question for the hapless contestant who could answer no other. A consolation for the ignorant, if you will. Groucho probably did not intend to disparage the final resting place of the Civil War hero. In years past, the public might not have tolerated the sacred space serving as a punchline, but in the 1950s, most found the joke hysterical. Not everyone, though. E. V. Durling from the *Milwaukee Sentinel* offered this criticism: "I don't think that running gag of—'Who is buried in Grant's tomb?'—is so funny. In fact, it seems in bad taste."7 Probably even Groucho would have been surprised by its lasting impact: the line would be remembered decades after its origin was forgotten by most. Many even forgot that it was a joke rather than a conundrum, leading more than a few to wonder if Grant really is buried in Grant's Tomb. If not Grant, then who?

For some, lighthearted jabs were replaced by outright hostility. A New Yorker who frequently walked past Riverside sent a letter to the custodian in 1954 to ask if Grant's Tomb was intentionally designed to look "like a cut phallus." The author sardonically compared the "symbol of circumcision of the Jews" to Grant's "savage" act, by which he meant General Order No. 11 of 1862 in which Grant expelled Jewish citizens from the Department of the Tennessee (the territory included parts of Kentucky, Mississippi, and Tennessee) to curtail black-market sales of Southern cotton.[8]

The 1950s also brought massive social changes in America. Elvis Presley debuted on *The Ed Sullivan Show* in 1956 to thrilled teenagers and their frightened, conservative parents. Rebellious teen movies hit the screens, such as Marlon Brando's *The Wild One* (1953) and James Dean's *Rebel Without a Cause* (1955). Whether reality imitated art or vice versa, the decade really did see the rise of youth gangs in urban cities. While Grant's Tomb was being transferred to the federal government, New York City was changing in myriad previously unfathomable ways. The area by the tomb, once one of the nicest in the city, had degenerated. As the buildings got older, wealthy residents moved out and poorer immigrants moved in. On June 11, 1955, New Yorkers opened their morning paper to find the shocking headline, GANG BATTLE FOR PARK AVERTED NEAR GRANT'S TOMB.[9] In one of the biggest brawls in the city's history up to that point, two hundred boys from six rival gangs, "many armed with zip guns and chains," fought behind Grant's Tomb to claim dominance over Riverside Park.[10]

Upon taking ownership of the monument, the National Park Service embarked upon a deep, almost philosophical debate on how Grant's Tomb should be interpreted. The question was as old as the idea for the tomb itself, but it was still relevant and pertinent. The meaning and interpretation of the tomb, as of the man, had changed much in the intervening years. It had once inspired feelings of patriotism, nationalism, unity, and reverence, but the important question was what it meant to the current generation. In an extensive analytical report titled "General Grant National Memorial: Its History and Possible Development," Dr. Thomas Pitkin, supervisory historian of the tomb, wrote of how it could be interpreted as either a final resting place or a national memorial. A later historian wondered aloud, "It is not entirely clear why Pitkin and so many others within the [National Park] Service found the two roles—tomb and national memorial—so incompatible." While seemingly inconsequential to the layman, to those at the National Park Service who spend careers making such distinctions, the difference was anything but. The direction Pitkin established was to interpret the site as a national memorial, explaining that the National Park Service was not tasked with "administering Grant's Tomb, but General Grant National Memorial."[11] This decision to consider Grant's Tomb as a tourist attraction would soon enough play out in very apparent ways, and, as a later historian stated, "was to have a number of unfortunate and unforeseen results."[12]

The National Park Service made one of its first changes in 1961. Display panels, which superintendent Newell H. Foster claimed were "repetitious and monotonous," were changed to "colorful and informative."[13] Color remained a theme the following year, when marble mosaics and other attempts to add vibrancy to the interior were proposed "to modify the prevailing dead white." Efforts were also made to allay the fears of a public alarmed by the newly rebellious youth. Floodlights were installed outside the tomb to "discourage the gathering of juveniles on the portico on summer nights. Such gatherings," it was reported, had "become a persistent problem."[14]

One aspect that did not change was the preoccupation with the equestrian statue. Like a cherry atop an ice cream sundae, many could not see Grant's Tomb as complete without it. More than thirty

Grant's Tomb from 1964. (Courtesy of the Library of Congress)

years after he was originally engaged, sculptor Paul Manship was again contacted. His new estimate was $100,000 to $200,000 (compared to a 1929 price of $75,000). The National Park Service came to the same realization in 1962 as the Grant Monument Association had years earlier, admitting that "the project was going badly, and that the necessary money did not seem to be available."[15]

The equestrian statue was abandoned, but a different addition to the tomb would have lasting impact. In 1964, the Grant Monument Association drained most of its accounts and transferred $20,000 to the National Park Service to fund two murals depicting Civil War battle scenes (to complete the set, a third was funded by the National Park Service). This gesture was among the last from the flailing association. After several years struggling to gain new members, the decision was made to terminate the eighty-year-old organization in March 1965. On April 7 of that same year, a "Certificate of

Dissolution" was issued. The Grant Monument Association ceased to exist as a legal entity. Its remaining $9,095.50 was donated to purchase Paul Manship's equestrian model, which was put on display inside the tomb (today it is beneath plexiglass in the visitor center). The gesture in miniature served as a dual symbolic death knell for both the Grant Monument Association and the long-desired statue of Grant on horseback.

On August 31, 1964, a contract was signed with artist Allyn Cox to create murals within the lunettes (arched spaces within the domed ceiling). A decade earlier, Cox had been hired to complete murals in the rotunda frieze at the United States Capitol Building, and in 1959 he had also completed a painting of Henry Clay for the Senate Reception Room.[16] Over the next year Cox worked on the first of the paintings, which interpreted Grant's epitaph engraved about the entrance: LET US HAVE PEACE. It depicted Grant and Robert E. Lee at Appomattox and was hung on April 1, 1965. A century after the Civil War, Grant's Tomb was still celebrating reunification.

Exactly a year later, the other two murals, depicting Grant's victories at Vicksburg and Chattanooga, were hung. At noon on May 26, 1966, a dedication ceremony was held for the three works of art, with remarks delivered by Major General Ulysses S. Grant III. Grant's descendant praised the murals: "My grandfather loved the outdoors, the greenery of life. He would have appreciated the color that has been added. Heretofore, there was lacking that touch of color which is so important in life. Now there is color."[17] While the murals remain one of the more memorable features of the tomb, they were not considered Cox's best effort. One historian commented, "Cox's work cannot be called altogether successful, His figures are stiff, the compositions dry and uninteresting. The men in combat look like rows of toy soldiers." But the biggest complaint had nothing to do with the depictions. "Perhaps most disturbing of all is their intense chromatic range, which clashes with the general austerity of the interior."[18]

The loud pastel colors of the Cox murals, so much a part of the Pop Art of the sixties, were embraced at the same time that appreciation for the historic value of other items within the tomb diminished. Several of the William Dean Fausett murals painted three decades earlier came to an undignified end. They were still in fine shape; a National Park Service employee described them as "just beautiful, and in perfect condition except for a little surface dirt."[19] Despite their historic and artistic value, they were "obliterated" when they were painted over in jarring blue and raspberry colors that were out of character with the tomb. Two other Fausett murals were modified to add African American figures to the paintings. Bronze flag cases holding Civil War battle flags that had been displayed in the tomb throughout the years were now expendable. In March 1970, two National Park Service employees were dispatched to Grant's Tomb armed with sledgehammers to destroy the flag cases, which may have been designed by John Duncan himself. Original architectural drawings from the competitions (particularly 1888) were deemed not worth the expense to maintain. Despite the artifacts being almost a century old and of indisputable historic significance, they were sadly—and intentionally—destroyed. The letters donated by Fred after Julia's death had been stored in a box under the hot water heater—unsurprisingly, many were damaged. Other historic items seem to have disappeared during these years, such as copper boxes that held records of people who contributed to the tomb's construction. They may have been stolen, but it is entirely possible that nobody cared enough to keep track of them. The staff had disregarded the most fundamental principles of historic preservation. Perhaps they were not trained, or perhaps they were incompetent, but indisputably their "unfortunate decisions" did irreparable damage.[20]

By the 1960s, a sharp difference developed in public perception of the tomb. With the centennial anniversary of the Civil War taking place amid tumultuous, eventful years in the Civil Rights movement, many found nothing particularly relevant in Grant's Tomb except that it marked how little progress had been made in the past century.

Another link to the past was broken on December 30, 1965 when George G. Burnside retired. After thirty-three years as curator, Burnside was given a gold watch and honored with a dinner at Longchamps on February 4. His father, George D. Burnside, who taught his son the ropes, had started working at Grant's Tomb in 1891, a year before the cornerstone was even laid.[21] George D.'s cousin was Ambrose Burnside, who had served under Ulysses S. Grant in the overland campaign a century earlier in 1864 and commanded troops in the battles of the Wilderness, Spotsylvania Court House, and Cold Harbor.

In the final years of the Grant Monument Association's ownership at the end of the 1950s, about 300,000 people visited annually. Attendance remained strong for the first six years of National Park Service stewardship, when the site averaged 286,467 people a year.[22] But in 1966, there was a dramatic downturn to only 120,100 people. Despite the honor of being added to the National Register of Historic Places that same year, attendance continued to decline.

While the 1950s sowed the seeds of rebellious youth culture, the 1960s spawned a full-blown revolution. Morals were changing, hair was longer, drug use was rampant, crime was rising, and the Yankees were in last place. The demographics of American society had also changed. As one reporter noted, "millions of immigrants arrived, many of whom knew little and cared less for Grant and the legacy of America's bloodiest conflict."[23]

All crime statistics increased, but perhaps there is no more powerful indicator than the murder rate in New York City. As it rose from 4.6 murders per 100,000 New York citizens in 1965 to 7.2 by the end of the decade, attendance at the tomb plummeted from 253,200 to 95,300 during the same years. Floodlights were installed outside the tomb in 1970 to help curtail crime, but more than illumination was required to combat the deteriorating conditions. The two statistics—crime and visitation—continued to trend in opposing directions throughout the 1970s.

More than any other presidential grave, Grant's Tomb became the grim poster child for urban decay, falling from its onetime place as New York City's most popular tourist attraction to one of its least visited and most dangerous sites. It was located only two blocks from the western edge of Harlem, an area that had suffered disproportionately and had become one of the roughest not only in New York, but in the entire country.

On April 27, 1972, there was a ceremony at the site to commemorate Grant's 150th birthday. In the middle of an unpopular war in Vietnam, the American public was disillusioned with the military and not eager to celebrate one of its leaders, especially one with as diminished relevance as Grant. While most chose to remain home and stay safe, about two dozen brave die-hards attended. They mingled with teenage members of the Young Aces and Junior Aces gangs, who made up about a third of the crowd that day. One Associated Press reporter asked a street tough from the Young Aces what he thought about the tomb. The defiant youth declared, "it was their territory," adding, "It's nice sitting around here playing congas at night. We have fights here too, if another club starts trouble."[24]

The National Park Service tried desperately to maintain the tomb's relevance, proposing radical ideas such as tie-dyeing festivals and outdoor movies shown on its side.[25] In 1972, tomb administrators partnered with a New York public arts group for a project that, on the surface, was undertaken to commemorate Grant's establishment of Yellowstone as the first national park in America a century earlier. When local artist Pedro Silva had an idea for mosaic benches, the National Park Service urged the public "come and help us complete it."[26] They hoped community engagement would curtail crime and vandalism and provided an estimated $20,000 worth of materials for the project. A diverse group of New Yorkers joined

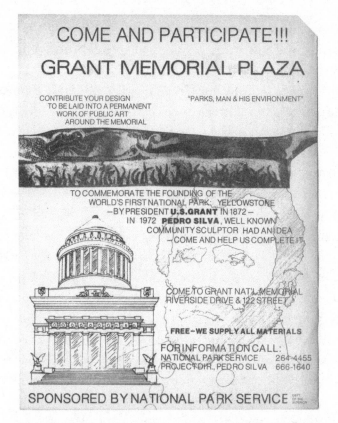

Invitational flyer used to solicit participation in the Memorial Bench Project. (Courtesy of the National Park Service, Manhattan Historic Sites Archive)

the effort, and Silva later recalled, "We had graffiti artists elbow to elbow with professors from Columbia." What slowly emerged from the unrestrained artistic collaboration were continuous fanciful-shaped forms in a psychedelic serpentine pattern that encircled the tomb on three sides. Each is covered in colorful, garish mosaics that feature dreamlike scenes such as a police officer issuing a ticket to a cab driver in a yellow Volkswagen Beetle (a popular 1970s staple), as well as an inverted elephant, an owl, penguins, mythological scenes featuring dragons, a princess and castle, an ice cream cone and a guitar, Disney stalwarts Donald Duck and Mickey Mouse, President Abraham Lincoln, and yes, a depiction of Grant. Truth be told, despite the fact that you can sit on some (but not all) parts, one would be hard-pressed to identify the structures as benches in any traditional sense.

The National Park Service made several more valiant efforts to attract visitors during these lean years. On September 7, 1974, a seven-hour multicultural marathon event to celebrate the end of summer and usher in autumn featured eclectic "musicians, square dancers, magicians, clowns, crafts, potters, puppeteers, belly dancers, children's theater, sitars, guitars, empanadas, artists, folksingers, eggrolls, jewelry, soul rock, modern dancers, health foods, balloons and people."[27] By this time the benches, started two years earlier, were almost complete, and the public was urged to "join in . . . as Pedro Silva continues piecing together the intricate designs for the mosaic benches that snake around the tomb."[28]

Depending on how one measures the results, the benches were either a soaring success or an abject failure. Viewing through the lens of the goal of community engagement, approximately 2,500 people were reportedly involved in the project in one form or another.[29] Certainly, they created a lasting work of folk art that embodies the free-spirited avant-garde style of the time. But the benches did not, as hoped, curb graffiti and the desecration of the tomb. Vandalism actually increased (although the benches were rarely targeted), visitation was not boosted, and the project ran wildly over budget to $50,000. But the biggest problem is that the benches were in 1974, and remain so today, ridiculously anachronistic at a tomb, which, despite the passage of time and evolution of attitudes, remains a solemn and sacred space. While the benches have been delicately called "quite controversial," they have also been roasted as unattractive, tasteless, and absurd.[30] Grant's great-granddaughter, Edith Grant Griffiths, complained, "I thought they were entirely inappropriate. They might be all right somewhere else, but they certainly clash with that severe and dignified building." From Chicago, the president of the Ulysses S. Grant Association opined, "It's like having

A view of the controversial mosaic benches from the rear of Grant's Tomb. The inscription reads, Grant Memorial Plaza by Pedro P. Silva and the Community 1972–1974. (Author's collection)

a roller-coaster ride running up and down the Lincoln Memorial. It may be fun, but it's not history."[31] The *New York Times* later observed, "The exquisitely detailed works look as if they would be more at home in a fanciful public park in Barcelona, where Antoni Gaudí is the architect most associated with the city, than surrounding a presidential mausoleum."[32]

The National Park Service continued to schedule alternative events at the tomb, such as a jazz concert in August 1975, but they were engaged in an uphill struggle.[33] A year after the Watergate scandal that forced President Richard Nixon to resign, the public was disillusioned. Traditional heroes like George Washington and Ulysses S. Grant, who were already tarnished, had lost even more of their luster. To make matters worse, in 1975 New York City teetered on the brink of bankruptcy. As insolvency approached, Congress considered providing funds for the city, but when President Gerald Ford made it clear he would not support a federal bailout, city residents awoke to find an alarming headline splashed across the *New*

York Daily News: FORD TO CITY: DROP DEAD.[34] Without the funds, the city was forced to lay off 50,000 employees from the New York City Police Department at a time when drugs, prostitution, and crime were rampant. Things were tough all over.

Later that year, the tomb was included in the New York City landmark register.[35] The designation was part of a larger American architectural trend that had played out in the decades when the tomb was so drastically altered. Going into the 1960s, there was a general sentiment that "old" was bad and required modernization. While perception began to change in the federal government with the 1966 Historic Preservation Act, it would take almost another decade for the architecture of the late 1800s to be better appreciated, when neoclassical structures were featured in exhibitions at the Museum of Modern Art and the Brooklyn Museum. But by that time the damage was done, and one only need see the tomb's out-of-character mosaic benches to realize the unfortunate impact.

In 1979, *New York Times* reporter Paul Goldberger lambasted Grant's Tomb as a "hopelessly solemn architecture" before adding that it was "pompous beyond even the requirements of a Mausoleum for a national hero. It is heavy and dry, utterly humorless, and while there is a pleasing interior, with an especially grand approach up a majestic flight of steps, there is nothing in this architecture to inspire true warmth."[36] While it is unclear why Goldberger expected a mausoleum to be humorous, he did love the benches, praising them as "surely Manhattan's finest piece of folk art of our time." He added a peculiar warning that appears to justify the years of vandalism: "It seems no accident that the benches have been free of graffiti while the monument has become tarred with it in recent years: there is a lesson in this, and one hopes that the lesson will be learned and the benches left where they belong."[37]

That same year, *The Warriors* was an unexpected box office hit. It featured an apocalyptic New York City, where hundreds of gangs battled for territory and ordinary citizens were terrorized

Graffiti on Grant's Tomb. The image is undated but is probably from the 1970s or 1980s. (Courtesy of the National Park Service)

indiscriminately. The film was not futuristic but instead set in the here and now, with dirty streets, graffiti-covered buildings, and danger lurking around every corner. It opens with rival gangs gathered in a park, tension thick and violence imminent, as the gang leader Cyrus appeals to them to put aside their petty turf battles and join forces to take over the city from the police. As he crescendos with a bellowing "Can you dig it?" a shot rings out and the only hope of peace within gangland dies along with Cyrus. The scene was filmed in Riverside Park, and the entire movie was shot on location in New York City. Years later the *Village Voice* noted that when *The Warriors* was being filmed, "an atmosphere of danger hung menacingly over the city."[38] The year *The Warriors* was released, the murder rate climbed to a disturbing 11.90 murders per 100,000 citizens, and attendance bottomed out when only 35,117 brave souls dared visit Grant's Tomb.[39]

The following year, the National Park Service commissioned a critical self-assessment. In *General Grant National Memorial Historical Resource Study*, author David M. Kahn lamented, "The public seems to have largely forgotten Grant."[40] The National Park Service was experiencing an existential crisis. Twenty years after taking over administration of the tomb, it was "struggling with the question of what to do with it." The author candidly observed, "No cohesive policy or interpretive program has emerged, regardless of what . . . official documents may say."[41] Kahn also lambasted the recent efforts to make the site relevant to 1970s America, such as the psychedelic benches and marathon culture festivals. At best, they were "totally unsuccessful in increasing visitation or in achieving the Park Service's larger goal of commemorating Ulysses S. Grant." At worst, they were "unacceptable sacrifices in the historic integrity of the site."[42] Another National Park Service report issued the same year (this one coauthored by Kahn) suggested the benches either be moved or "demolished, thus saving the expense of relocating them to another site."[43]

Conditions at the tomb and city did not fare any better in the 1980s. Hip-hop supplanted the rock and roll and disco music of the previous two decades, and with roots in the streets of New York, perhaps no early artist captured the inner-city experience better than its own Grandmaster Flash and the Furious Five. The raw lyrics of their 1982 hit "The Message" describe a dystopian, gritty, urban landscape: "Broken glass everywhere / People pissin' on the stairs, you know they just don't care / I can't take the smell, can't take the noise / Got no money to move out, I guess I got no choice." They might very well have been describing Grant's Tomb; that same year, a shocked visitor reported that the "graffiti and abandoned wrecked out cars surrounding the tomb . . . are deplorable"[44] In 1978 alone, the *New York Times* reported more than 79,000 "rusting, jagged-edged, litterstrewn vehicles" throughout the city, many north of 100th Street in the area of Grant's Tomb.[45] As for the tomb itself, officials tried to erase the defacement, but "like a blackboard wiped clean, it provided a clean slate for the next wave of graffiti vandals." A reporter lamented, "Grant's Tomb is better known as a joke than a national memorial."[46]

The sad and startling truth was that the conditions at Grant's

Tomb had become normalized, and some practically celebrated the depravity as one of its unique features. Vandals attacked the flagpoles, outdoor electrical outlets, and overhead wires. As soon as the National Park Service funded repairs, they were destroyed again.[47] The downward spiral continued: "The spot is a hangout for muggers. Homeless men sleep in the surrounding park. Drug dealers make nighttime sales nearby. And graffiti has to be sandblasted regularly from the tomb's walls and columns." A *Chicago Tribune* staff reporter lamented, "Few mentions of the monument are found in tourist brochures. Visitors to the site, which is open only five days a week, find nothing but a few plaques. The lighting is poor, the roof is leaky, there are no tour guides and no bathrooms."[48] While respectful visitors did not have access to a bathroom (the one installed in 1910 had since closed), vagrants regularly turned the tomb itself into one.

In 1990, there was renewed interest in Grant following the release of the wildly popular and successful five-part PBS documentary *The Civil War* by Ken Burns, which was initially broadcast September 23 to 28 and subsequently rerun. In 1990 and 1991, the average attendance jumped 25 percent from the previous two years to 86,311 annually. But the "Ken Burns effect" was not enough to overcome the public's revulsion at the pitiful conditions, and visitation again went into freefall. In 1992, the same year a vandal blew the beak off one of the eagles adorning the entrance with a firecracker, attendance dropped to 70,888. (Sadly, this was not even the first time the beak had been destroyed. This amputation occurred so frequently that the National Park Service had a cache of replacement beaks at the ready.) The following year, the *Los Angeles Times* reported that Grant's Tomb had become "a hangout for drunks, dope smokers, the dispossessed." Visitation plummeted to an anemic 37,272, the worst year in over a decade.[49]

The customary offenders were now joined by skateboarders. The hobby that started in California exploded in the 1970s and '80s, but

Evidence of homeless people using the portico of Grant's Tomb for shelter, 1994. (Courtesy of Frank Scaturro, Grant Monument Association)

in the years before skate parks were built, youths would practice wherever they could. The 1985 blockbuster *Back to the Future* introduced the sport to impressionable young people across the country and furthered the boom. Grant's Tomb, with its lack of security, alluring granite steps, and expansive pavement, proved to be the perfect place for skaters. But while they were enjoying their sport, they damaged the tomb in the process and added another insult to a long chain of offenses. In the 1950s and '60s, Groucho Marx had made Grant's Tomb a punchline, but now the tomb itself was the joke, and there was nothing funny about it. The National Park Service and the city of New York were not living up to their responsibilities.

Once again, Grant's Tomb was featured in a movie. *New Jack City* was a critically acclaimed 1991 film about a Harlem crack drug lord played by Wesley Snipes. Instead of the romantic or patriotic setting seen in *Personal* or *Mr. Deeds Goes to Town*, it was now the backdrop for a violent gangland murder that leaves dead bodies strewn about the bloodstained memorial. (A scene of a gang member getting crucified at the tomb was thankfully left on the editing floor.)[50]

While murder was perhaps the only crime not actually committed at Grant's Tomb—at least none is known to have occurred—the movie's depiction of desolation and squalor were true enough.[51] Newspapers regularly provided lurid descriptions of the depravity that had become commonplace at the tomb. In an article reprinted across the country, the Associated Press offered this description: "Makeshift beds of plastic bags, newspapers and blankets lie beside a pile of trash. There's a bottle of Thunderbird wine, just up the deteriorating steps from a bottle of malt liquor. Around the corner is an empty $10 bag of marijuana." The reporter noted sardonically: "The name of one vandal, 'Rase,' is visible three times on the tomb. Grant's name does not appear at all."[52]

Tourists had stayed away from the site for a generation, but now even employees were scarce. Only three workers were on hand at the tomb normally—two janitors and one brave soul to hand out pamphlets. Guided tours were canceled. To compound the deplorable conditions outside the tomb, inside was just as bad. Shoddy displays were rife with inaccuracies. One egregious example was a large photograph of Grant, but the problem was that it wasn't him! Even after a National Park Service ranger acknowledged the error to a reporter, the errant photograph remained in place. Artifacts, such as a rare photograph from 1843, were neglected and stolen.

Compared to Robert E. Lee's crypt within a small chapel on the campus of Washington and Lee University in Lexington, Virginia, the differences could not have been more striking. While Lee lost the Civil War in life, he clearly won the battle for public memory in death. Told about the conditions at Grant's Tomb and asked if anything similar happened at Lee Chapel, the director quickly replied, "No, no, no. If we caught them, we'd break their arms. . . . I've never seen anything like that. People come in here very respectful."[53] Grant's reputation also suffered by comparison. Grant was forgotten at best and blasted as a butcher general and inept president at worst, while Lee's stature had risen with the perception of his dignity in defeat. A generation earlier, President Dwight Eisenhower had hung a portrait of Lee in the Oval Office along with Washington, Franklin, and Lincoln, an alternate-reality Mount Rushmore of sorts.

Patriotic citizens valiantly tried to lend support and save the tomb. One such individual was George Craig. In 1993, the seventy-eight-year-old retired Port Authority employee founded the Friends of Grant's Tomb to raise money to make much-needed repairs: rebuild the leaky roof, install better lighting, create educational exhibits, and install bathrooms. Craig contacted Civil War groups across the country for support. But there was a steep price tag. After consulting with National Park Service officials, it was determined that a whopping $11.5 million was required. But, although Craig's intentions were good, his efforts were futile, as he admitted to a *Chicago Tribune* reporter: "If I've got $250, I'm lucky."[54]

While crime and hopelessness were rampant at Grant's Tomb, other sites in the vicinity fared much better, such as Columbia University's buildings and nearby churches, which remained graffiti-free. The problem, according to many observers, was that after thirty years of stewardship, the National Park Service had abdicated its responsibility. With no security and a scared staff, troublemakers had carte blanche to congregate at the unguarded site. The executive director of the Ulysses S. Grant Association, John Y. Simon, declared, "In effect, they have been given Grant's Tomb."[55]

Nature also began to reclaim the tomb. Weeds and grass—clearly visible in *New Jack City*—sprouted from the cracked granite. Grant's Tomb had lingered in a desperate state for almost three decades, but if there was a rock bottom, it occurred one morning in May 1993. Workers arrived that day to find a scene that was simultaneously repulsive and ridiculous. Looking down, they saw someone had defecated at the tomb entrance. Glancing up to the New York sky, they spied a garbage pail atop the flagpole. It was if the pirate dregs of society had commandeered the tomb and claimed it for themselves.[56]

All this desecration and decades of neglect begged the question: *Was the tomb worth saving?* In the years immediately after it was built, Grant's Tomb was a site for reconciliation, patriotism, and education. But what did it mean to people in the later years of the twentieth century? In an increasingly fractured society, people from the North and South, whether black or white, could still look to Grant, savior of the Union, as the embodiment of ideals worth fighting for—and therefore, some argued, his tomb was too. A reporter for the *Chicago Tribune* captured this modern reunification spirit: "His tomb is not just some obscure 'dead' building with no meaning for today. It is a monument to ideals of increasing importance to increasing numbers of people. Even as we face staggering social problems and cultural schisms, E Pluribus Unum is not dead."[57]

While all seemed hopeless, one person was not ready to concede the battle. Frank Scaturro, a student from nearby Columbia University, had been interested in presidential history since he was seven years old: "I devoured everything that I could about history, starting with the presidents." Several years later, the young boy from Long Island began to focus his attention on Ulysses S. Grant. Scaturro believed the Civil War general was misunderstood and underappreciated by historians. He would later write a highly regarded reassessment of Grant's presidency, *President Grant Reconsidered*. Serendipitously, Scaturro chose to study at Columbia University, just a few blocks away from the tomb. Shortly after moving into his dorm in August 1990, the eighteen-year-old became a frequent visitor.

The staff got to know him well and he inquired about volunteering at the tomb. When the bureaucratic process proved slow and a few months had passed with no response, he decided to take things into his own hands. On Grant's birthday, April 27, 1991, Scaturro visited the tomb. "I just started giving tours!" he recalled years later. "That's when my volunteer career began." His position was soon made official. As a frequent visitor both during and after hours, Scaturro witnessed the problems firsthand: "I knew it had suffered some rough times, but it was only when I worked there that I found out from a maintenance worker just how bad it was." While the graffiti was apparent, Scaturro learned that the custodian had to sweep debris away daily, as it would reappear the next morning. The worker would valiantly remove drug paraphernalia, garbage, and human waste, but the urine stench could not be so easily eliminated. "It was hard to identify a disrespectful activity that did not take place," Scaturro lamented. He even found evidence of animal sacrifice.[58]

Scaturro did research of internal reports such as the one that Kahn wrote and discovered additional problems. The repeated and intentional disregard and occasional destruction of artifacts related to the tomb dated back to almost immediately after the National Park Service had taken authority more than three decades earlier. Incidents such as painting over the Fausett murals horrified the young volunteer. Scaturro added, "Destruction of the bronze trophy cases was inexcusable."[59]

Between 1991 and 1993, Scaturro wrote to formally notify his superiors of the conditions. He respected the chain of command and wrote the National Park Service superintendent a "diplomatic and honest" listing of problems at the site. When things did not change, he wrote more. "At the height, I was sending weekly memos," he recalls. Despite warnings of reprisal, Scaturro persisted. Scaturro also requested twenty-four-hour security, since it was under the cover of night that most of the desecration occurred. His repeated requests "almost became a running joke," and he came to realize that "it's just never going to happen"[60]

During the summer, out of class, Scaturro could work full-time with the National Park Service. Perhaps he was becoming a thorn in the side of the powers that be. In 1993, he was relocated to Castle Clinton, located almost nine miles south in Battery Park, literally the farthest possible site the National Park Service could have reassigned him to on the island of Manhattan. That didn't stop him from visiting the tomb and observing that despite his complaints, there was not even a modicum of improvement.

By the fall of 1993, Scaturro, now a senior at Columbia, felt compelled to take a more drastic measure. He later recalled, "I didn't think too much about it. I just felt like this was something that needed to be done."[61] That something was a weighty 325-page report. Starting on September 29 and over the next few days, he mailed or hand-delivered copies to any New York media outlet he could think of. In addition, he sent copies to "virtually every elected official from President Bill Clinton on down," including Secretary of the Interior Bruce Babbitt.[62] In his scathing report, he took direct aim at the National Park Service for dereliction of duty. He chronicled the infractions at the site in detail: the cracks in the granite, a leaking roof, sandblasting stains, the disfigured eagle statue, but also much worse: "On virtually a daily basis Grant's Tomb had been used as shelter and bathroom for homeless people. A urine stench persisted throughout the day. We found marijuana bags and crack vials. It was a place where people felt they could go to get stoned."[63]

Scaturro's report drew the attention of Channel 4, the local NBC television station. In November 1993, Scaturro appeared on the early morning *Sunday Today in New York* show. He pointed out the Fausett murals that had been painted over as well as the other, more desperate problems. The reporter, Steve Dunlop, showed viewers graphic footage of the horrid conditions outside the tomb. As so few people had visited in recent years, this was the first time many had seen the deplorable conditions. The reporter also spoke to the custodian, who confirmed that homeless people were treating the tomb as a bathroom on a daily basis.

The situation escalated quickly. If Secretary Babbitt had not been aware of the tomb's horrendous condition beforehand, he certainly knew now. He also learned of a disturbing report that a brave young volunteer was let go for exposing the dismal conditions.

While the National Park Service had been slow to react to Scaturro's memos, they were lightning quick to respond to the broadcast. The same day as the *Sunday Today in New York* segment, the National Park Service held an emergency meeting, in which they undoubtedly discussed damage control. Unsurprisingly, they also decided that they no longer needed the services of the young whistleblowing volunteer. Scaturro was dismissed. The National Park Service claimed the official reason was that "he had failed to go through proper channels to lodge his complaints."[64]

Attention snowballed, but the avalanche began in earnest on January 2, 1994, when the *New York Times* picked up the story in an editorial titled "Dishonor for a Hero President." It was a brief article, a mere 426 words, but its impact was immense. "Ulysses S. Grant may rank as a disappointing President, but he was a hugely popular and widely respected war hero," the editorial began, before unequivocally stating its opinion: "His remains deserve better treatment than they get from the National Park Service."[65] While the article represented the culmination of three years of effort to raise awareness of the tomb's conditions, Scaturro's attention was elsewhere. His father passed away on the same day the *New York Times* article was published.

After the *Times* article, there was a dramatic shift. Instead of Scaturro frantically waving for media attention, news outlets were pursuing him. Even after he was fired, Scaturro would continue to frequent the tomb: "But by this point I was visiting with reporters, since I was no longer authorized to give tours." The site manager was not so friendly to the former volunteer. Scaturro criticized the National Park Service supervisors by name, and their responses would range from ignoring him to open hostility.

That same year, Scaturro moved to resurrect the Grant Monument Association, previously dissolved in 1965, to galvanize support for the restoration of the tomb. He contacted several of Grant's descendants from the New York area and sought support from citizens.

Scaturro also tracked down the last surviving member of the original association before it disbanded, Oren Root, grandnephew of Elihu Root, who had served in the cabinet of Theodore Roosevelt and whose daughter Edith had married Grant's grandson Ulysses III in 1907. With Oren's blessing as well as the support of Grant's descendants, Scaturro felt he could proceed. He received additional help from an attorney named Ed Hochman, who had contacted Scaturro out of the blue after reading the *New York Times* editorial to offer his legal services pro bono. The new Grant Monument Association was incorporated with nearly identical bylaws as the original. Despite its reestablishment, the reincarnated association was of course not involved in an official capacity.

At the same time Scaturro was making his stand, Illinois State Senator and Civil War buff Judy Baar Topinka also took notice. Topinka introduced a resolution, reminiscent of efforts made a century earlier, to move Grant's body out of New York to her home state, where Grant had briefly lived in Galena. She gave an ultimatum: "Either the National Park Service has to fix [the tomb] up, or they should let us take him home and bury him in a proper and respectful way."[66] Her assessment was also blunt: "Whether you liked him or not, he was a U.S. President, and you don't desecrate their grave site." Criticism from a young college student was one thing, but a rebuke from a state senator drew much more attention. This was a major embarrassment for the National Park Service. Topinka could claim Grant himself in support of her resolution, for he had listed the state as one of the three places he wished to be buried when he wrote, "Galena, or some other place in Illinois." Topinka proposed Grant Park in Chicago or beside Lincoln in Springfield, observing that Grant "would be better off anywhere than New York, but my argument is not with New York; it's with the National Park Service."

A hearing held on March 30, 1994, entered the realm of the surreal when Paul LeGreco, a toy store owner and Grant impersonator from Galena, spoke to the state senators. His unique perspective as the embodiment of Grant for two decades apparently qualified him to speak on behalf of the resolution. "I believe we should maintain a fitting tribute to Ulysses S. Grant. If it can't be done in New York, it should be done in Illinois." The resolution was later passed unanimously.

Soon the Illinois resolution escalated the issue from the state to the national level. On May 17, 1994, a resolution was proposed by Henry J. Hyde from Illinois in the House of Representatives. Hyde, like Topinka, gave an ultimatum: "If the maintenance of Grant's tomb is too burdensome, the State of Illinois would then request that the City of New York and the State of New York petition the National Park Service to be free of the burden of Grant's tomb and that the State of Illinois be allowed to appropriately honor this great hero so that he and his wife might find a final resting place with all due respect and tranquility, in a hallowed space in Illinois selected by the Illinois General Assembly in consultation with the Historic Preservation Agency; and be it further Resolved, That if the National Park Service agrees to move Grant's tomb to a site in Illinois, the cost shall be borne privately; and be it further Resolved, That Illinois is fully capable of honorably caring for its war heroes and former Presidents' resting places as is illustrated by the outstanding condition of Abraham Lincoln's tomb, located in Springfield, Illinois."[67]

Illinois was not the only contender for Grant's remains, as Ohio, Grant's birthplace, also joined the fray. Senator Eugene J. Watts argued, "If Grant's tomb is relocated, it absolutely should be in Ohio. . . . Our claim is as strong, if not stronger, than Illinois's." A visitor from Ohio voiced a familiar complaint: "The last time I was there, it was awful. Whiskey bottles, graffiti, marijuana bags and human waste."[68]

Another concern was raised from an important and influential source, one perhaps more weighty than any government official:

the descendants of Ulysses S. Grant. For them, it was not just a national figure whose grave was disgraced, it was their ancestor. One direct descendant, who happened to be the only one of his generation to share the potent, famous name, emerged as the most vocal: Grant's great-great-grandson, Ulysses Grant Dietz. Dietz's parents first brought him to Grant's Tomb in the early 1960s, when he was a young boy and only faintly aware of his important connection. He later recalled, "We had really come to New York to see the Bronx Zoo, but I remember the Tomb in the vaguest, most dreamlike sort of way. I recall being introduced to the park ranger on duty because my name was Ulysses, even though my parents called me Grant. The ranger seemed very pleased to meet me."[69] The next time Dietz visited Grant's Tomb was in 1987, when he was invited by the National Park Service to speak at a ceremony on Grant's birthday. At the time, he admits, he was not fully aware of Grant's legacy and significance in American history, but that day at Grant's Tomb changed him. "Growing up, I had all those myths [of Grant's tarnished reputation] browbeat into me. The tomb became the turning point when I began to realize I needed to learn what the truth was." In succeeding years, as he further embraced his famous ancestor, Dietz became a regular attendee at the annual events.[70] After connecting with Scaturro, Dietz voiced his disappointment at the dire state of the national and familial site to the press when he complained, "It's a presidential tomb, and it's being treated as a subway station."[71]

With growing pressure, Congress was spurred into action. While some in Ohio were demanding Grant's Tomb for their state, another Ohioan acted to secure the tomb's fate right where it was when Senator John Glenn pledged federal support. Reporters from the *Toledo Blade* were initially optimistic and declared, "Better days lie ahead for Grant's Tomb."[72] The National Park Service developed a plan to restore the tomb and published it on the symbolic date of April 27, 1994, which would have been Grant's 172nd birthday.

The National Park Service plan included funding for roof repairs, nighttime security, and expanded staff to permit the tomb to stay open seven days a week.[73] It set aside $400,000 for immediate needs and an additional $450,000 the following year. The amount was substantial when compared to the $323,000 annual budget (which covered salaries, maintenance, and operating costs), but minuscule beside the $11.5 million that the National Park Service had estimated as needed for restorations only six months earlier. Scaturro criticized these efforts as "token gestures."[74] Ulysses Grant Dietz, who spoke for family members, fired back at the National Park Service: "The government is basically throwing nickels and dimes at the site."[75]

Courtesy of Attorney Ed Hochman's free legal services, in late April 1994 Scaturro and the Grant family filed suit against the federal government to "restore the national historic site" to its 1959 condition and to keep it maintained "in perpetuity."[76] Dietz also warned, "The Grant family does have the legal power to reinter their ancestors if they so choose. The federal government cannot disregard the will of the Grant family."[77] To help galvanize public support, Scaturro wrote to the editorial page of the *New York Times*: "If Congress dumps Grant's Tomb, it will be back in the hands of vandals."[78]

The lawsuit and unenviable prospect of contending with a direct descendant's wishes to relocate the tomb finally spurred action when $1.8 million was appropriated over three years for restorations. After years of complacency, the National Park Service now went about the restoration with gusto. The first phase focused on the exterior. The tomb was cleaned top to bottom, the leaking roof sealed, and joints repaired. The next phase focused on the interior, which was repainted and cleaned. The National Park Service also sought to right past wrongs. They replaced the flag cases they had intentionally destroyed a quarter century earlier and placed historic flags within, and the murals that had survived the previous purge were restored. While the price tag was triple the original cost of the tomb, Superintendent Joseph T. Avery called the expense "well worth it."[79]

But something else was happening that year too. Murder rates that had peaked in 1990, with a shocking rate of 14.5 victims per 100,000 citizens of New York City, began to decline. At first the change was imperceptible: 14.2 in 1991, 13.2 in 1992, and 13.3 in 1993, when attendance cratered. In 1994 Rudolph W. Giuliani was elected mayor of New York City. As a United States attorney, he had gone after the New York mafia, and as mayor he and his police commissioners applied the "broken windows theory" of policing. Giuliani described this law enforcement approach by claiming, "A seemingly minor matter like broken windows in abandoned buildings leads directly to a more serious deterioration of neighborhoods. Someone who wouldn't normally throw a rock at an intact building is less reluctant to break a second window in a building that already has one broken." The snowball effect: "Someone emboldened by all the second broken windows may do even worse damage if he senses no one is around to prevent lawlessness."[80]

In 1994, as the tomb's funding was being debated in Congress amid threats to move the remains, murders had dropped precipitously to 11.1 victims per 100,000 New Yorkers. This was the single largest year-over-year drop since the authority of Grant's Tomb had passed to the National Park Service. The following year, 1995, saw another sharp decline to only 8.5 victims per 100,000. This was the lowest rate since 1970, which also happened to be the last year attendance topped 100,000 visitors. Scaturro recalled, "While there was an undeniable dramatic change in New York, what was happening at the tomb was largely its own quirky individual circumstance. Even in the early 1990s the neighborhood by the tomb was not bad. The tomb was adjoined by expensive fashionable Riverside Drive apartments that were in great shape."[81] But the difference was that they had security. The surrounding buildings did not suffer from vandalism anywhere near the extent that the tomb did. The most significant change was enhanced security measures that included round-the-clock guards and a barricade, so no one could get past the steps during off-hours.

Grant's Tomb was rebounding quickly. In 1994, crime and bad press kept attendance down to only 54,540 visitors. But in 1995, with positive attention and progress underway, attendance more than doubled to 115,800, and thousands more flocked to summer concerts hosted by the Jazzmobile on the tomb grounds.[82] That same year, the New York City Parks Department opened the Riverside Skate Park. Located just fourteen blocks south of the tomb, it offered skateboarders a legal and more ethical location to sharpen their shredding skills.[83]

"If the Old Guy Were Alive, He Might Have Enjoyed It"

A TOMB REDEDICATION ceremony was scheduled for April 27, 1997, on what would have been Grant's 175th birthday, a century since the original dedication. While the tomb had been ignored by the public for years, now it was the center of attention. The National Park Service proclaimed, "Due to the overwhelmingly enthusiastic response we have received, our plans for the event have grown well beyond our original expectations."[1] The event was expanded to two days. On April 26, Civil War reenactors hosted living history demonstrations. Just a few years earlier, the nights at Grant's Tomb belonged to gangs, drug addicts, and prostitutes, but now attendees were invited to camp at the site. While the National Park Service had been widely criticized in the dark years, on this day they could rightly look back on the recent progress and bask in a job well done. They had regained authority and stewardship of the General Grant National Memorial.

On April 27, at 11:30 a.m., a procession began at Riverside Drive at 103rd Street. Reminiscent of the commemorations of a century before, military units, veterans, bands, and patriotic organizations—1,300 people altogether—joined the mile-long parade that passed a reviewing stand as it approached the tomb. At 3:00 p.m., the formal ceremonies began.[2] Mayor Giuliani spoke, recalling: "On August 8, 1885, tens of thousands of people followed President

Grant's funeral procession to this very spot, to say farewell to their hero and loyal friend. This massive stone monument so aptly reflects the stoic strength he exhibited during the greatest crisis in our nation's history. As we rededicate this great structure today, let us remember Grant's legacy: that honesty, hard work and determination can carry a humble, ordinary person to greatness."[3] One of the many Grant descendants in attendance that day was Ulysses Grant Dietz, who had expressed his disappointment at the condition of the tomb three years earlier. Dietz spoke eloquently of the tomb's enduring meaning: "I believe that Grant's Tomb could easily inspire that same sense of sympathy and hope and pride [as it did in 1897] in a modern-day audience . . . an audience far bigger and far more complicated that the one a century ago." He added, "As the great-great-grandson of Ulysses and Julia Grant, all I really care about is that the tomb remains as you see it today: clean, fresh, well-maintained, and a fitting resting place for my revered ancestors."[4]

While not formally invited to the ceremonies, Scaturro, who by this time was a law student at the University of Pennsylvania, was in attendance as Dietz's guest.

In the closing years of the millennium, New York City continued its resurgence. Pornographic shops and peep shows in Times Square were supplanted by the Disney Store, Madame Tussauds, and the Hard Rock Café. Prostitutes and drug peddlers were replaced by people in Mickey Mouse and Spiderman costumes who convinced naïve tourists to pose for a picture with them for a tip.

It appeared better times lay ahead for Grant's Tomb, once again a safe, family-friendly attraction. But would the tourists return? In 1997, 126,432 people visited Grant's Tomb, the highest number since 1965. For the rest of the 1990s, annual attendance remained over 100,000.

In recent years, Grant's presidency has experienced a resurgence. Few defended his presidency at the time of his death, and he has regularly been relegated to among the worst of all time. In a 1982

A view from the sunken crypt (Grant's sarcophagus is on the left). Above is the Allyn Cox painting (from 1965) of Grant accepting Confederate General Robert E. Lee's surrender at Appomattox. (Author's collection)

Siena College Research Institute Presidential Ranking Survey, Grant was near the bottom, at thirty-sixth of thirty-nine presidents. His administration was considered better than only those of James Buchanan, Andrew Johnson, and Warren G. Harding. He retained his fourth-from-worst position when the survey was repeated in 1990 and again in 1994. Not coincidentally, these years were among the worst at Grant's Tomb, when both his legacy and his final resting place were figuratively—and for the tomb, literally—in the toilet.[5]

But when the tomb rebounded in the late 1990s, his legacy followed. One reason is the changing view of Reconstruction, the period after the Civil War when former slaves were struggling to gain their citizenship in the South. For years, the perception of this understudied and misunderstood period of our history was shaped by Columbia professor William A. Dunning, who taught in the early decades of the twentieth century, coinciding with the release of *The Birth of a Nation* and the proliferation of Confederate monuments. Dunning placed blame for a failed Reconstruction program squarely on the shoulders of Northern scalawags and carpetbaggers under Grant's presidency. But more recently historians, most notably another Columbia professor, Eric Foner, have reevaluated Reconstruction as the pursuit of a noble cause of equality and have placed Grant as being "on the right side of history."[6] A word of support also came from the top, when President Bill Clinton said, "I always thought old Grant got a bad rap in history."[7] By 2000, Grant had climbed to thirty-third of forty-one presidents. His rehabilitation continued, and in 2009 he ranked twenty-third of forty-two, which was the biggest single jump of any president. In the latest polling from 2018, Grant rests at twenty-fourth among forty-four presidents. While he remains the lowest-ranked president who

A view of Grant's Tomb from across the Hudson River in New Jersey. (Author's collection)

served a full two terms, he has moved ahead of Jimmy Carter (twenty-six), Gerald Ford (twenty-seven), Calvin Coolidge (thirty-one), and fellow Civil War generals Rutherford B. Hayes (thirty-two) and Benjamin Harrison (thirty-five).[8]

In the new millennium, attendance at Grant's Tomb hovers around 100,000 annually, some years above, but more often below.[9] In this century, though, many use different barometers to evaluate popularity, and as of this writing Grant's Tomb ranks number 130 out of 1,282 "Things to Do in New York City" on the popular travel website Tripadvisor.[10] While it's not the must-see stop for international tourists it once was, it still attracts many foreign visitors. In a recent visit, this author noted twelve of the previous eighteen visitors were international, hailing from Italy, Australia, and the Netherlands. No longer the revered site it was at the start of the last millennium, neither is it the disgraced and defiled one it later became. Safety and security are not a major issue, but the site still has its share of problems; some are new, and others reminiscent of its dark past.

Since even before construction began, Grant's Tomb symbolized, more than any other monument, reunification of a country that had been fractured by Civil War. As the Civil War generation faded away, the meaning ascribed to Grant's Tomb changed. In his book *Present Pasts*, Andreas Huyssen claims, "We have come to read . . . monuments as transformable and transitory, and sculptures subject to the vicissitudes of time."[11] For many people, Grant's Tomb reminds us that without the heroic actions and magnanimity of one man and the sacrifice of millions more, our nation could have been torn asunder.

But in the wake of racially charged violence that erupted in Charlottesville, Virginia, in August 2017, when a Unite the Right rally protested the removal of Confederate statues, many other monuments have come under unexpected scrutiny. Grant's Tomb is no exception. For a few, it has become a symbol of religious intolerance.

At a press conference in New York City, Marcia Kramer, political reporter for the local CBS station, confronted New York Mayor Bill de Blasio: "In 1862, he signed General Order number 11, which expelled Jews from Kentucky, Tennessee, and Mississippi. I wonder if you think that somebody who did that, given the large number of Jews who live in New York, should be buried here in New York?" A flummoxed de Blasio replied, "Marcia, I'm not familiar with that history. Obviously, I take it very seriously, but I'm just not familiar with it. You know, we don't tolerate anti–Semitism in New York City. . . . We have to look at each one of these cases. We'll have a commission. They'll come up with some universal rules."[12] None of that materialized, and by 2019, Grant's Tomb received strong federal support when New York Senator Chuck Schumer unequivocally stated, "There is no doubt: President Grant's gravesite is in need of major upkeep to preserve his story and America's rich history. I am proud to stand with the Grant Monument Association in calling attention to the needs of his plot and will press the federal government to deliver the dollars needed."[13]

Schumer's strong statement of moral and financial support indicates another problem that faces Grant's Tomb today. For a building completed in 1897 and restored in 1997, time has again taken its toll. Grant's Tomb requires regular maintenance, its problems surely exacerbated by its having been neglected for so long. Cracks in the pavement, water damage, a rusted flagpole, and peeling paint all require funds to repair. Grant's Tomb is competing with more than four hundred other sites in the National Park Service system for a minuscule sliver of the federal budget.[14]

During the February 2019 government shutdown, as if waiting two decades for their opportunity, vandals spray-painted graffiti on the tomb, demonstrating how easily it could slip back to the deplorable conditions from a generation ago. Frank Scaturro is still leading the charge. As president of the Grant Monument Association, Scaturro wrote President Donald Trump and Mayor de Blasio on

March 28, 2019. In addition to an appeal for funding for security, maintenance, and enhancements, Scaturro also resurrected a proposal long believed abandoned, requesting federal assistance "for the completion of Grant's Tomb with a crowning allegorical finial representing peace at its apex and an equestrian statue in its front plaza."[15] Perhaps the extraordinary story of Grant's Tomb has yet to achieve its culmination.

While solemn commemorations and patriotic celebrations were once held on Grant's birthday, today April 27 is a date to remind the public of why his tomb is important and worthy of their tax dollars. Funding also requires that Grant's Tomb remain in the public consciousness, and to do this the National Park Service continues to seek interesting and innovative ways to draw the public's attention. On July 4, 2003, the tomb was used as a patriotic backdrop for a musical performance in *Macy's 4th of July Spectacular.* In the show, nationally televised on NBC, Beyoncé Knowles sang her hit "Baby Boy." While it surely provided Grant's Tomb with a national audience, the event also sparked a controversy about appropriate use of a historically significant and solemn site. Scaturro lambasted the "lascivious choreography" and criticized Beyoncé's performance as "patently inappropriate . . . At that location, a certain decorum should have been observed from which popular entertainers are not exempt."[16] But not everyone was upset. Chapman Foster Grant, Ulysses S. Grant's great-great-grandson, commented, "It's kind of nice that he gets even a little exposure. . . . Who knows? If the old guy were alive, he might have enjoyed it."[17]

ACKNOWLEDGMENTS

IN WRITING THIS book, I was delighted to realize that I had something in common with Ulysses S. Grant. As Grant received help in writing his *Memoirs* from the likes of Mark Twain, Harrison Tyrrell, and Horace Porter, I could not have written this book without help from many people along the way. Some assisted knowingly, while others were unaware.

For starters, I would like to thank you—yes, you with the book in your hands. For your interest in one of the greatest men in American history and the monumental tomb created in his honor, you deserve to be commended. For taking your precious time to read my book, you have my sincere appreciation.

While on the journey of writing this book, I began teaching history at William Paterson University in Wayne, New Jersey. Many professors have helped me both in practice and through example, but I want to especially thank Lucia McMahon, Dewar MacLeod, Barbara Krasner, and George Robb.

A special thank-you to my sister, Rosemarie Flood, for her thoughtful proofreading. As this is the third book to which she has lent her literary expertise and expert eye to ferret out typos and sharpen prose, she could easily join the presidential lecture circuit.

I would like to acknowledge and recommend the rich archives of the Library of Congress, the *New York Times*, National Park Service, Newspapers.com, the Manhattan Historic Sites Archives, *Harper's*

Weekly, the Brooklyn Public Library, the New York Historical Society Museum & Library, the Museum of the City of New York, the American Presidency Project, JSTOR, and the NYS Historic Newspapers project, to name a few. I also owe a debt of gratitude to scholars who came before me and provided such insightful and valuable works including Joan Waugh, Ronald C. White, David M. Kahn, Geoffrey Perret, Geoffrey Ward, Dr. Thomas Pitkin, Ron Chernow, Eric Foner, Scott Martelle, John Y. Simon, and Mark Perry.

Thank you, Matthew Algeo, for your timely advice that helped make this a better book.

I would also like to tip my cap to the dedicated staff at the General Grant National Memorial. While online sources have surely made the historian's trade much easier, I am an old soul and prefer the gumshoe style of historic research. I am a quick train ride from New York City, and in researching this book, I visited Grant's Tomb more times than I can recall. I have seen the majestic structure in winter, spring, summer, and fall and have never found anyone on the staff anything but friendly, knowledgeable, and accommodating.

We all owe a large debt of gratitude to the past and current members of the Grant Monument Association. Thanks to their dedication and vigilance, this generation has an important and majestic treasure and a solemn and sacred space.

Thanks to Ulysses Grant Dietz, great-great-grandson of President Ulysses S. Grant, for sharing his story with candor and humor, and for the instrumental role he played that led to the restoration of Grant's Tomb.

I have researched dozens of sites where we commemorate the presidents, whether birthplaces, homes, or gravesites. But I can think of no other time in history when one person did so much to save an important piece of presidential—and American—history from a likely tragic ending. Thank you to Frank Scaturro for sharing your story with me. For your tireless crusade to rescue Grant's Tomb from ruin, we all owe you a debt of gratitude.

A special thank-you to the incredible people from Arcade and Skyhorse Publishing, including production editor Kirsten Dalley and cover designer Erin Seaward-Hiatt. This is the second book in which I have had the pleasure to work with Executive Editor Cal Barksdale, and I am once again blown away by his talent, courtesy, collaboration, expertise, and insight that only a true New Yorker could offer.

Finally, and most importantly, I owe everything else to my First Lady, Francesca, and our two wonderful sons, Vincent and Leonardo. During the time I have worked on this book, they have endured my frequent ramblings about Grant and his tomb: most often with interest (real or feigned), sometimes with understandable exasperation, but always with good humor. As with Beyoncé, I am confident that if the old guy were alive, he would have enjoyed them too.

NOTES

Chapter 1 "General Grant Is Doomed"

1. Joan Waugh, *U. S. Grant: American Hero, American Myth* (Chapel Hill, NC: University of North Carolina Press, 2009), 50.
2. Ronald C. White, *American Ulysses: A Life of Ulysses S. Grant* (New York: Random House, 2006), 23.
3. White, *American Ulysses*, 85.
4. Ron Chernow, *Grant* (New York: Penguin Press, 2017), 182.
5. White, *American Ulysses*, 251–252.
6. "March 4, 1869: First Inaugural Address," Miller Center, accessed June 8, 2020. https://millercenter.org/the-presidency/presidential-speeches/march-4-1869-first-inaugural-address.
7. Chernow, *Grant*, 862; "Reception by Ex-President Grant," *New York Herald*, May 15, 1877.
8. Geoffrey Perret, *Ulysses S. Grant: Soldier & President* (New York: Random House, 1997), 449.
9. White, *American Ulysses*, 594. Grant first used the phrase "Let us have peace" in his acceptance letter of the 1868 Republican candidacy for president.
10. "Gen. Grant's Tomb," *Gouverneur Free Press*, April 14, 1897.
11. White, *American Ulysses*, 609–610. Grant was apparently as impressed with the Japanese as they were with him. He later wrote, "my visit to Japan has been the most pleasant of all my travels." John Y. Simon, ed., *The Papers of Ulysses S. Grant: October 1, 1878–September 30, 1880* (Carbondale: Southern Illinois University Press, 2008), 192–193.
12. White, *American Ulysses*, 604.
13. "Grant Again in America" *New York Times*, September 21, 1879; "Gen. Grant's Travels," *New York Times*, September 21, 1879; Lucius Beebe and Charles Clegg, *The American West: The Pictorial Epic of a Continent* (New York: Bonanza Books, 1955), 144–145.

14. "Breaking Up General Grant," University of Virginia, accessed August 7, 2019. http://twain.lib.virginia.edu/onstage/babies.html.

15. "A Majority for Grant," *New York Times*, June 1, 1880.

16. Mark Twain and Harriet Elinor Smith, ed., *Autobiography of Mark Twain, Volume 1: The Complete and Authoritative Edition* (Berkeley: University of California Press, 2010), 76.

17. Esther Crain, *The Gilded Age in New York* (New York: Black Dog & Leventhal, 2016), 41.

18. "The Peabody Dinner," *New York Times*, March 23, 1867.

19. Mark Perry, *Grant and Twain: The Story of an American Friendship* (New York: Random House, 2005), 247.

20. White, *American Ulysses*, 624.

21. Perry, *Grant and Twain*, 116.

22. White, *American Ulysses*, 627.

23. White, 628.

24. Geoffrey C. Ward, *A Disposition to Be Rich* (New York: Vintage Books, 2012), 140.

25. White, *American Ulysses*, 629.

26. White, 548.

27. White, 569.

28. "A criminal scheme of the 1880s brought presidential treasures to the Smithsonian," Smithsonian, posted December 9, 2016. https://american history.si.edu/blog/criminal-scheme-presidential-treasures. *Harper's Weekly* cartoonist Thomas Nast was also ensnared in the fraud.

29. Ward, *A Disposition to Be Rich*, 212–213.

30. N. W. Ayer & Son, *Our Great Commander* (Philadelphia: Press of N. W. Ayer & Son, 1910).

31. Waugh, *U. S. Grant: American Hero, American Myth*, 54–55.

32. Federal Writers' Project of the Works Progress Administration of the State of New Jersey, *Entertaining A Nation: The Career of Long Branch* (Bayonne, NJ: The Jersey Printing Company, 1940), 3.

33. Waugh, *U. S. Grant: American Hero, American Myth*, 171–172.

34. White, *American Ulysses*, 634.

35. Morris S. Daniels, *The Story of Ocean Grove Related in the Year of its Golden Jubilee 1869–1919* (New York and Cincinnati: The Methodist Book Concern, 1919), 206. Palmer, it was reported, may have been the youngest member of the Union Army, having enlisted in the summer of 1861 at the tender age of fourteen and a half.

36. Daniels, *The Story of Ocean Grove Related in the Year of its Golden Jubilee 1869–1919*, 203.

37. "The Dead Hero," *Meriden Daily Republican*, July 24, 1885.

38. "Gen. Grant's Will," *New York Times*, August 17, 1885. Morton was rector of the St. James Protestant Episcopal Church.

39. Howard A. Kelly and Walter L. Burrage, eds., *American Medical Biographies* (Baltimore: The Norman, Remington Company, 1920), 60–62.

40. White, *American Ulysses*, 636–637.

41. Perry, *Grant and Twain*, 65.

42. George Frederick Shrady, *General Grant's Last Days* (New York: Privately Printed, 1908), 2.

43. Hamlin Garland, *Ulysses S. Grant: His Life and Character* (New York: Double & McClure Co., 1898), 509.

Chapter 2 "It Is All Over"

1. John Adams was the first president to attempt an autobiography, but it was unfinished at the time of his death. Martin Van Buren was the first to complete his autobiography during his lifetime, but it remained unpublished until 1920. Like Buchanan's book, Van Buren's was hardly a bestseller. Craig Fehrman, *Author in Chief: The Untold Story of Our Presidents and the Books They Wrote* (New York: Avid Reader Press, 2020); W. E., "The Autobiography of Martin Van Buren." *Tennessee Historical Magazine*, vol. 6, no. 3, 1920, 145–165.

2. Brian Matthew Jordan, *Marching Home: Union Veterans and Their Unending Civil War* (New York: Liveright Publishing, 2015), 88–89.

3. Mark Perry, *Grant and Twain: The Story of an American Friendship* (New York: Random House, 2005), 164–165.

4. Horace Porter, *Campaigning with Grant* (New York: The Century Co., 1906), 71.

5. Perry, *Grant and Twain*, 124.

6. Perry, 139.

7. George William Childs, *Recollections of General Grant: With an Account of the Presentation of the Portraits of Generals Grant, Sherman, and Sheridan* (Philadelphia: Collins Printing House, 1890), 43.

8. Later he would defend the doctors for its use: "[Cocaine] has never been given to me as a medicine. It has only been administered as an application to stop pain." Perry, *Grant and Twain*, 190.

9. "Gen. Grant Dying Slowly," *Indianapolis Journal*, March 1, 1885.

10. Perry, *Grant and Twain*, 225.

11. "Gen. Grant Dying Slowly," *Indianapolis Journal*, March 1, 1885.

12. "General Grant Dying," *Indianapolis Journal*, March 2, 1885.

13. *Harper's Weekly*, April 4, 1885; *Harper's Weekly*, April 11, 1885; and *Harper's Weekly*, April 18, 1885.

14. It's also worth noting that the presidents who followed Grant—Rutherford B. Hayes, James Garfield, Chester Arthur, Grover Cleveland, Benjamin Harrison, Grover Cleveland (again), and William McKinley—while able men, had not captured the nation's imagination or received their veneration as did Grant.

15. Ronald C. White, *American Ulysses: A Life of Ulysses S. Grant* (New York: Random House, 2006), 641.

16. "Rare Historical Foresight Preserved Grant's Upstate N.Y. Cottage," *Daily Gazette*, May 28, 1990.

17. "The Nation's Gratitude to General Grant," *Harper's Weekly*, March 21, 1885. Grover Cleveland signed the commission shortly after taking office, reportedly the second official act of his presidency. N. W. Ayer & Son, *Our Great Commander* (Philadelphia: Press of N. W. Ayer & Son, 1910).

18. William M. Thayer, *From Tannery to the White House: Story of the Life of Ulysses S. Grant, his Boyhood, Youth, Manhood, Public and Private Life and Services* (London: Thomas Nelson and Sons, 1885), 373.

19. "Gen. Grant Dying Slowly," *Indianapolis Journal*, March 1, 1885.

20. "Generous Californians," *Savannah Morning News*, March 5, 1885.

21. "Letter from the Clinton Avenue Institute to General Ulysses S. Grant, April 10, 1885," Manhattan Historic Sites Archive, accessed June 16, 2019. http://mhsarchive.com/item.aspx?rID=GEGR%20%20%20%20%20625.0015&db=objects&dir=CR%20GEGR.

22. "Letter from the Excelsior Club to General Ulysses S. Grant, March 6, 1885," Manhattan Historic Sites Archive, accessed June 16, 2019. http://mhsarchive.com/item.aspx?rID=GEGR%20%20%20%20%20625.0014&db=objects&dir=CR%20GEGR.

23. David M. Kahn, *General Grant National Memorial Historical Resource Study* (National Park Service, 1980), 6.

24. White, *American Ulysses*, 470.

25. Perry, *Grant and Twain*, 180–181. According to Newman, Grant consented to the baptism, but other accounts have Newman covertly baptizing Grant in his sleep. Geoffrey Perrett, *Ulysses S. Grant Soldier & President* (New York: Modern Library, 1998), 473–478.

26. White, *American Ulysses*, 642.

27. George Frederick Shrady, *General Grant's Last Days* (New York: Privately Printed, 1908), 61.

28. *Southern Historical Society Papers* (Richmond, VA: Wm. Ellis Jones, 1885), 360.

29. Joan Waugh, *U. S. Grant: American Hero, American Myth* (Chapel Hill, NC: University of North Carolina Press, 2009), 185.

30. "Joseph W. Drexel Dead," *New York Times*, March 26, 1888. Coincidentally, when Drexel died three years after Grant, he was tended by Dr. Fordyce Barker on his deathbed.

31. Esther Crain, *The Gilded Age in New York* (New York: Black Dog & Leventhal, 2016), 64.

32. "U. S. Grant's Ties to Spa City the Subject of History Talk," *Saratogian*, March 9, 2017.

33. *Albany Evening Journal*, June 19, 1885, as referenced in Perry, *Grant and Twain*, 209.

34. "Grant at McGregor," *Salt Lake Evening Democrat*, June 16, 1885.

35. "General Grant's Last Days by Frank W. Mack," *Saturday Evening Post*, February 26, 1910.

36. "General Grant's Last Days," *Saturday Evening Post*.

37. "Grant at McGregor," *Salt Lake Evening Democrat*, June 16, 1885.

38. "This day in history," History Channel, last updated July 28, 2019. https://www.history.com/this-day-in-history/statue-of-liberty-arrives-in-new-york-harbor. The disassembled statue consisted of 350 pieces.

39. "Resolution from the Colored Citizens of Chicago, June 23, 1885," Manhattan Historic Sites Archive, accessed July 7, 2019. http://mhsarchive.com/item.aspx?rID=GEGR%20%20%20%20%20120&db=objects&dir=CR%20GEGR.

40. "The Future of the Grants," *Indianapolis Journal*, July 5, 1885.

41. White, *American Ulysses*, 319.

42. Grant's reconciliatory attitude was also evident in his presidential appointments when he chose Confederate general James Longstreet to be the surveyor of customs, a very important and profitable position, at the port of New Orleans.

43. White, *American Ulysses*, 650.

44. "Buckner's Tribute to Grant," *New York Times*, August 8, 1885.

45. "On Death Watch Duty," *Daily True American*, February 25, 1891.

46. "The Day at Mt. McGregor," *Indianapolis Journal*, June 23, 1885.

47. "The Day at Mt. McGregor," *Indianapolis Journal*.

48. "A Hero Finds Rest. Ulysses S. Grant's Painless, Peaceful Death. The End Coming in the Early Morning," *New York Times*, July 24, 1885.

49. George William Childs, *Recollections of General Grant: With an Account of the Presentation of the Portraits of Generals Grant, Sherman, and Sheridan* (Philadelphia: Collins Printing House, 1890), 46.

50. Childs, 45.

51. Thayer, *From Tannery to the White House*, 381.

52. *Century Illustrated Monthly Magazine November 1885 to April 1886*. New York: The Century Co., 1886. 124–125.

53. Perry, *Grant and Twain*, 225–226.

54. Perry, 225–227.

55. White, *American Ulysses*, 650.

56. Richard Wightman Fox, *Lincoln's Body: A Cultural History* (New York: W. W. Norton & Company, 2015), 29–30.

57. Louis L. Picone, *The President Is Dead! The Extraordinary Stories of the Presidential Deaths, Final Days, Burials, and Beyond* (New York: Skyhorse Publishing, 2016).

58. "A Hero Finds Rest. Ulysses S. Grant's Painless, Peaceful Death. The End Coming in the Early Morning," *New York Times*, July 24, 1885.

59. George Frederick Shrady, *General Grant's Last Days*, 74.

60. "A Hero Finds Rest. Ulysses S. Grant's Painless, Peaceful Death. The End Coming in The Early Morning," *New York Times*, July 24, 1885.

61. "A Hero Finds Rest," *New York Times*.

62. "Sleeping, General Grant is at Rest," *Maryville Times* (Tennessee), July 30, 1885.

63. Thomas M. Pitkin, *The Captain Departs: Ulysses S. Grant's Last Campaign*. Carbondale, IL: Southern Illinois University Press, 1973, 93.

Chapter 3 "Mother Takes Riverside"

1. Mark Perry, *Grant and Twain: The Story of an American Friendship* (New York: Random House, 2005), 225–228.

2. "The Dead Hero," *Meriden Daily Republican*, July 24, 1885. Gerhardt later charged the family an exorbitant $17,000 for the death mask and refused to give it to the widow until he was paid. An embarrassed Twain paid Gerhardt $10,000 to settle the matter. Perry, *Grant and Twain*, 225–237.

3. Grover Cleveland, "Proclamation 270—Announcing the Death of Ulysses S. Grant," July 23, 1885. Online by Gerhard Peters and John T. Woolley, The American Presidency Project. https://www.presidency.ucsb.edu/node/205034.

4. "A Hero Finds Rest. Ulysses S. Grant's Painless, Peaceful Death. The End Coming in the Early Morning," *New York Times*, July 24, 1885.

5. "Grant's Tomb: Three Sites Offered the Family To-day," *Brooklyn Daily Eagle*, July 24, 1885.

6. When this author last visited in 2017, the site was a Manhattan Eyeworks, but the external architecture retains its integrity from when it was Stephen Merritt Burial & Cremation Company. As early as the 1940s,

the company continued to highlight their famous funeral in their advertising, boasting, "We Buried General Grant" in the *New Yorker* in 1947 and "We Conducted His Funeral!" on a poster in a subway in 1953 beneath an image of Grant's Tomb. At the time, a flag that had been placed on Grant's coffin still hung proudly in the company offices. *The New Yorker*, September 27, 1947; "Who's Buried in Grant's Tomb? A Funeral Company Advertises Its Part in It," *Milwaukee Journal*, December 31, 1953.

7. David M. Kahn, *General Grant National Memorial Historical Resource Study* (National Park Service, 1980), 23.

8. Campbell Gibson and Kay Jung, *Historical Census Statistics on Population Totals by Race, 1790 to 1990, and by Hispanic Origin, 1970 to 1990, For Large Cities and Other Urban Places in the United States* (Washington, DC: US Census Bureau, 2005). Note census data is collected every ten years, but since the events in the comparison fall approximately midway between the decades, an average of the previous and subsequent decades is used to determine the point-in-time population (using table 33). In 1885, the estimated population of 1,360,800 is based on 1880 (1,206,299) and 1890 (1,515,301). In 1964, the estimated population of 7,838,423 (now including Brooklyn, which merged into New York City in 1898) is based on 1960 (7,781,984) and 1970 (7,894,862). Playing this statistical game a little further, if one factors in attendance along with population differences, more than *eighteen times* as many people viewed the empty casket of President Grant than viewed the casket containing the body of President Hoover. One could go to the next level by including how many hours the viewing was open, but it is unknown how long Stephen Merritt allowed mourners to file past Grant's coffin.

9. Thomas M. Pitkin, *The Captain Departs: Ulysses S. Grant's Last Campaign* (Carbondale, IL: Southern Illinois University Press, 1973), 103.

10. "Grant's Obsequies, Services at Mt. McGregor," *Ithaca Democrat*, August 6, 1885.

11. As quoted in "The Dead Hero," *Meriden Daily Republican* (CT), July 24, 1885.

12. "Letter from Robert Todd Lincoln and the Bar Association of Chicago to Julia Dent Grant, August 6, 1885," Manhattan Historic Sites Archive, accessed June 16, 2019. http://mhsarchive.com/item.aspx?rID=GEGR%20%20%20%20%20625.0019&db=objects&dir=CR%20GEGR.

13. "Letter from the Woman's Relief Corps of Iowa to Julia Dent Grant and Nellie Grant Sartoris, July 27, 1885," Manhattan Historic Sites Archive, accessed June 16, 2019. http://mhsarchive.com/item.aspx?rID

=GEGR%20%20%20%20%20625.0017&db=objects&dir=CR%20
NPNYH.

14. "Letter from the Essex County Trades Assembly of Newark to the Grant
    family, July 27, 1885," Manhattan Historic Sites Archive, accessed June
    16, 2019. http://mhsarchive.com/item.aspx?rID=GEGR%20%20%20
    %20%20625.0016&db=objects&dir=CR%20NPNYH; "Letter from
    W. H. Roosevelt, Secretary Officer of the Ohio Association of Union
    Ex-Prisoners of War, to Mrs. U. S. Grant, October 21, 1885," Manhattan
    Historic Sites Archive, accessed July 7, 2019. http://mhsarchive.com/item
    .aspx?rID=GEGR%20%20%20%20%20198&db=objects&dir=CR%20
    GEGR.

15. "General Grant National Memorial Cataloged Resolutions and Memorial
    Items, 1885," Manhattan Historic Sites Archive, accessed June 16, 2019.
    www.mhsarchive.org/collection.aspx?rID=GEGR.COLLECT.005&db
    =exhibt&dir=CR%20GEGR.

16. Kahn, *General Grant National Memorial Historical Resource Study*, 27.

17. "The National Sorrow," *New York Times*, August 3, 1885.

18. "Gen. Grant's Funeral," *New York Times*, August 5, 1885.

19. "A Confederate Reunion," *New York Times*, August 6, 1885.

20. "The Dead Hero," *Meriden Daily Republican*, July 24, 1885.

21. Donald E. Collins, *The Death and Resurrection of Jefferson Davis* (Lanham,
    Maryland: Rowman & Littlefield, 2005), 79.

22. "Jefferson Davis on Grant," *New York Times*, August 12, 1885.

23. Ronald C. White, *American Ulysses: A Life of Ulysses S. Grant* (New York:
    Random House, 2006), 654.

24. "The Dead Hero," *Meriden Daily Republican*, July 24, 1885.

25. "Grant's Tomb: Three Sites Offered the Family To-day," *Brooklyn Daily
    Eagle.,* July 24, 1885.

26. "Sleeping, General Grant is at Rest," *Maryville Times* (Tennessee), July
    30, 1885.

27. "The Dead Hero," *Meriden Daily Republican*, July 24, 1885.

28. After the Civil War ended, the United States military turned its attention
    to the Western frontier, where confrontations with Native Americans
    were becoming more frequent and violent with the construction of the
    Transcontinental Railroad. In 1867, while Grant remained Commanding
    General of the United States Army, he assigned Sheridan the task of
    pacifying the American West. Although its origins are debatable, the
    invective "The Only Good Indian Is a Dead Indian" is often credited to
    Philip Sheridan.

29. "Letter from P. H. Sheridan to Col. Frederick Grant, July 23, 1885,"

Manhattan Historic Sites Archive, accessed June 16, 2019. http://www
.mhsarchive.org/item.aspx?rID=GEGR%20%20%20%20%20
625.0007&db=objects&dir=CR%20GEGR.

30. "The Future of the Grants," *Indianapolis Journal*, July 5, 1885.

31. "Letter from Mayor Grace to Mrs. Grant proposing a memorial to President
Grant, July 23, 1885," Manhattan Historic Sites Archive, accessed June 16,
2019. http://www.mhsarchive.org/item.aspx?rID=GEGR%20%20%20
%20%20625.0001&db=objects&dir=CR%20GEGR.

32. "Grant's Tomb: Three Sites Offered the Family To-day," *Brooklyn Daily
Eagle*, July 24, 1885.

33. "Let Him Lie in New York," *New-York Tribune*, July 25, 1885.

34. Kahn, *General Grant National Memorial Historical Resource Study*, 14.

35. "Letter from Kurt Forsberg to the President and Committee of the Grant
Monument Association, August 15, 1885," Manhattan Historic Sites
Archive, accessed June 22, 2019. http://mhsarchive.com/item.aspx?rID
=GEGR%20%20%20%20%20622.0117&db=objects&dir=CR%20
GEGR.

36. Edwin G. Burrows and Mike Wallace, *Gotham: A History of New York
City to 1898* (New York: Oxford University Press, 1999), 1050.

37. "Riverside Park Chosen," *New York Times*, July 29, 1885.

38. Joan Waugh, *U. S. Grant: American Hero, American Myth* (Chapel Hill,
NC: University of North Carolina Press, 2009), 273.

39. "Riverside Park Chosen," *New York Times*, July 29, 1885.

40. "Letter from Mayor Grace to a memorial to President Grant, July
23, 1885," Manhattan Historic Sites Archive, accessed June 16, 2019.
http://mhsarchive.com/item.aspx?rID=GEGR%20%20%20%20%20
625.0001&db=objects&dir=CR%20NPNYH.

41. "Belvedere Castle," Centralpark.com, accessed August 15, 2019. http:
//www.centralpark.com/guide/attractions/belvedere-castle.html.

42. "Riverside Park Chosen," *New York Times*, July 29, 1885.

43. "A Hero Finds Rest. Ulysses S. Grant's Painless, Peaceful Death. The End
Coming in the Early Morning," *New York Times*, July 24, 1885.

44. *The Magazine of American History with Notes and Queries, Volume 14*,
September 1885, 225.

45. *Magazine of American History with Notes and Queries, Volume 14*, 226.

46. "By Telegraph," *Deseret News*, August 5, 1885.

Chapter 4 "A Colossal and Memorable Demonstration"

1. "Death of General Grant," *Colonist* (volume XXVIII, issue 4229), August
29, 1885.

2. David M. Kahn, *General Grant National Memorial Historical Resource Study* (National Park Service, 1980), 34.

3. "Riverside Park Chosen," *New York Times*, July 29, 1885.

4. "The Dead General," *New York Evening Post*, July 29, 1885.

5. "Grant and Lincoln Park," *Inter Ocean* (Chicago), July 26, 1885.

6. "Riverside Park Chosen," *New York Times*, July 29, 1885.

7. "Riverside Park Chosen," *New York Times*.

8. Garfield, originally critical of Grant's presidency, later stated, "[Grant's] power of staying, his imperturbability, has been of incalculable value to the nation, and will be prized more and more as his career recedes." Ronald C. White, *American Ulysses: A Life of Ulysses S. Grant* (New York: Random House, 2006), 583.

9. The story of the 1880 election is expertly recounted in Benjamin T. Arrington's *The Last Lincoln Republican: The Presidential Election of 1880* (Lawrence: University Press of Kansas, 2020).

10. "The March to City Hall," *New York Times*, August 8, 1885.

11. "Fallen Heroes: Decoration Day Exercises in Brooklyn," *Brooklyn Daily Eagle*, May 31, 1884.

12. "Riverside Park Chosen," *New York Times*, July 29, 1885. The thirteen were Hiram Myers, Augustus Lippitt, Thomas Murray, William L. Young, Enos B. Vail, Chester T. Kenney, F. E. Miller, James B. Pringle, George G. Peavey, John Hemphill, O. W. Marvin, Marshal J. Corbett, and George W. Van Mater.

13. "Riverside Park Chosen," *New York Times*.

14. "Grant's Obsequies, Services at Mt. McGregor," *Ithaca Democrat*, August 6, 1885; William M. Thayer, *From Tannery to the White House: Story of the Life of Ulysses S. Grant, His Boyhood, Youth, Manhood, Public and Private Life and Services* (London: Thomas Nelson and Sons, 1885), 391.

15. "The Journey to the Tomb," *New York Times*, August 5, 1885.

16. "Leaving Mount McGregor," *Times Union* (Brooklyn), August 31, 1885.

17. The following year, the same car was used in the funeral train that carried Chester Arthur's remains from New York City to Albany.

18. "Toward the Grave," *Democrat and Chronicle* (Rochester, NY), August 5, 1885.

19. William Henry Harrison's remains were also briefly placed on a train in 1841, but that was almost four months after his death as he was temporarily placed in a crypt in Congressional Cemetery in Washington, DC. John Quincy Adams's remains also resided in the same temporary crypt before a train brought him for permanent interment in Quincy,

Massachusetts. As Adams's transport was less than two weeks after his death, it more resembled the modern funeral train.

20. "Preparations in Albany," *New York Times*, August 2, 1885.

21. "THE OBSEQUIES; Sombre Grandeur of the Funeral Pageant," *New York Times*, April 26, 1865.

22. "The Grant Funeral Cortege in Albany," *Brooklyn Daily Eagle*, August 5, 1885.

23. "Grant's Obsequies, Services at Mt. McGregor," *Ithaca Democrat*, August 6, 1885.

24. "The Grant Funeral Cortege in Albany," *Brooklyn Daily Eagle*, August 5, 1885.

25. "Albany Population Statistics," New York State Museum, last updated May 11, 2012. http://exhibitions.nysm.nysed.gov//albany/population.html.

26. "Albany to New York, The Remains of General Grant Taken from Albany to New York," *Dubuque Sunday Herald*, August 6, 1885.

27. "The March to the City Hall," *New York Times*, August 6, 1885.

28. "Waiting for the Body," *New York Times*, August 5, 1885.

29. "The March to the City Hall," *New York Times*, August 6, 1885.

30. "At the City Hall; Nearly 40,000 Persons View The Body Before 1 O'clock This Morning," *New York Times*, August 6, 1885.

31. Kahn, *General Grant National Memorial Historical Resource Study*, 24.

32. "At the City Hall; Nearly 40,000 Persons View The Body Before 1 O'clock This Morning," *New York Times*, August 6, 1885.

33. "At the City Hall; Nearly 40,000 Persons View The Body Before 1 O'clock This Morning," *New York Times*.

34. "Grant's Obsequies, Services at Mt. McGregor," *Ithaca Democrat*, August 6, 1885. While Abner Doubleday is often associated with the invention of baseball, in fact this is a myth. There is no evidence he had anything to do with the creation of our national pastime.

35. "The City's Floral Gift," *New York Times*, August 7, 1885.

36. Kahn, *General Grant National Memorial Historical Resource Study*, 22.

37. "Grant Album Brochure, August 8, 1885," Manhattan Historic Sites Archive, accessed June 18, 2019. http://mhsarchive.com/item.aspx?rID=GEGR%20%20%20%20%20622.0005&db=objects&dir=CR%20GEGR; "Incandescent Gas Light and Fuel Company Storefront, 1885," Manhattan Historic Sites Archive, accessed July 7, 2019. http://www.mhsarchive.org/item.aspx?rID=GEGR%20%20%20%20%20216&db=objects&dir=CR%20GEGR.

38. Kahn, *General Grant National Memorial Historical Resource Study*, 22.

39. "The Burial-Place of General Grant," *Harper's Weekly*, August 8, 1885.

40. James Monroe Gregory, *Frederick Douglass the Orator: Containing An Account Of His Life; His Eminent Public Services; His Brilliant Career As Orator; Selections From His Speeches And Writings* (Springfield, MA: Willey Company, 1893), 170.

41. Clarence D. Long, *Wages and Earnings in the United States, 1860–1890* (Princeton, NJ: Princeton University Press, 1960), 41.

42. Joan Waugh, *U. S. Grant: American Hero, American Myth* (Chapel Hill, NC: University of North Carolina Press, 2009), 234–236.

43. George Frederick Shrady, *General Grant's Last Days* (New York: Privately Printed, 1908), 33.

44. "Buckner's Tribute to Grant," *New York Times*, August 8, 1885.

45. "The Hero's Pall Bearers," *New York Times*, July 31, 1885.

46. "Who's Buried in Grant's Tomb? A Funeral Company Advertises Its Part in It," *Milwaukee Journal*, December 31, 1953.

47. Original estimates published shortly after Grant's death of 100,000 to 125,000 marchers, including 30,000 Grand Army veterans, were wildly overblown. "The Dead General," New York *Evening Post*, July 29, 1885.

48. *The Magazine of American History with Notes and Queries, Volume 14,* September 1885, 247.

49. "The Burial of Grant," *New York Times*, August 9, 1885.

50. Rudyard Kipling, *The Writings in Prose and Verse of Rudyard Kipling Letters of Travel 1892–1913* (New York: Charles Scribner's Sons, 1920), 18.

51. "The Burial of the Chieftain Yesterday," *Brooklyn Daily Eagle*, August 9, 1885.

52. *Within Are the Names of the Guests of the Fifth Avenue Hotel, on the Occasion of the Obsequies of General U. S. Grant August 8, 1885* (New York: Hitchcock, Darling & Co., 1885). The list is staggering and includes the president's cabinet, the pallbearers, Grant Monument Association members, and dozens of congressmen. It must have been quite a gathering that few would miss. Consider that Chester Arthur's home was only a half mile from the hotel at 123 Lexington Avenue.

53. Williams, Charles Richard, ed., *Diary and Letters of Rutherford Birchard Hayes, Volume 4, 1881–1893* (Ohio State Archaeological and Historical Society, 1925), 230–231. Hayes shared opinions on the two presidents he met that day. "President Arthur came in and we met in a friendly way. No reserve or embarrassment on either side." As for President Cleveland, "Found him plain, sensible, natural; in all respects well-appearing. His talk was friendly and assuring. He lacks experience, is not a great man, but he intends and anxiously wishes to do well."

54. "Grant Obsequies, Catafalque, August 8, 1885," Manhattan Historic Sites

Archive, accessed June 18, 2019. http://mhsarchive.com/item.aspx?rID=GEGR%20%20%20%20%20507&db=objects&dir=CR%20GEGR.

55. "Evacuation-Day," *Harper's Weekly*, December 1, 1883.

56. "Washington in Wall Street," *Harper's Weekly*, December 8, 1883.

57. "A Great Day," *Harper's Weekly*, December 8, 1883. As referenced in Karol Ann Marling, *George Washington Slept Here: Colonial Revivals and American Culture, 1876–1986* (Cambridge, MA: Harvard University Press, 1988), 101.

58. "A Nation at a Tomb, Scenes in Riverside Park," *New York Times*, August 9, 1885.

59. Williams, Charles Richard, ed., *Diary and Letters of Rutherford Birchard Hayes, Volume 4, 1881–1893* (Ohio State Archaeological and Historical Society, 1925), 231. Hayes commented, "President Arthur proved an excellent companion for such a drive—five hours."

60. "Who's Buried in Grant's Tomb? A Funeral Company Advertises Its Part in It," *Milwaukee Journal*, December 31,1953.

61. Kahn, *General Grant National Memorial Historical Resource Study*, 16.

62. Today the site is near 123rd Street, but in 1885 that street had not yet been completed.

63. "A Nation at a Tomb, Scenes in Riverside Park," *New York Times*, August 9, 1885.

64. "Grave of General Grant," *New York Times*, February 21, 1897. Due to the lack of mature flora at Riverside Park in 1885, the story of the providential oak tree does invite skepticism, including from a National Park Ranger I spoke with during a research visit.

65. Kahn, *General Grant National Memorial Historical Resource Study*, 17.

66. "A Nation at a Tomb, Scenes in Riverside Park," *New York Times*, August 9, 1885.

67. "A Nation at a Tomb, The Closing Scenes," *New York Times*, August 9, 1885.

68. *Seven Mile Funeral Cortège of Genl. Grant in New York Aug. 8, 1885* (Boston: The U.S. Instantaneous Photographic Co.), 1886.

69. "Tomb of General Grant to be Finished at Last," *New York Times*, February 17, 1929.

70. "Letter from Chauncey H. Burnett to George Burnside, February 1, 1944," Manhattan Historic Sites Archive, accessed June 18, 2019. http://mhsarchive.com/item.aspx?rID=GEGR%20%20%20%20%20622.0149&db=objects&dir=CR%20NPNYH. In 1944 the man's nephew, seventy-one years old at the time, admitted to his uncle's crime and returned the tassel to the Grant Monument Association.

71. Malcolm Townsend, *U.S. An Index to the United States of America* (Boston, MA: D Lothrop Company, 1890).

72. "Ulysses S. Grant's Temporary Tomb, August 1885," Manhattan Historic Sites Archive, accessed June 18, 2019. http://mhsarchive.com/item.aspx?rID =GEGR%20%20%20%20%20361&db=objects&dir=CR%20NPNYH.

73. Samuel D. Page, *The Riverside Souvenir: A Memorial Volume Illustrating the Nation's Tribute to General U. S. Grant* (New York: J. C. Derby, 1886).

74. Page, *The Riverside Souvenir.*

75. *Magazine of American History with Notes and Queries, Volume 14,* September 1885, 246.

Chapter 5 "A Sacred Duty"

1. "Grant's Memorial: What Shall It Be?" *North American Review,* September 1885.

2. "Riverside Park Chosen," *New York Times,* July 29, 1885.

3. David M. Kahn, *General Grant National Memorial Historical Resource Study* (National Park Service, 1980), 28.

4. Kahn, *General Grant National Memorial Historical Resource Study,* 28.

5. "Grant Monument Association Minute Book No. 1, 1885," Manhattan Historic Sites Archive, accessed June 18, 2019. http://mhsarchive.com /item.aspx?rID=GEGR%20%20%20%20%20622.0008&db=objects&dir =CR%20GEGR.

6. Kahn, *General Grant National Memorial Historical Resource Study,* 29.

7. "The Grant Monument Association," *New York Evening Post,* July 29, 1885.

8. Biographical information from "First Black Alumnus's Papers Found," *Harvard Magazine,* March 21, 2012. http://harvardmagazine.com/2012/03 /greener-papers-found. Greener quote about Grant from Kahn, *General Grant National Memorial Historical Resource Study,* 31.

9. Kahn, *General Grant National Memorial Historical Resource Study,* 29. Despite being first, her donation was the third recorded in the Association ledger on April 28. It is preceded by two donations totaling $1.50 that came through Chester Arthur.

10. The story of Eleanor Fletcher Bishop is an interesting one indeed, and it is doubtful she ever intended to pay the princely sum she had promised. Although she was wealthy, the following year she was arrested for stealing $1,500 in furniture. She was most notable, however, as the mother of Washington Irving Bishop, a popular mentalist who collapsed, exhausted, after one of his performances. He was declared dead and an autopsy was performed, but Mrs. Bishop believed her son was not deceased and that those who performed the autopsy knew this but cut up her son while

still alive so they could examine his brain. She wrote of her suspicions in a book, *A Synopsis of the Butchery of the Late Sir Washington Irving Bishop* (Philadelphia: Seldon & Marion, 1889); "Eleanor F. Bishop Arrested," *Sun*, January 29, 1886.

11. Kahn, *General Grant National Memorial Historical Resource Study*, 30.
12. "Grant Monument Fund," *New York Times*, August 1, 1885.
13. "Burdette Declines," *Butte Weekly Miner*, August 1, 1885.
14. "The Grand Army of the Republic and Kindred Societies," Library of Congress, posted September 13, 2011, https://www.loc.gov/rr/main/gar /garintro.html.
15. "The Monument Committee," *New York Times*, August 1, 1885.
16. "Account Moneys Received, 1886," Manhattan Historic Sites Archive, accessed June 7, 2019. http://www.mhsarchive.org/item.aspx?rID =GEGR%20%20%20%20%20622.0055&db=objects&dir=CR%20 GEGR. The association was just as meticulous about tracking expenses, which, in addition to stamps, telegrams, and paper, also included 88 cents for "ice for month," $4.50 for a hat rack, and $200 for Greener's monthly salary. "Expense Account Report 1885," Manhattan Historic Sites Archive, accessed June 7, 2019. http://mhsarchive.com/item.aspx?rID =GEGR%20%20%20%20%20622.0056&db=objects&dir=CR%20 GEGR.
17. "The Monument Committee, Their Headquarters to Be in the Old Mutual Life Insurance Building," *New York Times*, August 1, 1885.
18. James B. Bell and Richard I. Abrams, *In Search of Liberty: The Story of the Statue of Liberty and Ellis Island* (New York: Doubleday & Company, 1984), 36–37.
19. "Send in Your Money," *New York Times*, November 11, 1885.
20. "The Grant Monument Fund," *New York Times*, August 3, 1885.
21. "The Grant Monument Fund," *New York Times*, August 5, 1885.
22. "The Grant Monument Fund," *New York Times*, August 6, 1885.
23. "The Grant Monument Fund," *New York Times*, August 25, 1885.
24. "In and About the City," *New York Times*, August 18, 1885.
25. "Colored People Support Grant," *New York Times*, August 11, 1885.
26. "For the Grant Monument," *New York Times*, August 22, 1885.
27. "Twenty-five Days' Work," *New York Times*, August 27, 1885.
28. "Mounting Up Rapidly," *New York Times*, August 30, 1885. The children were eventually mollified once they learned their names would appear in the *New York Times*.
29. "Gen. Grant's Resting Place," *New York Times*, August 15, 1885.
30. "Subscription list of D. H. McAlpin Co. Tobacco Manufactures and

Employees, August 15, 1885," Manhattan Historic Sites Archive, accessed July 6, 2019. http://mhsarchive.com/item.aspx?rID=GEGR%20%20%20%20%20622.0179&db=objects&dir=CR%20GEGR.

31. "In and About the City," *New York Times*, August 18, 1885.

32. "For the Grant Monument," *New York Times*, August 22, 1885.

33. Kahn, *General Grant National Memorial Historical Resource Study*, 31.

34. "Subscriptions Pouring In," *New York Times*, August 23, 1885.

35. "The Races at Saratoga," *New York Times*, August 6, 1885.

36. "For the Grant Memorial," *New York Times*, August 26, 1885.

37. "A Crowd in Riverside Park," *New York Times*, August 17, 1885.

38. "Adding to the Fund," *New York Times*, August 25, 1885.

39. "Increasing Day by Day," *New York Times*, August 29, 1885.

40. "Twenty-five Days' Work," *New York Times*, August 27, 1885. While the reporter was referring to photographs, his comment can be applied in general as the chances of donations were indeed slipping away.

41. "Adding to Fund," *New York Times*, August 25, 1885. Funds rebounded, but only temporarily. By August 27, the paper reported $64,708.30. "Twenty-Five Days' Work," *New York Times*, August 27, 1885. By August 29, the total reached 67,183.05. "Increasing Day by Day," *New York Times*, August 29, 1885.

42. "Increasing Day by Day," *New York Times*, August 29, 1885.

43. "Steadily Pouring In," *New York Times*, August 28, 1885.

44. "Increasing Day by Day," *New York Times*, August 29, 1885.

45. Williams, Charles Richard, ed., *Diary and Letters of Rutherford Birchard Hayes, Volume 4, 1881–1893* (Ohio State Archaeological and Historical Society, 1925), 233.

46. "Proposed Monument in Illinois," *New York Evening Post*, July 29, 1885.

47. "Grant Monument Fund in Kansas," *New York Times*, August 14, 1885. Grant had visited Fort Leavenworth, Kansas, in June 1868. Along with his son Buck and fellow Civil War generals William Tecumseh Sherman and Philip Sheridan, the four departed Fort Leavenworth to take a two-week trip through the Western plains. Ronald C. White, *American Ulysses: A Life of Ulysses S. Grant* (New York: Random House, 2006), 463.

48. Thomas M. Pitkin, *The Captain Departs: Ulysses S. Grant's Last Campaign* (Carbondale, IL: Southern Illinois University Press, 1973), 117–118. Note that this proposal was made more than fifty years before Mount Rushmore was completed.

49. "Finish the New York Monument," *St. Lawrence Republican and Ogdensburgh Weekly Journal*, September 16, 1885.

50. *Architect and Building News*, September 5, 1885.

51. "Mounting Up Rapidly," *New York Times*, August 30, 1885.

52. "To Guard Camp Grant," *New York Times*, January 17, 1886.

53. "The Riverside Tomb," *Miamisburg Bulletin*, September 4, 1885.

54. Kahn, *General Grant National Memorial Historical Resource Study*, 39–40.

55. "The Tribute of Flowers," *New York Times*, August 12, 1885.

56. As the gravestone reads "ERECTED TO THE MEMORY / OF AN AMIABLE CHILD / ST. CLAIRE POLLOCK / DIED 15 JULY 1797/IN THE FIFTH YEAR OF HIS AGE," it has since become known as the Amiable Child Memorial. The gravestone still exists (a few hundred feet northwest of the tomb) and is today protected by an iron fence. "Amiable Child Memorial," NYC Parks, accessed August 11, 2019. https://www.nycgovparks.org/parks/riverside-park /monuments/1206.

57. "Albany to New York, The Remains of General Grant Taken from Albany to New York," *Dubuque Sunday Herald*, August 6, 1885.

58. "Pilgrims to the Tomb," *New York Times*, August 11, 1885. The reporter noted that the requestor "was not gratified."

59. "The Riverside Tomb," *Miamisburg Bulletin*, September 4, 1885.

60. "Grave of General Grant," *New York Times*, February 21, 1897.

61. Kahn, *General Grant National Memorial Historical Resource Study*, 26–27.

62. "Visitors at Riverside," *New York Times*, August 13, 1885.

63. "The Storm at Riverside," *New York Times*, August 14, 1885.

64. "At Gen. Grant's Tomb," *New York Times*, August 23, 1885.

65. "The Riverside Tomb," *Miamisburg Bulletin*, September 4, 1885.

66. "Pilgrims to the Tomb," *New York Times*, August 11, 1885.

67. *The Guide for Strangers: General Grant's Tomb in Riverside Park* (New York: Published by the Magazine of American History by Historical Publication Co., 1886).

68. Kahn, *General Grant National Memorial Historical Resource Study*, 34.

69. "Let Him Lie in New York," *Mechanicville Mercury*, August 21, 1885.

70. "Solicitation Form Letter, September 1885," Manhattan Historic Sites Archive, accessed July 6, 2019. http://mhsarchive.com/item.aspx?rID =GEGR%20%20%20%20%20622.0066&db=objects&dir=CR%20 GEGR.

71. "Baseball Ticket, September 26, 1885," Manhattan Historic Sites Archive, accessed June 16, 2019. http://mhsarchive.com/item.aspx?rID=GEGR %20%20%20%20%20622.0075&db=objects&dir=CR%20GEGR.

72. Kahn, *General Grant National Memorial Historical Resource Study*, 37.

73. Kahn, 32.

74. "Letter and enclosures from J. W. Merriam to Chester A. Arthur, July

21, 1886," Manhattan Historic Sites Archive, accessed June 18, 2019. http://mhsarchive.com/item.aspx?rID=GEGR%20%20%20%20%20 622.0071&db=objects&dir=CR%20GEGR.

75. "Letter from 'Little Carrie' to William R. Grace, August 25, 1885," Manhattan Historic Sites Archive, accessed December 26, 2019. http://mhsarchive.com/item.aspx?rID=GEGR%20%20%20%20%20 622.0108&db=objects&dir=CR%20NPNYH.

76. Kahn, *General Grant National Memorial Historical Resource Study*, 36–37. Note that the proposed fair location was not the current Madison Square Garden, but its initial predecessor built in 1879 at the corner of Twenty-Sixth Street and Madison Avenue.

77. "Skeptical Spiritualists," *New York Times*, August 10, 1885.

78. "The Riverside Tomb," *Miamisburg Bulletin*, September 4, 1885.

79. "Grant Monument Fund Subscription List of the People's Bank of Manchester, Mich, October 3, 1885," Manhattan Historic Sites Archive, accessed December 26, 2019. http://mhsarchive.com/item.aspx?rID =GEGR%20%20%20%20%20622.0060&db=objects&dir=CR%20 NPNYH.

80. Kahn, *General Grant National Memorial Historical Resource Study*, 33.

81. "Letter from Lew Morrill to Richard T. Greener, September 11, 1885," Manhattan Historic Sites Archive, accessed July 8, 2019. http: //www.mhsarchive.org/item.aspx?rID=GEGR%20%20%20%20%20 596&db=objects&dir=CR%20GEGR.

82. "Grant Monument Fund Donation August 3, 1885," Manhattan Historic Sites Archive, accessed June 16, 2019. http://mhsarchive.com/item.aspx? rID=GEGR%20%20%20%20%20622.0064&db=objects&dir=CR%20 GEGR.

83. "National Mourning," *Weekly Schuyler Sun* (Nebraska), August 6, 1885.

84. "Gen. Grant's Will," *Critic* (Washington, DC), August 24, 1885.

85. "Minor Notes," *Oshkosh Northwestern,* August 31, 1885.

86. Samuel D. Page, *The Riverside Souvenir: A Memorial Volume Illustrating the Nation's Tribute to General U. S. Grant* (New York: J. C. Derby, 1886).

87. "Letter from Mrs. Grant to Mayor Grace, October 29, 1885," Manhattan Historic Sites Archive, accessed June 16, 2019. http://www .mhsarchive.org/item.aspx?rID=GEGR%20%20%20%20%20 625.0003&db=objects&dir=CR%20GEGR.

88. "Letter from Horace L. Hotchkiss to Col. Thomas Denny, 1925," Manhattan Historic Sites Archive, accessed June 16, 2019. http://mhsarchive .com/item.aspx?rID=GEGR%20%20%20%20%20622.0175&db=objects &dir=CR%20GEGR. Note that Hotchkiss's letter references the board

of trustees, which was not formed until the Grant Monument Association was incorporated in February 1886.

89. "The Corsair Compact," JP Morgan, accessed June 3, 2019. https://www .jpmorgan.com/country/US/en/jpmorgan/about/history/month/jul.

90. "Work to Be More Active," *New York Times*, November 1, 1885.

91. "The Grant Monument Fund," *New York Times*, November 3, 1885.

92. "The Monument," *New York Times*, August 6, 1885, "the honor of having the tomb of Gen. Grant in our city imposes on our people a sacred duty."

93. "The Money to Be Raised," *New York Times*, August 21, 1885; "Sidney Dillon's Contribution," *Miltonvale News* (Kansas), November 19, 1885.

94. "News and Comment," *Rutland Daily Herald*, December 16, 1885.

95. Kahn, *General Grant National Memorial Historical Resource Study*, 36.

96. "Send in Your Money!" *New York Times*, November 27, 1885.

97. Kahn, *General Grant National Memorial Historical Resource Study*, 38.

98. "Barracks at Camp Grant," *New York Times*, November 10, 1885.

99. "A Soldier Worsted," *New York Times*, February 17, 1886. Some of the wounds were reported as severe, but Kavanagh's fate is unknown to this author.

100. Ben Perley Poore, ed. *Message of the President of the United States to the two Houses of Congress, at the Commencement of the Second Session of the Forty-ninth Congress* (Washington, DC: Washington Government Printing Office, 1886).

101. "By-laws 1892." Manhattan Historic Sites Archive, accessed December 26, 2019. http://mhsarchive.com/item.aspx?rID=GEGR%20%20%20 %20%20622.0054&db=objects&dir=CR%20NPNYH.

102. From Articles of Incorporation, Section 1, the full roster of twenty-nine trustees includes President Chester Arthur, Hamilton Fish, Alonzo Barton Cornell, the president of the J. Pierpont Morgan, Brayton Ives, Adolph L. Sanger, Sidney Dillon, Samuel L. M. Barlow, Oliver Hoyt, Cornelius N. Bliss (dry goods businessman), Cornelius O'Reilly, Cornelius Vanderbilt, William Lummis, Frederick R. Coudert, Whitelaw Reid (from the *New-York Tribune*), James Gordon Bennett, Charles M. Vail, Wesley Harper, Richard T. Greener, Benjamin Wood, Oswald Ottendorfer, Charles A. Dana, Peter A. Cassidy, George Ehret, William H. Wickham, George Jones, Seth Low, and Joseph Pulitzer. Four ex-officio trustees were listed in Section 2 by position, not by name, and included the mayor of New York, the mayor of Brooklyn, the governor of New York, and the president of the New York Department of Public Parks. "Grant Monument Association Articles of Incorporation February 6, 1886," Manhattan Historic Sites Archive, accessed June 18,

2019. http://mhsarchive.com/item.aspx?rID=GEGR%20%20%20%20%20622.0053&db=objects&dir=CR%20GEGR.

103. "Letter from Chester A. Arthur to Richard T. Greener, March 23, 1886," Manhattan Historic Sites Archive, accessed June 18, 2019. http://mhsarchive.com/item.aspx?rID=GEGR%20%20%20%20%20622.0044&db=objects&dir=CR%20GEGR. Like Grant's, Arthur's funeral was held in New York City, but besides honoring former presidents, the two events could not have been more different. Only a year and a half out of office, the amiable fifty-seven-year-old Arthur was widely forgotten by the city. Policemen, remembering Grant's funeral, braced themselves for crowds that never came. A reporter sardonically noted, "The number of would-be sight-seers was infinitesimal when compared with that which attended the last Presidential Funeral." *Annual Record, Issue 249 by Ancient and Honorable Artillery Company of Massachusetts 1886–7*, 1887, 24.

104. "The Day of Days Comes to New York," *Los Angeles Evening Express*, April 27, 1897.

105. "Letter from Abraham Dowdney to Richard T. Greener, July 28, 1886," Manhattan Historic Sites Archive, accessed June 16, 2019. http://mhsarchive.com/item.aspx?rID=GEGR%20%20%20%20%20622.0028&db=objects&dir=CR%20GEGR.

106. "Grant's Decorated Temporary Tomb, Decoration Day, May 31, 1885," Manhattan Historic Sites Archive, accessed July 6, 2019. http://mhsarchive.com/item.aspx?rID=GEGR%20%20%20%20%20357&db=objects&dir=CR%20GEGR.

107. "*Hermit of Cashel* Ticket, September 30, 1886," Manhattan Historic Sites Archive, accessed June 16, 2019. http://mhsarchive.com/item.aspx?rID=GEGR%20%20%20%20%20622.0074&db=objects&dir=CR%20NPNYH.

108. "Letter from Colonel Frederick Grant to George Jones, Esq., January 14, 1887," Manhattan Historic Sites Archive, accessed June 16, 2019. http://www.mhsarchive.org/item.aspx?rID=GEGR%20%20%20%20%20625.0009&db=objects&dir=CR%20GEGR.

109. "General Grant's Memoirs Selling Like Hot Cakes," *Boston Globe*, December 3, 1885.

110. "Gen. Grant's Memoirs," *Omaha Daily Bee*, March 8, 1886.

111. "About People and Things," *Indianapolis Journal*, May 14, 1887.

112. "Recent Literature," *Brooklyn Daily Eagle,* December 13, 1885.

113. "Gen. Grant's Memoirs," *Wichita Beacon*, January 4, 1886.

114. "The Ghost That Haunts Grant's Memoirs," *New York Times*, October 13, 2017.

115. "A Conversation with Former President Bill Clinton May 28, 2003," John F. Kennedy Presidential Library and Museum, accessed June 15, 2020. https://www.jfklibrary.org/events-and-awards/forums/past-forums /transcripts/a-conversation-with-former-president-bill-clinton.

116. David W. Blight, *Race and Reunion: The Civil War in American Memory* (Cambridge, MA: Harvard University Press, 2001), 211.

117. Ulysses Simpson Grant, *Personal Memoirs of U. S. Grant* (New York: Dover Publications, 1995), 435.

118. Kahn, *General Grant National Memorial Historical Resource Study*, 102; "The Day of Days Comes to New York," *Los Angeles Evening Express*, April 27, 1897.

119. "Letter from Cornelius Vanderbilt to Greener, April 4, 1887," Manhattan Historic Sites Archive, accessed June 16, 2019. http://mhsarchive.com /item.aspx?rID=GEGR%20%20%20%20%20622.0045&db=objects &dir=CR%20GEGR; "Letter from Cornelius Vanderbilt to Richard T. Greener, April 8, 1887," Manhattan Historic Sites Archive, accessed June 16, 2019. http://mhsarchive.com/item.aspx?rID=GEGR%20%20%20 %20%20622.0046&db=objects&dir=CR%20GEGR.

120. "*Judge*'s Grand Word Contest, Announcement and Rules, 1887," Manhattan Historic Sites Archive, accessed July 7, 2019. http://www .mhsarchive.org/item.aspx?rID=GEGR%20%20%20%20%20388&db =objects&dir=CR%20GEGR' "The Grant Monument," *New York Times,* February 24, 1887.

121. Kahn, *General Grant National Memorial Historical Resource Study*, 41.

122. "The Day of Days Comes to New York," *Los Angeles Evening Express*, April 27, 1897.

123. Ishbel Ross, *The General's Wife: The Life of Mrs. Ulysses S Grant* (New York: Dodd, Mead, 1959), 320.

124. Kahn, *General Grant National Memorial Historical Resource Study*, 11.

Chapter 6 "An American Pantheon"

1. "Increasing Day by Day," *New York Times*, August 29, 1885.

2. David M. Kahn, *General Grant National Memorial Historical Resource Study* (National Park Service, 1980), 37.

3. "Style and the Monument," *North American Review* 141, no. 348, 1885, 443.

4. "Letter from Mrs. Clarry A. Sheafor to the Grant Monument Association, August 21, 1885," Manhattan Historic Sites Archive, accessed June 22, 2019.

http://mhsarchive.com/item.aspx?rID=GEGR%20%20%20%20%20
622.0116&db=objects&dir=CR%20GEGR.

5. "Style and the Monument," *North American Review* 141, no. 348, 1885, 448.

6. "Style and the Monument," *North American Review*, 443, 451.

7. John C. Rives, *The Congressional Globe: Containing the Debates and Proceedings of the Second Session of the Thirty-Seventh Congress, Volume 26* (Washington, DC, 1853), 324.

8. "In and About the City," *New York Times*, August 18, 1885.

9. "The Grant Memorial," *Century Magazine*, April 1886. The prospect of a woman designing the memorial is intriguing. However, the idea would not have been unheard of. Louise "Jennie" Blanchard Bethune (1856–1913) was the first professional female architect in America. Along with her husband, they established a firm in Buffalo in 1883. Johanna Hays, *Louise Blanchard Bethune: America's First Female Professional Architect* (Jefferson, NC: McFarland, 2014).

10. "Letter from William J. Eames and Thomas C. Young to Chester A. Arthur, July 31, 1885," Manhattan Historic Sites Archive, accessed July 6, 2019. http://mhsarchive.com/item.aspx?rID=GEGR%20%20%20%20%20622.0118&db=objects&dir=CR%20GEGR.

11. "Letter from William J. Eames and Thomas C. Young to Chester A. Arthur, July 31, 1885."

12. *American Architect and Building News*, August 1, 1885.

13. "Competition for a Design for a Memorial to General Grant," *American Architect and Building News*, August 8, 1885.

14. Kahn, *General Grant National Memorial Historical Resource Study*, 45.

15. "To the Editors of the American Architect," *American Architect and Building News*, October 10, 1885.

16. *American Architect and Building News*, August 1, 1885. Reporters at the New York *Evening Post* took umbrage with the description of the park as "neglected and remote," and a heated exchange ensued between the two publications. After the *Evening Post* decried their assessment as a "grotesque attack upon the Riverside Park," the architects responded in print: "to justify the *Evening Post's* unfavorable opinion of our veracity, we made a visit to Riverside Park a few days ago, only to find our previous idea confirmed." *American Architect and Building News*, August 15, 1885.

17. *American Architect and Building News*, August 1, 1885.

18. "Our Great Dead," *Hartford Courant*, September 29, 1885.

19. "A Canvas of the City," *New York Times*, November 10, 1885.

20. "A Canvas of the City," *New York Times*.

21. Kahn, *General Grant National Memorial Historical Resource Study*, 48.
22. Kahn, 48.
23. "The Proposed Grant Monument," *Voice* (New York), June 16, 1887.
24. Kahn, *General Grant National Memorial Historical Resource Study*, 50.
25. "The Grant Monument," *Brooklyn Daily Eagle*, November 4, 1887.
26. Despite the lackluster fundraising for the tomb, the national interest in Grant had not waned. In 1888, the humble cabin in which Grant was born in Point Pleasant, Ohio, was purchased by a Captain Powers. He loaded it on a barge and transported the home around the Midwest to display at fairs, including the Ohio Centennial Exposition in Cincinnati and later the 1893 World's Columbian Exposition in Chicago. Louis L. Picone, *Where the Presidents Were Born: The History & Preservation of the Presidential Birthplaces* (Atglen, PA: Schiffer Publishing, 2012), 78.
27. "The Grant Memorial," *New York Times*, February 5, 1888.
28. "To Artists, Architects and Sculptors, January 26, 1888," Manhattan Historic Sites Archive, accessed June 16, 2019. http://mhsarchive.com/item.aspx?rID=GEGR%20%20%20%20%20585&db=objects&dir=CR%20NPNYH.
29. Neil Harris, "The Battle for Grant's Tomb," *American Heritage* 56 (August–September 1985): 70–79.
30. "Letter from the American Institute of Architects to Alonzo B. Cornell and Richard T. Greener, March 15, 1888," Manhattan Historic Sites Archive, accessed July 5, 2019. http://mhsarchive.com/item.aspx?rID=GEGR%20%20%20%20%20622.0122&db=objects&dir=CR%20GEGR.
31. "Letter from the American Institute of Architects to Alonzo B. Cornell and Richard T. Greener, March 15, 1888."
32. "To Artist Decorators," *American Architect and Building News*, March 22, 1884.
33. Kahn, *General Grant National Memorial Historical Resource Study*, 54.
34. "Needed—An American Westminster," *Evening Star* (Washington, DC), August 1, 1885; "The Riverside Tomb," *Evening Bulletin* (Maysville, KY), September 2, 1885.
35. "Washington Monument History & Culture," National Park Service, accessed March 4, 2017, https://www.nps.gov/wamo/learn/historyculture/index.htm.
36. Harris, "The Battle for Grant's Tomb," 70–79.
37. "A Worthy Object," *City News* (Muscatine, IA), August 7, 1868.
38. John Carroll Power, *Abraham Lincoln: His Life, Public Services, Death and*

Great Funeral Cortege, With a History and Description of the National Lincoln Monument (Chicago: H. W. Rokker, 1889), 334.

39. "The Mania for Monuments," *Deseret News*, September 29, 1869.

40. Harris, "The Battle for Grant's Tomb," 70–79.

41. As quoted in Esther Crain, *The Gilded Age in New York* (New York: Black Dog & Leventhal, 2016), 158. This situation led to the rise of public bathhouses, which later were repurposed as recreational pools.

42. David W. Blight, *Race and Reunion: The Civil War in American Memory* (Cambridge, MA: Harvard University Press, 2001), 215.

43. The trend of mammoth memorial tombs would continue after William McKinley's assassination in 1901. However, the taste for oversized presidential tombs ran out of steam, perhaps later than it should have, when a massive memorial was erected for Warren G. Harding, who died in office in 1923 and whose legacy was already in tatters before the groundbreaking ceremony occurred.

44. "Cartoons and Comments," *Puck*, August 19, 1885.

45. The most expensive entry, "Let Us Have Peace," tops the list at $968,291. "Design submissions for the first competition for Grant's Tomb, 1889," Manhattan Historic Sites Archive, accessed June 16, 2019. http://mhsarchive .com/item.aspx?rID=GEGR%20%20%20%20%20622.0139&db =objects&dir=CR%20GEGR.

46. Kahn, *General Grant National Memorial Historical Resource Study*, 54.

47. *New York Times*, February 21, 1890.

48. Besides LeBrun, the other five consisted of three architects—James E. Ware (secretary), George B. Post, and James Renwick, Jr—and two professors, William R. Ware (Columbia University) and Solomon Woolf (City College).

49. "The Grant Monument Designs," *Harper's Weekly*, October 6, 1889.

50. "Report of the Design Competition Committee to Richard T. Greener, April 23, 1889," Manhattan Historic Sites Archive, accessed July 15, 2019. http://mhsarchive.com/item.aspx?rID=GEGR%20%20%20%20 %20622.0125&db=objects&dir=CR%20GEGR.

51. "Motto 1822, Design No. 19, 1889," Manhattan Historic Sites Archive, accessed July 6, 2019. http://mhsarchive.com/item.aspx?rID=GEGR%20 %20%20%20%20622.0137&db=objects&dir=CR%20GEGR.

52. Schweinfurth took umbrage at the comparison and in a letter to the Grant Monument Association demanded to be "cleared of the imputation." Kahn, *General Grant National Memorial Historical Resource Study*, 59.

53. "D.O.M., Design No. 27 1889," Manhattan Historic Sites Archive,

accessed June 16, 2019. http://mhsarchive.com/item.aspx?rID=GEGR%20%20%20%20%20622.0138&db=objects&dir=CR%20GEGR.

54. Kahn, *General Grant National Memorial Historical Resource Study*, 76.

55. "Letter from the Grant Monument Commission Board of Experts to the Executive Committee of the Grant Monument Association June 10, 1889," Manhattan Historic Sites Archive, accessed July 5, 2019. http://mhsarchive.com/item.aspx?rID=GEGR%20%20%20%20%20622.0126&db=objects&dir=CR%20GEGR.

56. Kahn, *General Grant National Memorial Historical Resource Study*, 62.

57. *New York Times*, February 21, 1890.

58. "The Grant Memorial," *New York Times*, March 28, 1890.

59. "The Grant Memorial," *New York Times*, March 28, 1890.

60. "Grant Monument Plans," *New York Times*, April 1, 1890.

61. Kahn, *General Grant National Memorial Historical Resource Study*, 62.

62. *Architecture and Building,* April 5, 1890.

63. Kahn, *General Grant National Memorial Historical Resource Study*, 72. Duncan's middle name was often mistaken for Hemingway.

64. "Grant Monument Association Executive Committee Report, 1890," Manhattan Historic Sites Archive, accessed December 26, 2019. http://mhsarchive.com/item.aspx?rID=GEGR%20%20%20%20%20622.0136&db=objects&dir=CR%20NPNYH.

65. "Letter from Ortgies & Co. to Albert Bierstadt, April 22, 1892," Manhattan Historic Sites Archive, accessed June 22, 2019. http://mhsarchive.com/item.aspx?rID=GEGR%20%20%20%20%20622.0078&db=objects&dir=CR%20GEGR.

66. Kahn, *General Grant National Memorial Historical Resource Study*, 102.

67. "Letter and program from Mr. Silas G. Pratt to Richard T. Greener, April 25, 1890," Manhattan Historic Sites Archive, accessed December 26, 2019. http://mhsarchive.com/item.aspx?rID=GEGR%20%20%20%20%20622.0077&db=objects&dir=CR%20NPNYH.

68. "Letter and program from Mr. Silas G. Pratt to Richard T. Greener, April 25, 1890."

69. Kahn, *General Grant National Memorial Historical Resource Study*, 65.

70. As quoted in Michael Kammen, *Mystic Chords of Memory: The Transformation of Tradition in American Culture* (New York: Knopf, 1991), 116.

71. "Telegram from William C. Wallace to Richard T. Greener, August 8, 1890," Manhattan Historic Sites Archive, accessed July 6, 2019. http://mhsarchive.com/item.aspx?rID=GEGR%20%20%20%20%20622.0029&db=objects&dir=CR%20GEGR.

72. "Descriptive design submission by John Ord, August 30, 1890," Manhattan

Historic Sites Archive, accessed June 18, 2019. http://mhsarchive
.com/item.aspx?rID=GEGR%20%20%20%20%20622.0135&db
=objects&dir=CR%20GEGR.

73. Kahn, *General Grant National Memorial Historical Resource Study*, 69.

74. "Design for the Monument to General Ulysses S Grant, 1890–1891,"
Manhattan Historic Sites Archive, accessed July 6, 2019. http://
mhsarchive.com/item.aspx?rID=GEGR%20%20%20%20%20
342&db=objects&dir=CR%20GEGR.

75. "Grant's Tomb Design Description, September 1, 1890," Manhattan Historic
Sites Archive, accessed June 18, 2019. http://mhsarchive.com/item.aspx?rID
=GEGR%20%20%20%20%20622.0180&db=objects&dir=CR%20
GEGR; "Competitive Design for the Proposed Grant Monument,
1890–1891," Manhattan Historic Sites Archive, accessed July 6, 2019. http:
//mhsarchive.com/item.aspx?rID=GEGR%20%20%20%20%20344&db
=objects&dir=CR%20GEGR.

76. "Grant's Tomb, the Plans Made Public by Exhibition To-day," *Brooklyn
Daily Eagle*, September 12, 1890.

77. "Grant Monument Competition, 1890–1891," Manhattan Historic Sites
Archive, accessed July 6, 2019. http://mhsarchive.com/item.aspx?rID=GEGR
%20%20%20%20%20343&db=objects&dir=CR%20GEGR; Kahn, *General
Grant National Memorial Historical Resource Study*, 70. John Phillip Rinn
also proposed topping the memorial with the world's largest electric light
in the 1889 competition for which he won second prize.

78. E. Merton Coulter, "A Name for the American War of 1861–1865." *The
Georgia Historical Quarterly* 36, no. 2 (1952): 109–131.

79. "Description of Competitive Design for The Grant Monument by John
H. Duncan, Architect, 1890," Manhattan Historic Sites Archive, accessed
June 18, 2019. http://mhsarchive.com/item.aspx?rID=GEGR%20%20
%20%20%20622.0140&db=objects&dir=CR%20NPNYH; "Grant's Tomb,
the Plans Made Public by Exhibition To-day," *Brooklyn Daily Eagle*,
September 12, 1890.

80. "Competitive design for a Monument to General Grant, October 1890,"
Manhattan Historic Sites Archive, accessed June 16, 2019. http://mhsarchive
.com/item.aspx?rID=GEGR%20%20%20%20%20410&db=objects&dir
=CR%20NPNYH.

81. "Centennial Commemoration Souvenir Program, April 27, 1997," Manhattan
Historic Sites Archive, accessed June 16, 2019. http://mhsarchive.com/item
.aspx?rID=GEGR%20%20%20%20%20895.0008&db=objects&dir
=CR%20NPNYH.

82. Harris, "The Battle for Grant's Tomb," 75.

83. "Grant Design Accepted," *Evening World* (New York), September 9, 1890.

84. "Letter from Richard T. Greener to John H. Duncan, September 12, 1890," Manhattan Historic Sites Archive, accessed December 26, 2019. http://mhsarchive.com/item.aspx?rID=GEGR%20%20%20%20%20 602&db=objects&dir=CR%20NPNYH.

85. "Duncan's Design Adopted," *Sun*, September 12, 1890.

86. "The Grant Monument," *New York Times*, September 13, 1890.

87. "Our Parish and Beyond," *Ithaca Daily Journal*, April 29, 1897. The article states, "John H. Duncan, the designer of Grant's Tomb, is a native of Binghamton, leaving that city twenty-three years ago."

88. *The Centennial Celebration and Washington Monument at Newburgh, N.Y* (Washington, DC: Washington Government printing office, 1889), 97. Maurice J. Power was the commissioned architect whom Duncan aided. The tower, which stands fifty-three feet tall with an archway on each side of the base, was built by the site of George Washington's headquarters from 1782 to 1783 and was built from 1886 to 1887. Today the structure is known as Newburgh's Tower of Victory.

89. "The Lucky Man, A New Yorker Gets the Soldiers Work. The Experts Decide in Favor of John H. Duncan's Design for the Memorial Arch to be Erected by Brooklyn—It Will be the Next to the Highest Thing of Its Kind in the World," *Brooklyn Daily Eagle*, August 6, 1889.

90. "To Mark Washington's Victory," *Chicago Tribune*, May 24, 1891; "Trenton Battle Monument: Designing the Monument," New Jersey division of parks and forestry, updated June 29, 2007. http://www.state.nj.us/dep /parksandforests/historic/Trentonbattlemonument/designing.htm.

91. Kahn, *General Grant National Memorial Historical Resource Study*, 83; "Gossip Going Around," *World*, September 26, 1890; *Sun*, October 25, 1890.

92. "The Grant Monument," *New York Times*, September 13, 1890.

93. "The General's Tomb," *Brooklyn Citizen*, September 14, 1890.

94. Kahn, *General Grant National Memorial Historical Resource Study*, 143.

95. Kahn, 84.

96. "The Mausoleum at Halicarnassus," CNN, accessed January 3, 2017. http://www.cnn.com/TRAVEL/DESTINATIONS/9705/seven.wonders /mausoleum.html. The handful of stones are currently in a museum in London.

97. Kahn, *General Grant National Memorial Historical Resource Study*, 84.

98. Kahn, 88–89.

99. The horse stables Cutcheon referred to were part of the Claremont Inn located one block north. The Inn was erected in 1788 and torn down in 1950. Today there is a historic marker at its former location

Riverside Drive at 123rd Street. "Claremont Inn Tablet," NYC Parks, accessed December 4, 2019. https://www.nycgovparks.org/parks/riverside-park/monuments/262.

100. "Congressional Record, December 10, 1890," Manhattan Historic Sites Archive, accessed June 16, 2019. http://mhsarchive.com/item.aspx?rID=GEGR%20%20%20%20%20622.0030&db=objects&dir=CR%20NPNYH.

101. "Congressional Record, December 10, 1890."

102. "To Remain at Riverside," *New York Times*, December 10, 1890. One of the minority votes in support of moving the tomb was that of Ways and Means Committee member from Ohio, William McKinley.

103. "To Grant," *Brooklyn Daily Eagle*, September 13, 1890.

104. Scott Martelle, *The Admiral and the Ambassador: One Man's Obsessive Search for the Body of John Paul Jones* (Chicago: Chicago Review Press, 2014), 31.

105. "Letter from Charles H. T. Collis to Mayor William R. Grace, October 8., 1890," Manhattan Historic Sites Archive, accessed June 16, 2019. http://mhsarchive.com/item.aspx?rID=GEGR%20%20%20%20%20622.0019&db=objects&dir=CR%20GEGR.

106. Kahn, *General Grant National Memorial Historical Resource Study*, 94–95.

107. Horace Porter, *Campaigning with Grant* (New York: The Century Co., 1906), 5.

108. Ronald C. White, *American Ulysses: A Life of Ulysses S. Grant* (New York: Random House, 2006), 483.

109. "Ulysses S. Grant at His Home. General Horace Porter's Daily Sketch of the Sufferer's Daily Life," *New York Times*, March 25, 1885.

110. "The Grant Monument, Ground Broken for It at Riverside Park, New York," *Sullivan County Record*, May 8, 1891; "An Ode: To be sung on the occasion of breaking ground for the Mausoleum of General Grant, April 27, 1891," Manhattan Historic Sites Archive, accessed June 16, 2019. http://mhsarchive.com/item.aspx?rID=GEGR%20%20%20%20%20622.0003&db=objects&dir=CR%20NPNYH.

111. Crain, *The Gilded Age in New York*, 61.

Chapter 7 "The Humiliating Spectacle"

1. David M. Kahn, *General Grant National Memorial Historical Resource Study* (National Park Service, 1980), 98.

2. "Ronkonkoma Man Retires as Grant's Tomb Curator," *Long Island Advance*, February 17, 1966.

3. "A Monumental Engineering Feat," *Stone, A Journal for Producers, Workers and Users of Stone, Marble and Granite*, December 1891.

4. *American Architect and Building News*, November 14, 1891.

5. Kahn, *General Grant National Memorial Historical Resource Study*, 100.

6. "Grant Monument Association: Ex-Mayor Grace Will Have Nothing More to Do with It," *Richmond Item* (Indiana), November 27, 1891.

7. "Trustees in Turmoil," *Inter Ocean* (Chicago), February 3, 1892.

8. "The Grant Monument Association," *Sun*, February 18, 1892.

9. "Pugnacious Porter," *Saint Paul Daily Glove*, January 4, 1892. The article was reprinted from the *Chicago Evening Post*.

10. *Manhattan Nationalist* (Kansas), February 12, 1892.

11. "Letter from Horace Porter, 1892," Manhattan Historic Sites Archive, accessed June 20, 2019. http://mhsarchive.com/item.aspx?rID=GEGR%20%20%20%20%20622.0051&db=objects&dir=CR%20GEGR.

12. "Darius Ogden Mills," The Mills Building, accessed January 7, 2017. http://www.themillsbuilding.com/about-the-building/darius-ogden-mills.

13. Joan Waugh, *U. S. Grant: American Hero, American Myth* (Chapel Hill, NC: University of North Carolina Press, 2009), 288.

14. Kahn, *General Grant National Memorial Historical Resource Study*, 104.

15. Waugh, *U. S. Grant: American Hero, American Myth*, 286.

16. "Letter from Andrew Carnegie to General Horace Porter, March 29, 1892," Manhattan Historic Sites Archive, accessed June 16, 2019. http://mhsarchive.com/item.aspx?rID=GEGR%20%20%20%20%20622.0050&db=objects&dir=CR%20NPNYH; "Letter from Andrew Carnegie to General Horace Porter, May 21, 1892," http://mhsarchive.com/item.aspx?rID=GEGR%20%20%20%20%20622.0082&db=objects&dir=CR%20GEGR.

17. "Letter from Col. Frederick Grant to Gen. Horace Porter March 2, 1892," Manhattan Historic Sites Archive, accessed June 16, 2019. http://www.mhsarchive.org/item.aspx?rID=GEGR%20%20%20%20%20625.0011&db=objects&dir=CR%20GEGR.

18. "The Grant Monument," *Illustrated American*, April 9, 1892.

19. Kahn, *General Grant National Memorial Historical Resource Study*, 114.

20. Kahn, 115–116.

21. Kahn, 126.

22. " Unveiling of the Grant Statue," *Scranton Republican*, April 28, 1899.

23. Kahn, *General Grant National Memorial Historical Resource Study*, 126–127.

24. "Instructions to Post Commanders, May 12, 1892," Manhattan Historic Sites Archive, accessed June 18, 2019. http://mhsarchive.com/item.aspx?rID=GEGR%20%20%20%20%20622.0178&db=objects&dir=CR%20GEGR.

25. "General Porter to Colonel Cummings," *Brooklyn Daily Eagle*, April 20, 1892.

26. *Inter Ocean* (Chicago), September 20, 1903; "From the Churches," *Inter Ocean* (Chicago), April 28, 1889.

27. "To Urge Sunday Closing," *Chicago Tribune*, September 3, 1891.

28. *Inter Ocean* (Chicago), September 20, 1903.

29. Scott Martelle, *The Admiral and the Ambassador: One Man's Obsessive Search for the Body of John Paul Jones* (Chicago: Chicago Review Press, 2014), 31.

30. "Cragin wrote to Porter in February 1893 with an unconventional offer." The author is mistaken, as the offer must have been made in 1892. Martelle, *The Admiral and the Ambassador*, 32. "One of Porter [sic] Chicago acquaintances, James W. Cott, wrote to him recommending the services of one Edward F. Cragin." Kahn, *General Grant National Memorial Historical Resource Study*, 106.

31. Kahn, 106.

32. "Tribute to E. F. Cragin," *Chicago Tribune*, April 20, 1897.

33. "The Grant Monument," *Illustrated American*, April 9, 1892.

34. "Gen. Grant's Tomb," *New York Times*, March 21, 1892.

35. "President Horace Porter's speech, 1892," Manhattan Historic Sites Archive, accessed August 13, 2019. http://mhsarchive.com/item.aspx?rID=GEGR%20%20%20%20%20622.0088&db=objects&dir=CR%20GEGR.

36. "More Grant Monument Committees," *Sun*, April 14, 1892.

37. Kahn, *General Grant National Memorial Historical Resource Study*, 107.

38. "Letter from Horace Porter to the People of the City of New York," Manhattan Historic Sites Archive, accessed June 22, 2019. http://mhsarchive.com/item.aspx?rID=GEGR%20%20%20%20%20622.0076&db=objects&dir=CR%20GEGR.

39. Kahn, *General Grant National Memorial Historical Resource Study*, 108.

40. "Letter from George De Revere to James C. Reed, May 18, 1892," Manhattan Historic Sites Archive, accessed June 22, 2019. http://mhsarchive.com/item.aspx?rID=GEGR%20%20%20%20%20622.0104&db=objects&dir=CR%20GEGR.

41. Neil Harris, "The Battle for Grant's Tomb," *American Heritage* 56 (August–September 1985): 70–79.

42. *New York Times*, April 25, 1897.

43. "At Grant's Tomb, Laying the Corner-Stone of the Great General's Monument in Riverside Park," *New York Evening World*, April 27, 1892.

44. Kahn, *General Grant National Memorial Historical Resource Study*, 1.

45. "Grant's Tomb, The Cornerstone Laid with Impressive Ceremonies," *Brooklyn Daily Eagle*, April 27, 1892. Regarding the Civil War soldiers' age: "The average Union soldier was 25.8 years old; there is no definite

information on the average age of Confederate soldiers, but by the end of the war old men and young boys, who otherwise would have stayed home, were being pressed into service." "Civil War Facts," Civil War Trust, accessed June 13, 2020. http://www.civilwar.org/education /history/faq.

46. "Grant's Tomb, The Cornerstone Laid with Impressive Ceremonies," *Brooklyn Daily Eagle*, April 27, 1892. The bicycle would soon take hold in New York, prompting the first designated bike path in America, created in Brooklyn in 1892. "History of Bicycling: A Revolution in Parks, NYC Parks, accessed March 18, 2019. https://www.nycgovparks.org /about/history/bicycling.

47. "Grant's Tomb, The Cornerstone Laid with Impressive Ceremonies," *Brooklyn Daily Eagle*, April 27, 1892.

48. "Grant Monument," *Sacramento Daily Union*, April 27, 1892.

49. "Laid by the President," *New York Times*, April 28, 1892.

50. "Contents of copper box placed in cornerstone of Grant's Tomb, April 27, 1892," Manhattan Historic Sites Archive, accessed June 16, 2019. http://mhsarchive.com/item.aspx?rID=GEGR%20%20%20%20%20 622.0002&db=objects&dir=CR%20GEGR.

51. "Laid by the President," *New York Times*, April 28, 1892. Harrison was parsimonious with his words because he was eager to get back to Washington, DC. A week earlier he had written Greener that he regretted the ceremony ended at such a late time and that his "remarks would be exceedingly brief and not more than eight to ten sentences." "Letter from Benjamin Harrison to Horace Porter, April 21, 1892," Manhattan Historic Sites Archive, accessed June 16, 2019. http://mhsarchive.com/item.aspx? rID=GEGR%20%20%20%20%20622.0142&db=objects&dir=CR%20 GEGR.

52. "About 'Depewed' Noses," *Daily Leader* (Gloversville, NY), July 16, 1891.

53. Chauncey Mitchell Depew, *Orations, addresses and speeches of Chauncey M. Depew* (New York: Privately Printed, 1910), 108–112.

54. "Letter from Benjamin Harrison to Horace Porter, March 16, 1892," Manhattan Historic Sites Archive, accessed June 16, 2019. http://mhsarchive .com/item.aspx?rID=GEGR%20%20%20%20%20622.0141&db=objects&dir =CR%20GEGR.

55. "Letter from Levi P. Morton to Horace Porter, May 8, 1892," Manhattan Historic Sites Archive, accessed June 22, 2019. http://mhsarchive.com/item .aspx?rID=GEGR%20%20%20%20%20622.0079&db=objects&dir =CR%20GEGR.

56. It was won by Miss Ethel Stebbins from Normal College, which later became Hunter College. "Letter from John L. N. Hunt to Horace

Porter, June 23, 1892," Manhattan Historic Sites Archive, accessed June 22, 2019. http://mhsarchive.com/item.aspx?rID=GEGR%20%20%20%20%20622.0098&db=objects&dir=CR%20GEGR.

57. Carnegie felt guilty about the donation because he believed Grant would have preferred "so great a sum should have been used in a wholly different manner." Rockefeller, however, articulated no such compunction. "Letter from Andrew Carnegie to General Horace Porter, May 21, 1892," Manhattan Historic Sites Archive, accessed June 22, 2019. http://mhsarchive.com/item.aspx?rID=GEGR%20%20%20%20%20622.0050&db=objects&dir=CR%20GEGR; "Letter from John D. Rockefeller to Horace Porter, May 13, 1892," Manhattan Historic Sites Archive, accessed June 22, 2019. http://mhsarchive.com/item.aspx?rID=GEGR%20%20%20%20%20622.0081&db=objects&dir=CR%20GEGR.

58. "Letter from Horace Porter to the Members of Committees of the Grant Monument Association, May 23, 1892," Manhattan Historic Sites Archive, accessed June 22, 2019. http://mhsarchive.com/item.aspx?rID=GEGR%20%20%20%20%20622.0083&db=objects&dir=CR%20GEGR.

59. "Letter from W. F. Sanders to Horace Porter, May 26, 1892," Manhattan Historic Sites Archive, accessed August 13, 2019. http://mhsarchive.com/item.aspx?rID=GEGR%20%20%20%20%20622.0031&db=objects&dir=CR%20GEGR.

60. Harris, "The Battle for Grant's Tomb," 70–79.

61. "New York and the Grant Monument," *Buffalo Enquirer,* June 2, 1892.

62. "Letter from Isaac Lewis Peet to James C. Reed, June 1, 1892," Manhattan Historic Sites Archive, accessed June 22, 2019. http://mhsarchive.com/item.aspx?rID=GEGR%20%20%20%20%20622.0085&db=objects&dir=CR%20GEGR.

63. "In Honor of Gen. Grant," *Evening World,* April 28. 1893.

64. Kahn, *General Grant National Memorial Historical Resource Study,* 132.

65. *Bradstreet's, A Journal of Trade, Finance, and Public Economy,* May 21, 1892.

66. Later a tree was planted to commemorate the temporary tomb. The tree still stands in a gated enclosure behind the permanent tomb, though it is unclear how precisely the footprint of the enclosure corresponds to the actual temporary tomb location.

67. "The Tomb of Grant," *Fayetteville Recorder,* May 29, 1895.

68. "Granite Quarry Link to the Past," *Conway Daily Sun,* September 1, 2014.

69. Kahn, *General Grant National Memorial Historical Resource Study,* 117.

70. Kahn, 119.

71. "Letter from James C. Reed to General Horace Porter, March 1, 1893," Manhattan Historic Sites Archive, accessed June 22, 2019. http://mhsarchive.com/item.aspx?rID=GEGR%20%20%20%20%20 622.0052&db=objects&dir=CR%20GEGR.

72. Kahn, *General Grant National Memorial Historical Resource Study*, 121.

73. Gary Richardson and Tim Sablik, "Banking Panics of the Gilded Age," Federal Reserve History, December 4, 2015. https://www.federalreservehistory .org/essays/banking_panics_of_the_gilded_age.

74. The crisis continued for four years, finally ending in 1897, the same year Grant's Tomb was completed and dedicated.

75. "Free Bread Now," New York *World*, January 8. 1894.

76. Kahn, *General Grant National Memorial Historical Resource Study*, 121.

77. Kahn, 119.

78. "City Beautiful Movement," The New York Preservation Archive Project, accessed March 4, 2017. http://www.nypap.org/preservation-history/city -beautiful-movement.

79. *The Great Round World and What is Going on in It*, Vol. 1, No. 9, January 7, 1897, 282.

80. "About AHA," American Historical Association, accessed January 5, 2020. https://www.historians.org/about-aha-and-membership.

81. "Lee in Bronze," *Baltimore Sun*, May 30, 1890. As of this writing, plans are being discussed to remove the statue.

82. W. Fitzhugh Brundage, "I've studied the history of Confederate memorials. Here's what to do about them," VOX, August 18, 2017. https: //www.vox.com/the-big-idea/2017/8/18/16165160/confederate-monuments -history-charlottesville-white-supremacy.

83. "The Lee Monument Unveiling," *Richmond Planet*, May 31, 1890. In New England, a reporter declared that the Lee monument "affronted the patriotic sentiment of the country," *Vermont Phoenix*, June 6, 1890.

84. "The Tomb of Grant," *Fayetteville Recorder*, May 29, 1895.

85. "Grant's Monument," *Daily Leader* (Gloversville, NY), May 17, 1895.

86. "General Grant's Tomb," *Watertown Herald*, October 12, 1895.

87. Kahn, *General Grant National Memorial Historical Resource Study*, 132.

88. Kahn, 123.

89. Waugh, *U. S. Grant: American Hero, American Myth*, 293–294.

90. Kahn, *General Grant National Memorial Historical Resource Study*, 124–125.

91. "Grant Sarcophagus Here," *New York Times*, March 16, 1897.

92. Kahn, *General Grant National Memorial Historical Resource Study*, 131.

93. Kahn, 133.

94. James Garfield's beautiful Gothic memorial tomb is taller at 180 feet tall but is smaller in terms of square footage.
95. "Grave of General Grant," *New York Times*, February 21, 1897.
96. "Work on the Tomb Ended," *New York Times*, April 14, 1897.
97. "General Grant's Tomb," *Timely Topics*, April 30, 1897.
98. "Gen. Grant's Body Removed," *Salt Lake Tribune*, April 18, 1897.
99. James Monroe and John Quincy Adams were also reinterred; however, it was not the intention upon their death.
100. Martelle, *The Admiral and the Ambassador*, 281. A special acknowledgment to Martelle for his hard work scouring the Porter archives, many of which are yet to be digitized.

Chapter 8 "Let Us Have Peace"
1. Scott Martelle, *The Admiral and the Ambassador: One Man's Obsessive Search for the Body of John Paul Jones* (Chicago: Chicago Review Press, 2014), 7.
2. "Sub-Committees Named for Grant Monument Inauguration Ceremonies," *Brooklyn Daily Eagle*, February 21, 1897.
3. "Dodge, Grenville Mellen, (1831–1916)," Biographical Directory of the United States Congress, accessed February 2, 2017. http://bioguide.congress.gov/scripts/biodisplay.pl?index=D000395.
4. "Gen. Grant's Body Removed," *New York Times*, April 18, 1897.
5. "The President Invited," *New York Times*, March 16, 1897. Despite the title of this article, nowhere in this letter did Mayor Strong actually invite President McKinley to attend.
6. "The Grant Monument Dedication," *Evening Post*, March 29, 1897.
7. David M. Kahn, *General Grant National Memorial Historical Resource Study* (National Park Service, 1980), 136.
8. Kahn, *General Grant National Memorial Historical Resource Study*, 135–136. Several white bricks that were used within the inside of the tomb were donated by the Grant family to the Smithsonian on March 26, 1903. The bricks later made their way to the National Park Service, which now has three of these bricks in their collection, although none were on display in the small visitor center when I last visited in 2020.
9. "Topic of the Times," *New York Times*, April 6, 1897.
10. Kahn, *General Grant National Memorial Historical Resource Study*, 138.
11. "Death List of the Day," *New York Times*, April 24, 1897.
12. "James C. Reed's Illness," *New York Times*, April 18, 1897.
13. "The Grant Monument Dedication," *Northern Observer* (Massena, NY) March 18, 1897.
14. "Gen. Grant's Tomb," *Gouverneur Free Press*, April 14, 1897.

15. *"The Grant Memorial Day March and Two Step*, 1897," Manhattan Historic Sites Archive, accessed July 7, 2019. http://www.mhsarchive.org/item.aspx ?rID=GEGR%20%20%20%20%20516&db=objects&dir=CR%20 NPNYH; *"Here Sleeps the Hero*, 1897," Manhattan Historic Sites Archive, accessed July 7, 2019. http://www.mhsarchive.org/item.aspx?rID=GEGR %20%20%20%20%20499&db=objects&dir=CR%20GEGR.

16. "A Nation's Tribute to a Nation's Hero," *Kansas City Journal,* April 28, 1897.

17. Today in Madison Square can be seen a bronze statue of President Chester Arthur, sculpted by George Edwin Bissel and dedicated two years after the Grant's Tomb dedication ceremony, on June 13, 1899. In addition, you can see a tree transplanted in 1936 from James Madison's Montpelier estate. Before it sits a bronze marker that reads, "1836–1936 This Tree From The Virginia Estate Of Former President James Madison Presented To The City Of New York By The Fifth Avenue Association Inc. To Commemorate The First Centennial Of The Opening Of Madison Avenue."

18. "Tribute of The Nation," *Paterson Daily Press*, April 29, 1897.

19. "Grant Day," *Harper's Weekly*, May 1, 1897. Interestingly, an advertisement for Mark Twain's latest books for sale appears in the classified section of this issue.

20. Perhaps Governor Tanner had a point. As host, New York felt fit to disregard their own rules and place their own first in the march despite being the eleventh state to join the Union on July 26, 1788.

21. "Souvinier [sic] Programme of the U. S. Grant Memorial Parade and Cerimony [sic] at Riverside Park, April 27, 1897," Manhattan Historic Sites Archive, accessed February 2, 2017. http://www.mhsarchive.org/item .aspx?rID=GEGR%20%20%20%20%20447&db=objects&dir=CR%20 NPNYH.

22. "Streetscapes/The American Surety Building; An 1890's Skyscraper May Become a Landmark," *New York Times*, January 28, 1996.

23. *Real Estate Record and Builders' Guide* v. 53, no. 1,357 (March 17, 1894), 404.

24. Albert Rees and Donald P. Jacobs, *Real Wages in Manufacturing, 1890–1914* (Princeton, NJ: Princeton University Press, 1961), 121. Average wage research was produced for the National Bureau of Economic Research.

25. "Grant Monument Medal, April 23, 1897," Manhattan Historic Sites Archive, accessed July 6, 2019. http://www.mhsarchive.org/item.aspx? rID=GEGR%20%20%20%20%20503&db=objects&dir=CR%20 NPNYH.

26. "Tribute of The Nation," *Paterson Daily Press*, April 29, 1897.

27. George Frederick Shrady, *General Grant's Last Days* (New York: Privately Printed, 1908), 33.

28. *The Great Round World and What Is Going on in It*, vol. 1, no. 9, January 7, 1897, 282–283. Note that from an illustration included in the article, one can also see the flora was still quite sparse.

29. "Tribute of the Nation," *Paterson Daily Press*, April 29, 1897.

30. Kahn, *General Grant National Memorial Historical Resource Study*, 139.

31. "Fitting Tribute," *Daily-News Democrat* (Huntington, Indiana), April 28, 1897.

32. Martelle, *The Admiral and the Ambassador*, 112. The goodwill between these two nations ended the following year with the Spanish American War. The sinking of the *Maine* in February 1898 sparked the war (as well as the battle cry, "Remember the *Maine!*") and the *Infanta Maria Theresa* was sunk on July 3, 1898, in the Battle of Santiago de Cuba.

33. "Review of the Warships," *New York Times*, April 28, 1897.

34. "Thirteen Governors Here; Two More Are Expected to Arrive To-day to Take Part in the Ceremonies." *New York Times*, April 27, 1897. O'Ferrall was also a Confederate veteran.

35. "A Nation's Tribute to a Nation's Hero," *Kansas City Journal*, April 28, 1897.

36. "Tribute of the Nation," *Paterson Daily Press*, April 29, 1897.

37. Some time later Varina Davis wrote about the Grant dedication. She referenced her husband's own ceremony and spoke on behalf of the South: "The soldiers of the Confederacy who bore their own beloved leader from New Orleans to his final resting place in Richmond, would be the last to cavil at the enthusiasm of the North for their dead hero." Carol Berkin, *Civil War Wives: The Lives and Times of Angelina Grimké Weld, Varina Howell Davis and Julia Dent Grant* (New York: Random House, 2009), 214–215. The spirit of reunification manifested itself in many ways, some quite peculiar. Just four days after the dedication of Grant's Tomb, the purported log cabins where Abraham Lincoln and Confederate president Jefferson Davis were born were put on display side by side at the Tennessee Centennial Exposition that opened in Nashville on May 1, 1897, to somehow demonstrate the North and the South together again. The Davis cabin was authentic. The Lincoln cabin was not. The fair also held "United Confederate Veterans' Days" and "Grand Army of the Republic Day." Louis L. Picone, *Where the Presidents Were Born: The History & Preservation of the Presidential Birthplaces*. Atglen, PA: Schiffer Publishing, 2012, 64.

38. "Letter from John Winfield Scott to Mrs. Donald McLean, April 7, 1897," Manhattan Historic Sites Archive, accessed July 7, 2019. http://www.mhsarchive.org/item.aspx?rID=GEGR%20%20%20%20%20269&db=-objects&dir=CR%20GEGR. The flag was donated by the United States Bunting Company and the flagpole was donated by the newly formed New York City Chapter of the Daughters of the American Revolution.

39. "A Grand Tribute," *Sacramento Daily Union*, April 28, 1897; Alexander K. McClure and Charles Morris, *The Authentic Life of William McKinley, Our Third Martyr President: Together with a Life Sketch of Theodore Roosevelt* (Washington, DC: W. E. Scull, 1901), 222–223.

40. "At Riverside Park," *Indianapolis Journal*, April 28, 1897.

41. "Official Programme of the Exercises at the Dedication of the Monument and Tomb of General Ulysses S. Grant, April 27, 1897," Manhattan Historic Sites Archive, accessed June 16, 2019. http://mhsarchive.com/item.aspx?rID=GEGR%20%20%20%20%20228&db=objects&dir=CR%20GEGR.

42. Kahn, *General Grant National Memorial Historical Resource Study*, 3.

43. "A Nation's Tribute to a Nation's Hero," *Kansas City Journal*, April 28, 1897.

Chapter 9 "Long-range Good Hands"

1. "Few at Grant's Tomb," *New York Times*, May 3, 1897.

2. "An Insult to Erin," *Editor & Publisher*, January 8, 1921. Their embarrassment might have been slightly alleviated had they known that Grant received the same treatment when he visited China on his global tour.

3. *Fifth Avenue Events, A Brief Account of Some of the Most Interesting Events Which Have Occurred on the Avenue* (Boston: Walton Advertising and Printing Company, 1916), 35. The crowd might have been larger, but the Chinese population had plummeted in recent years since the passing of the Chinese Exclusion Act. This regrettable act barred all Chinese immigration to the United States, a ban which would not be lifted until 1943 (it was initially passed in an 1882 bill and was renewed in 1892). "Chinese Immigration and the Chinese Exclusion Acts," United States State Department Office of the Historian, accessed June 12, 2019. https://history.state.gov/milestones/1866-1898/chinese-immigration.

4. *The Critic, A Weekly Review of Literature and the Arts,* vol. 30 (New York: The Critic Company, 1897), 303.

5. "Repairing Grant's Tomb," *Pittsburgh Press*, December 30, 1904.

6. David M. Kahn, *General Grant National Memorial Historical Resource Study* (National Park Service, 1980), 145; *Laws of the State of New York: Passed*

at the One Hundred and Thirty-First Session of the Legislature, Volume 1 (Albany, NY: J. B. Lyon Company), 1908. 41–42.

7. "When Is Grant's Tomb not a Tomb?" *New York Tribune*, October 29, 1922. Buckner may have remained on the job even longer, but no record could be found of his employment at Grant's Tomb after 1922.

8. "When Is Grant's Tomb not a Tomb?" *New York Tribune.*

9. Kahn, *General Grant National Memorial Historical Resource Study*, 141. Kahn estimated 10,000 to 15,000 visited the day after the dedication.

10. As quoted in Esther Crain, *The Gilded Age in New York* (New York: Black Dog & Leventhal, 2016), 170.

11. "History of Bicycling: A Revolution in Parks," NYC Parks, accessed March 18, 2019. https://www.nycgovparks.org/about/history/bicycling.

12. Kahn, *General Grant National Memorial Historical Resource Study*, 148–149.

13. "Grant's Tomb to Be Guarded All the Time," *Deseret News*, February 1, 1909.

14. "The Automobile Parade," *New-York Tribune*, May 24, 1899.

15. "Danger at Grant's Tomb," *New York Times*, January 12, 1916.

16. Jay Maeder, *Big Town, Big Time: A New York Epic: 1898–1998* (New York: Sports Publishing LLC, 1998), 16; "Mrs. Grant's Funeral," *Indianapolis Journal*, December 21, 1902.

17. "Lee's Post Act," *Brooklyn Daily Eagle*, June 3, 1891.

18. "At Grant's Tomb: An Ex-Confederate Pays Hero of America a High Tribute," *Morning Astorian* (Oregon), May 31, 1902.

19. "Blue and the Gray," *Morning Astorian* (Oregon), April 29, 1905.

20. "At Grant's Tomb," *New-York Tribune*, May 31, 1905.

21. *Personal* lasts almost seven minutes. It begins with a lovesick Frenchman waiting at Grant's Tomb. First one woman arrives, and within a minute about ten more show up to compete for his affections. The viewer is then treated to a slapstick chase as the desperate women pursue the Frenchman through rural New York City (shot on location). Edison's rendition is longer at almost eleven minutes (shot in New Jersey). Besides footage of the Frenchman getting ready for his big meeting, the remainder is nearly identical, and by *nearly*, I mean almost *exactly identical*. In both films, first we see a close shot of the Doric columns, and then a wide view of the entire tomb. As well, both feature well-dressed, bonneted maidens chasing the top-hatted Frenchman from the tomb over a wooden bridge, down a sand dune, and over a fence. Edison adds a chase scene on a beach and a grand finale in which the Frenchman runs into a lake, which is apparently a test, as only his true love follows him into the water. The films are just plain silly, and despite their short

running time, laborious to watch given twenty-first-century sensibili-
ties and attention spans. From a historic perspective, however, the shots
(in both films) of the entire tomb are notable as they show a landscape
barren of trees or visible structures. In 1905, Biograph took Edison to
court for copyright infringement, but the judge sided with the Edison
cinematographer's argument that "My photograph is not a copy, but
an original." Robert Sklar, *Movie-Made America: A Cultural History of
American Movies* (New York: Vintage, 1994), 29; Siva Vaidhyanathan,
*Copyrights and Copywrongs: The Rise of Intellectual Property and How It
Threatens Creativity* (New York: New York University Press, 2001),
92. Both films are available on YouTube at "Personal (1904), accessed
November 9, 2020. https://www.youtube.com/watch?v=rmrprFJV1xg;
and "How a French Nobleman Got a Wife through the *New York Herald*
Personal Column," YouTube, accessed October 6, 2019. https://www.
youtube.com/watch?v=fhz4tonI864.

22. "Burial, Construction & Early History," Grant Monument Association,
    accessed September 10, 2020. https://grantstomb.org/burial-construction
    -early-history.

23. "Greetings from the Smithsonian, A Postcard History," Smithsonian
    Institution Archives, accessed August 21, 2019. https://siarchives.si.edu/
    history/featured-topics/postcard/postcard-history.

24. James Tobin, *To Conquer the Air: The Wright Brothers and the Great Race for
    Flight* (New York: Free Press, 2004), 345–355.

25. "Rough Trip for Curtiss," *Parsons Daily Eclipse* (Kansas), October 4, 1909.

26. "A Great Flight Made by Wright in Gotham Today," *Richmond Palladium
    and Sun-Telegram*, October 4, 1909.

27. "Suffragettes, Grant's tomb, 5/2/14," Library of Congress, accessed
    January 24, 2020. https://www.loc.gov/item/2014695737.

28. "Gen. Grant's Tomb," *New York Times*, July 31, 1910.

29. "When Is Grant's Tomb not a Tomb?" *New York Tribune*, October 29,
    1922.

30. "Ronkonkoma Man Retires as Grant's Tomb Curator," *Long Island
    Advance*, February 17, 1966.

31. Kahn, *General Grant National Memorial Historical Resource Study*, 150.

32. Joan Waugh, *U. S. Grant: American Hero, American Myth* (Chapel Hill,
    NC: University of North Carolina Press, 2009), 262.

33. "Fort George Amusement Park," Museum of the City of New York,
    published May 8, 2017. https://www.mcny.org/story/fort-george-amusement
    -park.

34. "How Harlem River Speedway Became Harlem River Drive," Museum

of the City of New York, published February 28, 2012. https://blog.mcny
.org/2012/02/28/how-harlem-river-speedway-became-harlem-river-drive.

35. "Hammerstein's Victoria," *New York Times*, March 3, 1899. The critic
raved, "The adornments are both rich and tasteful. There is not a touch
of grotesque in the auditorium."

36. "Theater District," New York Preservation Archive Project, accessed
March 18, 2019. http://www.nypap.org/preservation-history/theater
-district.

37. "Streetscapes: 1155 Broadway; The Birthplace of the Movies," *New York
Times*, February 9, 1992.

38. Kahn, *General Grant National Memorial Historical Resource Study*, 148.

39. "When Is Grant's Tomb not a Tomb?" *New York Tribune*, October 29,
1922.

40. "The Humor of J.F.K.," Niagara County Community College *Spirit*,
November 13, 1973.

41. "Joffre Salutes Grant as Hero Among Soldiers," *New York Tribune*, April
28, 1922.

42. Calls for an equestrian statue at the tomb site started almost immedi-
ately after Grant's death. Reverend Newman commented six days after
Grant's death, "There should be a fine equestrian statue in the park."
"Riverside Park Chosen," *New York Times*, July 29, 1885.

43. "In Grateful Memory," *New Haven Morning Journal and Courier*, April 28,
1897.

44. Kahn, *General Grant National Memorial Historical Resource Study*, 152.

45. Kahn, 151.

46. "Commercialism at Grant's Tomb," *New York Times*, August 12, 1932.
Today there is no souvenir shop in the tomb (it has been tactfully relocated
to the nearby visitor center), leaving James Garfield's tomb as the only
one with a gift shop within the premises.

47. A plea to potential donors read, "When the monument was erected a generation ago, the neighborhood comprised mainly undeveloped city blocks.
Stately buildings now cover these and emphasize the need for the completion and embellishment of one of the most superbly placed Monuments
in the world." "Fund-raising form letter, 1929," Manhattan Historic
Sites Archive, accessed June 18, 2019. http://mhsarchive.com/item.aspx-
?rID=GEGR%20%20%20%20%20622.0058&db=objects&dir=CR%20
GEGR.

48. "Tomb of General Grant to Be Finished at Last," *New York Times*,
February 17, 1929.

49. Kahn, *General Grant National Memorial Historical Resource Study*, 150–151.

50. "Wanted: 'A Man on Horseback,'" *New York Herald Tribune*, date unknown.

51. "The Final Tribute to General Grant," *New York Times Magazine*, March 17, 1929.

52. "Tomb of General Grant to Be Finished at Last," *New York Times*, February 17, 1929.

53. Kahn, *General Grant National Memorial Historical Resource Study*, 159.

54. Waugh, *U. S. Grant: American Hero, American Myth*, 210.

55. "Man Who Daubed Poetry on Grant's Tomb is Arrested," *Boston Globe*, October 21, 1932.

56. "Ronkonkoma Man Retires as Grant's Tomb Curator," *Long Island Advance*, February 17, 1966.

57. "Grant Monument Association, Charter, By-Laws, Officers and Trustees. April 1, 1934," Manhattan Historic Sites Archive, accessed June 18, 2019. http://mhsarchive.com/item.aspx?rID=GEGR%20%20%20%20%20 622.0172&db=objects&dir=CR%20GEGR.

58. Kahn, *General Grant National Memorial Historical Resource Study*, 162.

59. Ron Thomson and Marilyn Harper, *Telling the Stories: Planning Effective Interpretive Programs for Properties Listed in the National Register of Historic Places* (National Park Service, 2000), 8.

60. "Letter from Alexander MacGregor to William M. Mather, May 13, 1938," Manhattan Historic Sites Archive, accessed December 26, 2019. http://mhsarchive.com/item.aspx?rID=GEGR%20%20%20%20%20 622.0169&db=objects&dir=CR%20NPNYH.

61. "Letter from William M. Mather to Herbert L. Satterlee, February 2, 1938," Manhattan Historic Sites Archive, accessed February 11, 2017. http://www.mhsarchive.org/item.aspx?rID=GEGR%20%20%20%20 %20622.0170&db=objects&dir=CR%20NPNYH.

62. Kahn, *General Grant National Memorial Historical Resource Study*, 168.

63. "Experience America's Best Idea: National Park Getaways: General Grant National Memorial," National Park Service, accessed June 29, 2019. www.nps.gov/getaways/gegr.

64. "Eagle Sculpture, General Grant National Memorial, September 1982," Manhattan Historic Sites Archive, accessed February 12, 2017. http://www.mhsarchive.org/item.aspx?rID=GEGR%20%20%20%20%20 895.0043&db=objects&dir=CR%20NPNYH.

65. Scott Martelle, *The Admiral and the Ambassador: One Man's Obsessive Search for the Body of John Paul Jones* (Chicago: Chicago Review Press, 2014). Porter wanted no elaborate ceremony upon his death, instead requesting "the simplest funeral a man can have," to only include "A word, a song, and a prayer." But for the man so widely celebrated with saving Grant's

Tomb, the irony is that he himself is now buried beneath a humble stone in an under-maintained cemetery in Long Branch, New Jersey. On the day I visited in 2016, I was saddened to find weeds growing high and garbage, including dozens of tattered and trampled-upon flags, littering the cemetery.

66. *Mr. Deeds Goes to Town* (1936), IMDB, accessed December 4, 2019, https://www.imdb.com/title/tt0027996/characters/nm0000011. Two years earlier Grant's Tomb was also mentioned in *The Thin Man*, starring William Powell and Myrna Loy; however, there is no sentimentality or patriotism associated with it in this film. When Powell asks Loy what she thinks of Grant's Tomb, she deadpans, "It's lovely. I'm having a copy made for you."

67. "Moses Calls on Boro to Yield Grant Statue," *Brooklyn Daily Eagle*, June 6, 1941.

68. Kahn, *General Grant National Memorial Historical Resource Stud*, 173.

69. Kahn, 173.

70. "Letter from Herbert L. Satterlee to General William G. Bates, February 5, 1942," Manhattan Historic Sites Archive, accessed June 19, 2019. http://mhsarchive.com/item.aspx?rID=GEGR%20%20%20%20%20 622.0155&db=objects&dir=CR%20GEGR.

71. "Letter from William G. Bates to George G. Burnside, February 18, 1944," Manhattan Historic Sites Archive, accessed July 6, 2019. http://mhsarchive.com/item.aspx?rID=GEGR%20%20%20%20%20 622.0161&db=objects&dir=CR%20GEGR.

72. "Air raid and sabotage memorandum, February 9, 1942," Manhattan Historic Sites Archive, accessed June 16, 2019. http://mhsarchive.com/item.aspx?rID=GEGR%20%20%20%20%20622.0157&db=objects&dir=CR%20 NPNYH; "Letter from W. M. Mather toGeorge D. Burnside, February 9, 1942," Manhattan Historic Sites Archive, accessed July 6, 2019. http://mhsarchive.com/item.aspx?rID=GEGR%20%20%20%20%20 622.0158&db=objects&dir=CR%20GEGR.

73. Kahn, *General Grant National Memorial Historical Resource Study*, 175.

74. "Grant's Tomb Profitable," *New York Times*, June 4, 1952.

75. Kahn, *General Grant National Memorial Historical Resource Study*, 176.

76. "Muffled Roll for Grand Army," *Life* Magazine, August 20, 1956. Three other people who outlived Woolson claimed to be Confederate veterans, but none have been verified.

77. "Muffled Roll for Grand Army," *Life* Magazine.

78. "Grant Monument Association Certified Resolutions from the Annual and Special Meeting, October 23, 1958," Manhattan Historic Sites

Archive, accessed June 18, 2019. http://mhsarchive.com/item.aspx?rID=GEGR%20%20%20%20%20622.0168&db=objects&dir=CR%20NPNYH.

79. "Nation Takes Grant's Tomb," *Armored Sentinel*, May 8, 1959.

80. "Report on Transfer of the General Grant Memorial to the National Park Service, 1959," Manhattan Historic Sites Archive, accessed July 7, 2019. http://mhsarchive.com/item.aspx?rID=GEGR%20%20%20%20%20622.0016&db=objects&dir=CR%20NPNYH; "Land Ownership Record, Grant's Tomb Site, Deed No. 1, May 1, 1959," Manhattan Historic Sites Archive, accessed July 7, 2019. http://mhsarchive.com/item.aspx-?rID=GEGR%20%20%20%20%20895.0019&db=objects&dir=CR%20GEGR. Transferring the land to the federal government first required finding deeds from 1872, when the land was first acquired by the city through condemnation.

81. "Memorandum from Daniel J. Tobin to the Director of the National Park Service, April 10, 1959," Manhattan Historic Sites Archive, accessed July 7, 2019. http://mhsarchive.com/item.aspx?rID=GEGR%20%20%20%20%20895.0015&db=objects&dir=CR%20GEGR.

82. "Nation Takes Grant's Tomb," *Armored Sentinel*, May 8, 1959.

Chapter 10 "We Have Fights Here Too"

1. Joan Waugh, *U. S. Grant: American Hero, American Myth* (Chapel Hill, NC: University of North Carolina Press, 2009), 2.

2. "U. S. Grant was the great hero of the Civil War but lost favor with historians," *Washington Post*, April 24, 2014.

3. John Durant and Alice Durant, *The Pictorial History of the Presidents of the United States* (London: A. S. Barnes and Company), 1958, 145.

4. Durant and Durant, 154.

5. Harry S. Truman and Margaret Truman ed., *Where the Buck Stops: The Personal and Private Writings of Harry S. Truman* (New York: Grand Central Publishing, 1990).

6. "You Bet Your Life: The Best Episodes," National Public Radio, posted September 17, 2004. https://www.npr.org/templates/story/story.php?storyId=3923046. True experts in the field of presidential graves would know the answer is nobody is buried in Grant's Tomb. The Grant couple are interred above ground in the mausoleum; hence they are not buried under ground. Also note that *You Bet Your Life* first started as a radio show in 1947 before transitioning to television after three seasons.

7. "Better Groucho Should Bury Grant's Tomb Gag," *Milwaukee Sentinel*, December 12, 1953. While the line is so often credited to Groucho, he

may have actually pilfered it, as an earlier form of the joke was uttered by Shirley Temple in the 1933 short film *Dora's Dunkin Donuts*. At the 3:30 mark of the movie, the precocious five-year-old asks her teacher, "What general with five letters in his name was buried in Grant's Tomb?" *"Dora's Dunkin Donuts* (1933)–Classic Comedy Films," YouTube, accessed December 4, 2019. https://www.youtube.com/watch?v= g5JgL6lMpc.

8. "Letter from George Edelman to the Custodian of Grant's Tomb, January 16, 1954," Manhattan Historic Sites Archive, accessed June 22, 2019. http://mhsarchive.com/item.aspx?rID=GEGR%20%20%20%20%20 622.0152&db=objects&dir=CR%20NPNYH.

9. "Gang Battle for Park Averted Near Grant's Tomb. Cops Patrol Trouble Spot," *New York Journal American*, June 11, 1955. As quoted in Lewis Yablonsky, "The Delinquent Gang as a Near-Group." *Social Problems* 7, no. 2 (1959): 109.

10. "Fighting Gangs, Terror of the Past," *Columbia Spectator*, February 10, 1967.

11. David M. Kahn, *General Grant National Memorial Historical Resource Study* (National Park Service, 1980), 181.

12. Kahn, 177.

13. "Memorandum from Newell H. Foster to National Park Service Region Five Director, January 16, 1962," Manhattan Historic Sites Archive, accessed July 7, 2019. http://mhsarchive.com/item.aspx?rID=GEGR%20 %20%20%20%20895.0032&db=objects&dir=CR%20GEGR.

14. "National Park Service Planning and Development at General Grant National Memorial During the Calendar Year 1962," Manhattan Historic Sites Archive, accessed July 7, 2019. http://mhsarchive.com/item.aspx? rID=GEGR%20%20%20%20%20895.0018&db=objects&dir=CR%20 GEGR.

15. Kahn, *General Grant National Memorial Historical Resource Study*, 183.

16. "Cox Corridors," Architect of the Capitol, updated May 25, 2016. https: //www.aoc.gov/capitol-buildings/cox-corridors.

17. "Grant's Tomb Gets 3 Murals After 69 Yrs.," *New York Daily News*, May 27, 1966.

18. Kahn, *General Grant National Memorial Historical Resource Study*, 185.

19. Kahn, 189.

20. Frank Scaturro, telephone interview with author, June 21, 2017.

21. "Ronkonkoma Man Retires as Grant's Tomb Curator," *Long Island Advance*, February 17, 1966. On August 1, 1954, George G. Burnside was a contestant on the game show *What's My Line?* The panel, which included Dorothy Kilgallen, Steve Allen, Arlene Francis, and Bennett

Cerf, was unable to guess his occupation. "What's My Line?—Jayne Meadows (Aug 1, 1954)," YouTube, Posted September 24, 2015. https://www.youtube.com/watch?v=rTNrT2Fxd0Q.

22. "Grant's Tomb Goes to US Next Friday as National Shrine," *New York Times*, April 24, 1959. From a historian's perspective, one major advantage of the tomb being moved to the National Park Service is that we now have records of exact attendance statistics.

23. "In N.Y., Grant and His Tomb Get Little Respect," *Chicago Tribune*, November 7, 1993.

24. "Grant's Tomb Gang Territory," *Vancouver Sun*, April 28, 1972.

25. *Analysis of Management Alternatives including Environmental Assessment, General Grant National Monument* (New York: National Park Service, 1980), 24.

26. "Creation of Memorial Benches in Grant Memorial Plaza Flyer, 1972," Manhattan Historic Sites Archive, accessed August 6, 2019. http://mhsarchive.com/item.aspx?rID=GEGR%20%20%20%20%20895.0011&db=objects&dir=CR%20GEGR.

27. "Free Seven-Hour Celebration at Grant's Tomb, 1974," Manhattan Historic Sites Archive, accessed August 6, 2019. http://mhsarchive.com/item.aspx?rID=GEGR%20%20%20%20%20895.0035&db=objects&dir=CR%20GEGR.

28. "Free Seven-Hour Celebration at Grant's Tomb, 1974," Manhattan Historic Sites Archive.

29. "Echoes of Gaudí in a Place That Honors Grant," *New York Times*, July 20, 2008.

30. "Grant's Tomb, Then," *New York Times*, April 30, 1999.

31. "Skirmish at Grant's Tomb Over Benches," *New York Times*, July 23, 1979.

32. "Echoes of Gaudí in a Place That Honors Grant," *New York Times*, July 20, 2008.

33. "Jazzmobile Pays Tribute to WRVR," *Villager*, August 14, 1975.

34. "Ford to City: Drop Dead," *New York Daily News*, October 30, 1975.

35. "Letter and Designation Report from the Landmarks Preservation Commission, December 1, 1975," Manhattan Historic Sites Archive, accessed July 7, 2019. http://mhsarchive.com/item.aspx?rID=GEGR%20%20%20%20%20895.0006&db=objects&dir=CR%20GEGR.

36. "Design Notebook," *New York Times*, August 16, 1979.

37. "Design Notebook," *New York Times*.

38. "Remember the Warriors: Behind the Chaotic, Drug-Fueled, and Often Terrifying Making of a Cult Classic," *Village Voice*, September 8, 2015.

Popular films set in a New York City in moral and civic decline include *Midnight Cowboy* (1969), *Mean Streets* (1973), *Serpico* (1973), *Death Wish* (1974), *Taxi Driver* (1976), and *Escape From New York* (1981), among many others.

39. "NPS Stats: National Park Service Visitor Use Statistics," National Park Service, accessed December 3, 2019. https://irma.nps.gov/STATS/Reports /Park/GEGR.

40. Kahn, *General Grant National Memorial Historical Resource Study*, 3.

41. Kahn, 4.

42. Kahn, 4.

43. *Analysis of Management Alternatives including Environmental Assessment, General Grant National Monument*, 20. A memo the following year anticipated, and perhaps hoped, "that the bench could lose one-half of its tiles in ten years." National Park Service Memorandum, "Record of Decision, Finding of No Significant Impact, General Management Alternative Selection, General Grant National Memorial," April 3, 1981.

44. "Little Respect Given to Graves of Leaders," *Ocala Star-Banner*, March 27, 1983.

45. "Car Abandoning Believed Declining," *New York Times*, August 1, 1981.

46. "The Answer to Who is Buried in Grant's Tomb," *Press-Republican* (Plattsburg, NY), January 8, 1985.

47. *Analysis of Management Alternatives including Environmental Assessment, General Grant National Monument*, 31.

48. "In N.Y., Grant and His Tomb Get Little Respect," *Chicago Tribune*, November 7, 1993. The bathroom built in 1910 was renovated and reopened in 2011 as the National Park Visitor Center. Inside there are public bathrooms as well as a gift shop and auditorium. The words "Men" and "Women" are still visible, engraved above the exterior doors.

49. "Grant Won the Civil War, But His N.Y. Tomb Is Losing the Urban Wars, Monument: Resting Place of Civil War Victor Is Scarred by Vandals and Neglect, a Hangout for the Homeless. One Citizens' Group Is Fighting to Restore the Memorial to Its Glory," *Los Angeles Times*, December 19, 1993; "NPS Stats: National Park Service Visitor Use Statistics," National Park Service, accessed December 3, 2019. https://irma.nps.gov/STATS/ Reports/Park/GEGR.

50. *New Jack City* (1991), IMDB, accessed October 7, 2019. https://www.imdb .com/title/tt0102526. Roger Ebert wrote, "It's an original, in-depth look at this world, written and directed with concern—apparently after a lot of research and inside information." Regarding New York as a setting, Ebert adds, *New Jack City* has "an authentic and gritty feel: [director Mario

Van Peebles] shoots on location, he uses a lot of street slang, he allows his cast to sound like their street characters and not like guys from a TV cop show." "New Jack City," RogerEbert.com, May 1, 1991. https://www.rogerebert.com/reviews/new-jack-city-1991.

51. There was at least one suicide, however. In my research I found a fascinating, and eerily familiar, article from 1954. A boxer, Fred Picone (no known relation), was found dead, shot in the head and stabbed in the stomach, "lying in bushes near Grant's Tomb" after stabbing his wife to death in their apartment in a jealous rage. The reporter seems to add insult to injury by noting that Picone "never had much luck in the ring." "Boxer Fred Picone Found Shot, Stabbed," *Ottawa Journal*, November 5, 1954.

52. "Grant Won the Civil War, But His N.Y. Tomb Is Losing the Urban Wars," *Los Angeles Times*. The revolting reports are horrifying in their numbing redundancy. Another reporter noted, "Graffiti from 'Lov Boogie' and Jazzy' is far more visible than the Grant quotation 'Let Us Have Peace.'" "Graffiti, Budget Trouble Grant's Tomb," *Palladium Times*, December 13, 1991.

53. "Graffiti, Budget Trouble Grant's Tomb," *Palladium Times*.

54. "In N.Y., Grant and His Tomb Get Little Respect," *Chicago Tribune*, November 7, 1993.

55. "Grant Won the Civil War, But His N.Y. Tomb Is Losing the Urban Wars," *Los Angeles Times*. The "mission of the Ulysses S. Grant Association is to conduct research into the life of Ulysses S. Grant and preserve the knowledge of his importance in American history." Ulysses S. Grant Association, accessed March 18, 2017, http://www.usgrantassociation.org.

56. "Grant Won the Civil War, But His N.Y. Tomb Is Losing the Urban Wars," *Los Angeles Times*.

57. "Grant's Reputation, and Therefore His Tomb, Deserve Renovation," *Chicago Tribune*, April 7, 1994.

58. Frank Scaturro, telephone interview with author, June 21, 2017.

59. Scaturro, interview.

60. Scaturro, interview. Twenty-four-hour surveillance was included in the 1959 General Master Plan but was never followed through. It was again proposed in a 1980 National Park Service report, but once again, it was dismissed.

61. Scaturro, interview.

62. "Ceremony at Grant's Tomb Notes Gadfly's Triumph," *New York Times*, April 28, 1997.

63. "Who's Buried in Grant's Tomb? Soon, Maybe No One," *Baltimore Sun*, October 20, 1994.

64. "Ceremony at Grant's Tomb Notes Gadfly's Triumph," *New York Times*, April 28, 1997.

65. "Dishonor for a Hero President," *New York Times*, January 2, 1994.

66. "Illinois Lawmakers Want to Move Grant's Tomb," *Times of Northwest Indiana*, April 1, 1994.

67. "Congressional Record Volume 140, Number 62," Government Publishing Office, accessed March 19, 2017. https://www.gpo.gov/fdsys /pkg/CREC-1994-05-18/html/CREC-1994-05-18-pt1-PgE17.htm.

68. "3 States War for Grant's Remains," *Toledo Blade,* April 10, 1994.

69. Ulysses Grant Dietz, *A Walk in the Park with Rudy* (unpublished memoirs), 1.

70. Ulysses Grant Dietz, telephone interview with author, June 28, 2020.

71. "Once Grand, Grant's Tomb Now Grungy," *USA Today*, April 1, 1994.

72. "3 States War for Grant's Remains," *Toledo Blade,* April 10, 1994.

73. "Government to Refurbish Grant's Tomb," *Albany-Herald*, April 28, 1994.

74. Frank Scaturro, telephone interview with author, June 21, 2017.

75. "Guess Who May Be Moved from Ill-Kept Grant's Tomb?" *Chicago Tribune*, October 16, 1994.

76. "For Grant's Tomb, the Battle's in Court," *New York Times*, April 27, 1994.

77. "Guess Who May Be Moved from Ill-Kept Grant's Tomb?" *Chicago Tribune*, October 16, 1994.

78. "Grant's Tomb Nears an Uncertain Centennial," *New York Times*, April 22, 1995.

79. "Centennial Commemoration Souvenir Program, April 27, 1997," Manhattan Historic Sites Archive, accessed June 27, 2019. http: //mhsarchive.com/item.aspx?rID=GEGR%20%20%20%20%20 895.0008&db=objects&dir=CR%20NPNYH.

80. Rudolph W. Giuliani, *Leadership* (New York: Hyperion, 2002), 47.

81. Frank Scaturro, telephone interview with author, June 21, 2017. After substantial improvements were evident, the lawsuit filed by Scaturro and the Grant descendants in April 1994 was withdrawn without prejudice. This ended the litigation but kept open their right to refile if neglect resumed.

82. "New Life for Old Tomb U. S. Grant Monument Once Again Centerpiece," *New York Daily News*, April 26, 1997.

83. "Skate Park," Riverside Park Virtual Tour, accessed August 26, 2019. https://www.nycgovparks.org/facilities/skateparks.

Chapter 11 "If the Old Guy Were Alive, He Might Have Enjoyed It"

1. "Invitation form letter for Grant's Tomb Centennial Celebration, April 21, 1997," Manhattan Historic Sites Archive, accessed July 7, 2019. http://mhsarchive.com/item.aspx?rID=GEGR%20%20%20%20%20 895.0037&db=objects&dir=CR%20GEGR.

2. "Invitation form letter for Grant's Tomb Centennial Celebration, April 21, 1997," Manhattan Historic Sites Archive.

3. "Mayor Giuliani Takes Part in Celebration of 100th Anniversary of the Dedication of Grant's Tomb April 27, 1997," Archives of the Mayor's Press Office, accessed March 19, 2017. http://www.nyc.gov/html/om /html/97/sp219-97.html.

4. "President Grant's Tomb Rededication," C-SPAN, April 27, 1997. https: //www.c-span.org/video/?80923-1/president-grants-tomb-rededication.

5. "American President: Greatest and Worst, Siena's 5th Presidential Expert Poll 1982–2010," press release, Siena College Research Institute, July 1, 2010. https://s3.amazonaws.com/attachments.readmedia.com/files/16848 /original/Presidents_Release_2010_final.pdf?1291273777.

6. "Ulysses S. Grant Died 130 Years Ago. Racists Hate Him, But Historians No Longer Do," *Huffington Post,* July 23, 2015. http://www.huffingtonpost .com/entry/ulysses-s-grant-died-130-years-ago-today-racists-hated -him-but-historians-no-longer-do_55afe547e4b0a9b948535f6e? ncid=txtlnkusaolp00000592; "How Did Ulysses Grant Become a Caricature?" *Atlantic,* June 1, 2010.

7. "A Conversation with Former President Bill Clinton May 28, 2003," John F. Kennedy Presidential Library and Museum, accessed June 15, 2020. https://www.jfklibrary.org/events-and-awards/forums/past-forums /transcripts/a-conversation-with-former-president-bill-clinton.

8. "Siena's 6th Presidential Expert Poll 1982–2018," Siena College Research Institute, accessed June 15, 2020, https://scri.siena.edu/2019/02/13/sienas -6th-presidential-expert-poll-1982-2018/. Full transparency: I was among the "157 participating presidential scholars" who participated in the 2018 survey.

9. "NPS Stats: National Park Service Visitor Use Statistics," National Park Service, accessed December 3, 2019. https://irma.nps.gov/STATS/Reports /Park/GEGR.

10. "General Grant National Memorial," Tripadvisor, accessed August 30, 2020. https://www.tripadvisor.com/Attraction_Review-g60763-d105812 -Reviews-General_Grant_National_Memorial-New_York_City _New_York.html. While it long since ceased to be a competition, it is worth noting the Statue of Liberty ranked #14 on the same date.

11. Andreas Huyssen, *Present Pasts: Urban Palimpsests and the Politics of Memory* (Stanford, CA: Stanford University Press, 2003), 6–7.

12. "New York City 'Symbols of Hate' Purge Could Target Columbus Statue, Grant's Tomb," CBS New York, August 22, 2017. http://newyork.cbslocal.com/2017/08/22/new-york-city-statue-removal.

13. "Graffiti, peeling paint, stained ceilings: Ulysses S. Grant's final resting place needs a makeover and fast, with the 200th anniversary of his birth approaching," *New York Daily News*, April 28, 2019.

14. "Restore Grant's Tomb to Its Glory—And Other Treasures, Too," *New York Daily News*, April 26, 2017.

15. Grant Monument Association letter to President Donald J. Trump, New York mayor Bill de Blasio, Deb Haaland (House Subcommittee on National Parks, Forests, and Public Lands Committee on Natural Resources), Steve Daines (Chairman Senate Subcommittee on National Parks Committee on Energy and Natural Resources), Betty McCollum (Chairman House Subcommittee on Interior, Environment, and Related Agencies, Committee on Appropriations), and Lisa Murkowski (Chairman Senate Subcommittee on Interior, Environment, and Related Agencies, Committee on Appropriations), March 29, 2019.

16. "Grant Officials Take Offense," *Telegraph-Herald*, July 14, 2003.

17. "Taken for Granted Caretaker Rips Sexy Beyoncé Show at Tomb," *New York Daily News*, July 8, 2003.

BIBLIOGRAPHY

Blight, David W. *Race and Reunion: The Civil War in American Memory.* Cambridge, MA: Harvard University Press, 2001.

Burrows, Edwin G., and Mike Wallace. *Gotham: A History of New York City to 1898.* New York: Oxford University Press, 1999.

Chernow, Ron. *Grant.* New York: Penguin Press, 2017.

Childs, George William. *Recollections of General Grant: With an Account of the Presentation of the Portraits of Generals Grant, Sherman, and Sheridan.* Philadelphia: Collins Printing House, 1890.

Crain, Esther. *The Gilded Age in New York.* New York: Black Dog & Leventhal, 2016.

Doss, Erika. *Memorial Mania: Public Feeling in America.* Chicago: University of Chicago Press, 2010.

Fehrman, Craig. *Author in Chief: The Untold Story of Our Presidents and the Books They Wrote.* New York: Avid Reader Press, 2020.

Garland, Hamlin. *Ulysses S. Grant: His Life and Character.* New York: Double & McClure, 1898.

Grant, Ulysses Simpson. *Personal Memoirs of U. S. Grant.* New York: Dover Publications, 1995.

Gregory, James Monroe. *Frederick Douglass the Orator: Containing an Account of His Life; His Eminent Public Services; His Brilliant Career as Orator; Selections from His Speeches and Writings.* Springfield, MA: Willey, 1893.

Hufbauer, Benjamin. *Presidential Temples: How Memorials and Libraries*

Shape Public Memory. Lawrence, KS: University Press of Kansas, 2006.

Huyssen, Andreas. *Present Pasts: Urban Palimpsests and the Politics of Memory.* Stanford, CA: Stanford University Press, 2003.

Jordan, Brian Matthew. *Marching Home: Union Veterans and Their Unending Civil War.* New York: Liveright Publishing, 2015.

Kahn, David M. *General Grant National Memorial Historical Resource Study.* National Park Service, 1980.

Kammen, Michael. *Mystic Chords of Memory: The Transformation of Tradition in American Culture.* New York: Knopf, 1991.

Martelle, Scott. *The Admiral and the Ambassador: One Man's Obsessive Search for the Body of John Paul Jones.* Chicago: Chicago Review Press, 2014.

N. W. Ayer & Son. *Our Great Commander.* Philadelphia: Press of N. W. Ayer & Son, 1910.

Page, Samuel D. *The Riverside Souvenir. A Memorial Volume Illustrating the Nation's Tribute to General U. S. Grant.* New York: J. C. Derby, 1886.

Perret, Geoffrey. *Ulysses S. Grant: Soldier & President.* New York: Random House, 1997.

Perry, Mark. *Grant and Twain: The Story of an American Friendship.* New York: Random House, 2005.

Picone, Louis L. *The President Is Dead! The Extraordinary Stories of the Presidential Deaths, Final Days, Burials, and Beyond.* New York: Skyhorse Publishing, 2016.

———— *Where the Presidents Were Born: The History & Preservation of the Presidential Birthplaces.* Atglen, PA: Schiffer Publishing, 2012.

Pitkin, Thomas M. *The Captain Departs: Ulysses S. Grant's Last Campaign.* Carbondale, IL: Southern Illinois University Press, 1973.

———— *General Grant National Memorial: Its History and Possible Development.* National Park Service, 1959.

Porter, Horace. *Campaigning with Grant*. New York: The Century Company, 1906.

Ross, Ishbel. *The General's Wife: The Life of Mrs. Ulysses S Grant*. New York: Dodd, Mead, 1959.

Shrady, George Frederick. *General Grant's Last Days*. New York: Privately Printed, 1908.

Simon, John Y., ed. *The Papers of Ulysses S. Grant: October 1, 1878–September 30, 1880*. Carbondale, IL: Southern Illinois University Press, 2008.

Thayer, William M. *From Tannery to the White House: Story of the Life of Ulysses S. Grant, His Boyhood, Youth, Manhood, Public and Private Life and Services*. London: Thomas Nelson and Sons, 1885.

Tobin, James. *To Conquer the Air: The Wright Brothers and the Great Race for Flight*. New York: Free Press, 2004.

Twain, Mark and Elinor Smith, Harrier, ed. *Autobiography of Mark Twain, Volume 1: The Complete and Authoritative Edition*. Berkeley: University of California Press, 2010.

Ward, Geoffrey C. *A Disposition to Be Rich*. New York: Vintage Books, 2012.

Waugh, Joan. *U. S. Grant: American Hero, American Myth*. Chapel Hill, NC: University of North Carolina Press, 2009.

White, Ronald C. *American Ulysses: A Life of Ulysses S. Grant*. New York: Random House, 2016.

Wightman Fox, Richard. *Lincoln's Body: A Cultural History*. New York: W. W. Norton, 2015.

INDEX

stamps, 214

Standard Oil Trust (New York City), 50

Star Route postal ring scandal, 2

Statue of Liberty, 7, 31, 84, 87, 104, 150, 191, 196, 197

Steinway, William, 154

Stephen Merritt Burial and Cremation Company, 41, 43, 69
charges for funeral, 74

Stern Manufacturing Company (Rochester, New York), 41

Stokes, Reverend E. H., 15

Stone (Indianapolis periodical), 145

Stone Mountain (Georgia), 167

Stonewall Brigade, 71

Strong, William Lafayette, 175, 177, 186

Studer, Jacob, 94

Sunday Today in New York television show, 234, 235

Taft, William Howard, 195, 200

Tanner, John Riley, 180

Tarrytown, New York, 31

Taylor, Moses, 14

Taylor, Zachary, 3, 101, 120, 173
final words, 37

telephone, 72, 110

temporary tomb, 75–77, 87–88, 172
relocation (1891), 145
relocation (1892), 162

Territorial Enterprise, 7

Thomas, George H., 207

Tiffany and Company, 182

Tiffany, Charles S., 154, 175

Tiffany, Louis C., 154

Toledo Blade, 238

Topinka, Judy Baar, 236, 237

Transcontinental Railroad, 110

Traveler (Boston), 55

Treaty of Washington (1871), 6

Trenton Battle Monument (New Jersey), 137

Tripadvisor, 246

Troy Commercial Travelers baseball club, 94

Truman, Harry
views on Ulysses S. Grant, 214

Trump, Donald, 247

Turner, William L., 49

Twain, Mark, 7, 9, 11, 12, 20–21, 22, 26, 36, 105

Tweed, William M., 49

Tyler, John, 101, 120

typewriter, 110

Tyrrell, Harrison, 21, 39

Ulysses S. Grant Association, 223, 231

Ulysses S. Grant Memorial (Washington, DC), 200

Union Granite Company, 151

Union Hotel (New York City), 156

Union League Club of New York, 148

Union Pacific Railroad, 176

Unite the Right, 246

United Daughters of the Confederacy, 166, 167

United States Capitol Building, 111, 156, 218

United States Department of Justice, 2